The Language of Difference

CONTEMPORARY STUDIES IN PHILOSOPHY AND THE HUMAN SCIENCES

Series Editor: John Sallis, Loyola University of Chicago

Associate Editors: Hugh J. Silverman, SUNY-Stony Brook, David Farrell Krell, University of Essex

EDITORIAL BOARD

Edward Casey, SUNY-Stony Brook
Jacques Derrida, Ecole Normale Supérieure, Paris
Amedeo Giorgi, Duquesne University
Karsten Harries, Yale University
Don Ihde, SUNY-Stony Brook
Louis Marin, Ecole Pratique des Hautes Etudes, Paris

Wolfe Mays, University of Manchester
Otto Poggeler, Ruhr-Universität Bochum
Jacques Taminiaux, Université de Louvain-la-neuve
Bernhard Waldenfels, Ruhr-Universität Bochum
David Wood, University of Warwick

This new international book series explores recent developments in philosophy as they relate to foundational questions in the human sciences. The series stresses fundamental and pervasive issues, alternative methods, and current styles of thought. It constitutes a response to the emergence in England and America of widespread interest in the domains, intersections, and limits of questions arising from the human sciences within a climate inspired chiefly by Continental thought. Although primarily philosophical in orientation, the series cuts across the boundaries of traditional disciplines and will include volumes in such areas as phenomenology, structuralism, semiotics, post-structuralism, critical theory, hermeneutics, and contemporary cultural (literary and artistic) criticism.

Other Titles

DIALECTIC AND DIFFERENCE by Jacques Taminiaux, translated by James Decker and Roberts Crease
WHERE WORDS BREAK by Robert Bernasconi
UTOPICS: SPATIAL PLAY by Louis Marin
translated by Robert Vollrath
SEEING AND READING by Graeme Nicholson
BEYOND METAPHYSICS? by John Llewelyn
IN THE PRESENCE OF THE SENSUOUS by Mikel Dufrenne
translated by Mark Roberts and Dennis Gallagher
MARTIN HEIDEGGER'S PATH OF THINKING by Otto Pöggeler
translated by Daniel Magurshak and Sigmund Barber

The Language of Difference

Charles E. Scott

HUMANITIES PRESS INTERNATIONAL, INC.
Atlantic Highlands, NJ

First published in 1987 in the United States of America by HUMANITIES PRESS INTERNATIONAL, INC., Atlantic Highlands, NJ 07716

© Humanities Press International, Inc., 1987
Reprinted, 1988
Library of Congress Cataloging-in-Publication Data
Scott, Charles E.
    The language of difference.

    (Contemporary studies in philosophy and the human sciences)
    Includes index.
    1. Languages—Philosophy. 2. Ontology. 3. Time.
I. Title. II. Series.
P106.S345 1987   149'.94   86–7335
ISBN 0-391-03442-1

All rights reserved. No part of this publication may be reproduced or transmitted, in any form or by any means, without permission.

PRINTED IN THE UNITED STATES OF AMERICA

Contents

Preface	vii
1. A Beginning	1
2. Transvaluation in *Beyond Good and Evil*	9
1. Passing through the Prejudices of Philosophers	11
2. The Tensions of the Free Spirit	20
1.a "O Sancta Simplicitas!" (II.24)	20
b "Even if *language*, here as elsewhere, will not get over its awkwardness . . ."	22
2.a ". . . Go away. Flee into concealment." (II.25–26)	23
b "A serious word"	24
3.a Reversal of perspective (II.32)	24
b "The decisive value of an action lies precisely in what is *unintentional* in it."	26
4.a "A duty to suspicion" (II.34)	27
b "On the basis of perspective"	28
5.a "Thinking is merely a relation of . . . drives to each other" (II.36)	28
b A demand by the conscience of method	29
6.a "Whatever is profound loves masks" (II.40)	30
b "A questionable question"	31
7.a "New friends of 'truth'" (II.41–43)	31
b "*My* judgment is *my* judgment"	32
8.a "We free spirits" and "how the plant 'man' has so far grown most vigorously" (II.44)	32
b The free spirit and creation	33
3. Old Forces with New Force	34
1. "The range of inner human experiences reached so far . . ."	36
2. Why atheism today?	38
3. "Masked epilepsy": "a penitential spasm" (III.47)	40
4. "The philosopher as *we* understand him . . ."	42
4. A Discourse Overcoming Itself	46

3. The De-struction of *Being and Time* — 53

1. The Discipline of the Question — 55
2. ". . . if our Dasein is to be stirred by the question of Being." — 58
3. How the Question Stirs — 59
4. The Formulation of the Question of Being — 63
   a. De-structuring the Foundation — 63
   b. Foundation and Phenomenon — 65
5. The Whole of Dasein — 71
   a. Interpreting the Primordial Question Primordially — 71
   b. Existential Structures and Historicity — 75
6. Historicity — 81
   a. Posing the Issue of Historicity — 81
   b. The Middle Voice of Time and History — 83
   c. What Happens to History? — 85
   d. The Strife of the Question of Being — 87

4. Recurrences without Representation — 89

1. Variations on Deleuzian Themes: Thinking without Representing — 93
2. The Line of Recurrence: Transgression — 101
3. Genealogy — 106
4. The Loss of Man: The Emergence of a Different Life — 111
5. The Strife of Differences — 118

5. The Coming of Time Has No Shape — 121

1. A Beginning for Thought with the Passage of Strife — 124
2. Outside the Question of Being — 128
3. Looking Back to a Shaky Beginning — 136
4. A Modest Option — 145

6. "Différance" without Conclusion — 149

Index — 182

PREFACE

Jacques Derrida's works are found in traces throughout this book, but they are discussed primarily in notes and in the final chapter. There are two reasons for this peculiarity. First, if the discussion as a whole is persuasive, one will find that Derrida's emphases and tones are in a history that speaks through them, that a discourse comes to expression through his writing, that his genius is a variation on tones, functions, and ruptures that have been going on for some time. To speak of the language of difference today is necessarily to be indebted to his writing. But his language is also indebted—happily so—and we are dealing with the carrier, the debtor, the discourse that, as we return to it now, shows processes that go far beyond the intentions of any of the writers who have thought within it. Second, a direct discussion of what Derrida says, and of what is said and not said in the language that he writes, is reserved for another work. At present we shall follow a discourse of difference that has helped to make his and our writing and thinking, and in which possibilities, styles, and ideas are yielded through the thought of difference. This essay will have done its work if it follows an emergence of "difference" as a giver, in a remarkable middle voice, of a traceable way of thinking and speaking, and if it leaves open this language for supplementation, variation, pluralization, and demise.

Among the pleasures of writing this book have been the conversations and seminars in which some of its ideas developed. There have been times in which several people together, I among them, have been moved by processes of thinking to ideas that none of us had previously thought. Seminars and colleagues at Vanderbilt University, the Collegium Phenomenologicum in Perugia, Italy, and the Heidegger Circle have been especially effective in exploring some of the thoughts and movements of this book. Ed Casey, Alasdair MacIntyre, Graham Parks, Mary Rawlinson, and Don Reed read parts or all of the manuscript. I am indebted to them for their encouragement and critique. I am especially grateful to Holley Roberts for her editorial expertise. Chris Bastian and Stella Thompson worked with efficient good cheer in preparing the book's several versions. The Vanderbilt Research Council generously supported part of the book's research. To my family—Donna, Stuart, Rebecca, and Charles—goes appreciation, always in inadequate measure, for their support that went beyond kindness and respect, and that invariably found its way to the heart of the matter.

1

A Beginning

In the discourse that we call the language of difference, prefaces and introductions are frequently the occasion for an author to question the function of a book's beginning. Nietzsche said in his preface to the second edition of *The Gay Science* that if the reader has not lived through experiences similar to those of the book, the preface probably will not greatly help. Without a knowledge of gratitude—a knowledge of the *release* of gratitude after a long period without hope, as though one "were attacked by hope, the hope for health and the *intoxication* of convalescence"—without such knowledge the book's happy play of language and its gladness will not be comprehensible, regardless what the preface says. He then added sixty-three verses, which he entitled as a whole "Joke, Cunning, and Revenge," for his introduction. Heidegger wrote a considerable introduction for *Being and Time*, but soon afterward he would write only a few short, factual paragraphs to introduce his books, or he would give lectures with just a beginning paragraph or no introduction at all. Lacan and Derrida prefer to overturn the traditional function of introductions, to resist summary language and the expectation of summarizable conclusions. Foucault, however, liked introductions and used them to set a mood or to set the record straight about this or that. They were occasions for him to play.

Translators have less trouble with introductions. Most of Nietzsche's, Heidegger's, Derrida's, and Lacan's books in English have introductions by their translators. Probably the function of translating encourages talk about what goes on in the text, whereas many of the writers within the language of difference prefer to let the language go on outside the purview of commentary. Most of Foucault's translations into English do not have a translator's introduction. Perhaps that is because he brought introductions and his own language together satisfactorily, and left the translator with less to say.

Is talking about what is going on in a text prohibited by the language of difference, this way of speaking that is sometimes called, among other things, postmodern? Surely not, because all of the writers in this strand of discourse say a lot about other writers and thinkers. Rather, the use of summary language or reporting conclusions at the beginning seems to be the problem. How can we free ourselves from the image of a completed textual body that, once completed, can be well introduced and summarized as though it were finished? That image clearly violates the ongoing, open development of discourses as well as the polyvalence of language, its lack of comprehensible finality, its many simultaneous dimensions, and its play of meanings, possibilities, and sheer lack of meaning. If an introduction could counteract the images of completion, then . . .

How would that different kind of introductory language, free of the image of finality or completion, function? One strategy is to put words in play by which they cannot mean only what they are usually taken to mean. The history of a word that has contradictory meanings or that is used to signify very different things might be played out by punning or by naming different things by the same word. *Introduce*, for example, might be played in its senses of to make known, to insert, to cause to exist, to go inward, to open. How might an opening to the text as text, the text's threshold, make it known? As the text is put in play by playing with *introduce*, the playing would be an important part of the introduction. Or one might put a face on the text by raising expectations in the preface for thinking without conclusions, thus letting the text speak nonconclusively in the antonym for *conclusion, preface*. These kinds of play function to recall the sliding, fluid, nonconclusive, and nonintroductory element of language. As wordplays go on, participants' attitudes and expectations regarding speaking and writing often change. They experience the play of language, its remarkable richness, its own play of differences.

We shall emphasize in the text at hand, however, *functions* within which words take part rather than the history and meanings of particular words. As we follow the language of difference—the strand of discourse in which "difference" gains ascendancy over "identity" and develops, in that ascendancy, distinctive ways of speaking and thinking—functions will stand out more than individual words. The function of wordplay rather than the words being played, for example, attracts our attention. Traditional words can be used nontraditionally if the functions of a discourse are different from traditional discursive functions. When the idea of difference has controlling influence in a discourse, for example, *idea* need not mean primarily seeing by mental action and by means of mental forms. It might come to mean the repetition of a group of associated words. When "difference" functions with discursive dominance, as it does in the language of difference, the way "idea" departs from its own history and moves in a different element and context of thinking gives it a new hearing and breaks it loose from its previous associations. The process that it is undergoing differentiates it from its history in other discursive functions.

The functions of transvaluation in Nietzsche's writing and of destruction in Heidegger's have been significant forces in the development of the language of difference. In those functions discursive changes take place that override traditional meanings and significations. Those changes and their consequences take on a life of their own in the sense that in the language of difference they condition what can be said and what wants to be said. When a person follows those functions inside the discourse that they helped to develop, the person's feelings, beliefs, and ideas are developed—"yielded," we shall say—as the discourse's elements flow through words and thoughts, just as a person is developed by metaphysical elements in metaphysical discourses. We shall follow some of the discursive functions and transmutations that have effected, and that constitute, a way of thinking and speaking that is guided primarily by the idea of difference.

An introduction has a play all its own that is not totally dependent on what the word *introduction* means. How it picks up ideas and themes that are yet to come may be more or less explicit. Or what is not said may be, in the book's context, more significant than what is said. The book's mood, its style, its lightness or heaviness, its interests and compulsions may be announced or indicated or covered over.[1] The introduction in the text at hand is a threshold for a language that moves from extreme conflict to a flow of thought with decreasing violence by means of the increasing influence of "difference" in its functions and formations. Nietzsche's Dionysian preface for *The Gay Science*—he speaks of himself as a resurrected author—in which gratitude, parody, and irony work together with exuberance and without overpowering resentment or exhaustion: that preface is a good one for the language of difference. It foresees, in a language that is still conflicted with a history of repression, the development of a language of release from repression. As we mention his preface as a preface for our subject, we make an entry into a process that he helped to launch and one that he foresaw with painful hope as it left the confines of his own words and thinking.

This essay is about the formation of a strand of discourse, a way of speaking and thinking, that has developed largely in this century. It is a "strand" in the sense that it has not developed into a mainstream discourse, and it is alongside other similar strands that have different histories. A larger context for this discourse is the development and the crumbling of the large confederation of ideas and beliefs that we call metaphysics. In our discourse we find that epistemology and ethics decline in importance. They are recast; the philosophical bases of ethics and epistemology are rethought and rearranged so that they do not occur in this discourse. The ideas of substance and identity are broken apart, and the discursive edifices that house those ideas change. The principles and axioms that govern the relations and hierarchies of ideas change. With these changes, the intuitive certainties and criteria for intellectual good sense transmute. Sensibilities and styles emerge from different points of departure and with different trajectories.

That such changes have been going on in many fields and disciplines is generally recognized. The language and thought that constitute the recognition, however, are less often questioned. A conviction lingers from modern metaphysics that the power and accuracy of recognition, description, and analysis have something like neutral transcendence in relation to what is recognized. We are sometimes persuaded that accurate, coherent thought is in some sense outside of its own finite developmental course. Perhaps we expect philosophical rigor and good sense to represent more than their own language and discourse. Or we might think that, at its best, human action reflects or is related to something that invests it from "outside" with meaning and truth. In the discourse that we follow, those kinds of linkage with metaphysical ways of thinking change into different patterns that are governed by such ideas as difference rather than identity, fragment rather than whole, historical rather than transhistorical necessity, and the power of finite self-acceptance rather than disciplines of obedience regarding transcendent principles or forces.

The discourse we work with is new and involves experimenting with ways to speak and think. It often makes the most of its own uncertainty by giving priority to its deepest experiences of uncertainty. It is aware of its metaphysical reliances, and encourages its own processes of working through and away from those reliances. This essay is part of this process in its effort to understand in a few instances how the transforming, de-structuring, and realigning that gave the process its start continued in the emerging discourse. This essay attempts to think out of—in the wake of—those particular processes.

We begin with *Beyond Good and Evil* and *Being and Time* as texts that set themselves aside through processes that they initiate. These two books do not encourage the reader to turn them into definitive texts or normative presences. They encourage one, rather, by their processes of transvaluation and de-struction, to undergo them, to think through them, and to continue in whatever movements of thought and speech that they engender. In such a process, referral to the texts involves letting the texts work on themselves with transvaluing and de-structuring processes. By putting themselves in question and de-centering their place in the discourse they helped to develop, the text's transvaluation and de-struction have had a major impact on the strand of discourse that we call the language of difference. They are in processes of making differences that apply to the texts themselves as they are thought on their own terms. In the language of this essay, thinking can become a way of repeating textual functions in which both the texts and the thinking regarding them change through processes initiated by the texts. In such processes some of the repressive and hence violent aspects of traditional thinking are transmuted into ways of speaking and thinking that are released from those aspects and that repeat the nonviolent release in discourse-forming ways.

The next two chapters emphasize the functions of transvaluation and de-struction rather than dominant ideas in the books. Transvaluation and de-struction permitted the development of a discourse in which the idea of difference gains dominance over the idea of identity. Transvaluation also overrides the metaphysical ideas in *Beyond Good and Evil*, just as de-struction overrides the metaphysical ideas in *Being and Time*. *Beyond Good and Evil* becomes unsatisfactory on its own terms, however, when it is read in the effective power of transvaluation, because transvaluation pushes the ensuing discourse beyond the tensions and conflicts that run through Nietzsche's work. Similarly, *Being and Time* is inadequate to its own goals because of the accomplishments of de-struction in the essay that lead one beyond the confines of fundamental ontology. Each essay is characterized by a changing language and thought that invests each book with a type of conflict that each is designed to overcome by means of either transvaluation or de-struction. They lead to ways of thinking and speaking that are significantly different from those in the essays. When one returns to the essays in the language and thinking that they helped to effect, the essays are found to be transitional, and their ideas are more significant because of their conflicts and transitions than because of their specific, often literal claims.

One of our claims is that by virtue of the noted processes of transformation a discursive strand now functions that is neither metaphysical nor antimetaphysical. The transformation processes involved have increased the discursive power of the idea of difference, and we follow those processes in a language that is itself within the hegemony of difference. Another associated claim is that the power of representational thinking is diminished as one speaks in this discourse of difference. In the work of Foucault,

Heidegger, and Derrida, representational thinking is replaced with distinctive manners of thinking that we shall discuss. A third claim is that the language of difference initiates an expectation that differences can be organized and thought with the effects of experiences of release and play. Those experiences suggest the possibility of communication without the particular repressive violence of traditional, normative thought. This suggestion, however, is a developing one and is unclear in its implications.

When the idea of difference establishes relations among rules, those rules and relations have meaning only for the space that they define. One grouping can be replaced by another, as when a person comes to think and live in a language different from the one he learned first. There is always a significant carry-over of some rules and principles when a switch occurs. But if the transformations build on one another through switching and changing constellations of rules and so forth, a discourse can emerge that is quite different from a distant, earlier one; and although one can find similarities in them, the way those similarities function—how they govern and are governed in the discourses—can be different enough to constitute very different ways of thinking. The move from broadly metaphysical thinking through *Beyond Good and Evil*, for example, to Foucault's discourse of transgression is such a transformation. The movement through *Being and Time* to *Time and Being* or "Building, Dwelling, Thinking" is also one that moves from de-struction of metaphysics to a way of thinking that is neither antimetaphysical nor metaphysical.

We are writing within a small tributary of language—small in the vast element that has spawned it or that swells around it, or whatever language does around one of its strands. This essay speaks of a small flow of language that has come so far as to be different from the established, expected language that has taught us what to ask and how to answer. One way to work in this language is to circle back to the especially important texts, to find in the texts the remnants, the ideas and words, that connect them with their metaphysical heritage, to show the movement away from that heritage in a language that is no longer dominated by that heritage. Our choice is to follow the two discursive functions, transvaluation and de-structuring, that have changed their heritages and that have helped to give the idea of difference a new place in the formation of ideas, hierarchies, and affections. We then follow three ways of thinking that have come out of the transvaluing and de-structuring processes. Our attention is on the processes that take place as the idea of difference gains dominance over the idea of identity, and on the ways of thinking and speaking that emerge with these processes.

The language of difference is thoroughly unsatisfactory if it is viewed through language and ideas ordered by the priority of identity. The feelings that are part of our traditional discourses often are not part of the language ordered by difference. In metaphysical traditions, for example, a person wants to know what is real and what is not real. One feels obligated to find norms for judgment. One feels acutely the danger of despair if ultimate reality and meaning are threatened. These desires and feelings do not develop in the language of difference. Within it, a person feels no longing for ultimate reality and meaning. The idea of reality has lost its attractive force. One feels the exhaustion of traditional ideas and a sense of happiness in a new and freer, less certain flow of words, thoughts, and expectations. The traditional certainties often feel more dangerous for human survival and well-being than they feel like motivations for hope. The absence of metaphysical connections, whatever they might be, has a feeling of rightness connected with it, and the possibility for continued thinking in the aftermath of metaphysics feels attractive and promising.[2]

If this book succeeds thematically, the reader will follow the development of a language of difference and understand how one strand of thinking in our time has come to be through the increasing power of the idea of difference. If the book succeeds philosophically, the reader will be able to think in the increased power of difference as he or she thinks in the book's language and conceptuality.

Julia Kristeva speaks of psychoanalytic interpretation as "an encounter with the subject speaking to us which enables him to express himself at the point closest to his own destruction."[3] One part of that "point closest to his own destruction" before it achieves reflective clarity is language that is "unaware of repression." The repressions that are most thorough, most destructive, and most powerful are closely related to a nonreflective and unspeakable sense of death, to situations in which the living being senses overwhelming threat to his or her own life. The person's language loses emotion and empties itself of desire in those situations, and images and significations related to them lack strong affect. The life-endangered areas have been cast out of one's reflective alertness, as it were, and retrieval of those areas, communication with them, release from their threatening, repressed power are necessary for restored energy and desire.

The work before us has to do with transformation out of a philosophical language that developed strong senses of identity and rightness. Philosophical discourses demarcate their own limits. They define themselves. In their processes they develop a sharp intuitive sense for what cannot be said and for how speaking is to go on so that their own identities will survive. Because they speak of truth, life, meaning, death, order, sense, relation, and so forth, essential change in philosophical discourses looks and feels life-threatening within those discourses. Not only the discursive life is threatened when significant changes develop in the discourse; one's sense of life is also threatened. When conceptual organizations that are basic for a discourse change, the identity of the discourse changes, its sense of identity changes, and the ways of thinking and living of people related in the discourse change as well. The pain and disorientation that we expect in a person's upheaval occur on a large and equally subtle scale in discourses.

When the discursive changes occur "at the point closest to [its] own destruction," that is, when something repressed is released or when previously dominant meanings and values are made subservient to previously repressed meanings and values, the emerging new way of speaking and thinking will bring with it not only awareness of the repressiveness of the previous order. It will also bring with it thoughts and affects that are felt to be dangerous in the other discourse. Perhaps the perceived danger, however, will carry less repression, less of that kind of violence, and will develop with an expanded sense of life and vital diversity. Perhaps the language of difference will bring with it ways of speaking and thinking that carry in them affirmation of their own transformations. Perhaps its difference will be thinking in which the polarity of identity and difference does not exist. If that were the case, how would we speak and think?

2

Transvaluation in Beyond Good and Evil

Nietzsche transvalues his inherited language by combining countervailing, often contradictory words, ideas, desires, and beliefs. He arranges an interplay among them that produces transformed ideas, desires, beliefs, and associations among words. Transvaluation takes place as those interplays develop and proceed. Within the interplay different ideas, desires, and so forth struggle against each other through Nietzsche's irony, mockery, and reversals of standpoint as well as through his genealogies, which often make use of the very ideas and values that are being transformed in the genealogical process. His writing is a process in which the different words and ideas are so combined that their interaction produces ways of speaking and thinking that are distinct from those initial differences and their combinations: Nietzsche's writing initiates discursive processes that move away from his own thinking.

As we shall see, the idea of identity loses its discursive control through the force of transvaluation. In Nietzsche's writing things are interpreted as networks of forces, and those networks differentiate from other networks and from their own dominant hierarchies and patterns as they drive, combine, and exclude. Nietzsche perceives by reference to differences of power and ranking, and also by the different forces that constitute things and define their continuous changeability and replaceability. Hence the ideas and power that were formed under the influence of the idea of identity do not form a core of positive reference for Nietzsche. Those powers are continually transvalued, as we shall see, by combining their ideas with ideas hostile to them, by irony and mockery, and by undercutting the persuasion that differences depend on something substantial or subjective that gives differences an underlying sameness and identity in an otherwise chaotic play of forces. His discourse differentiates itself from the traditionally dominant influences by a transvaluing use of those influences. He finds in traditional thinking suppressed yet effective opposites that uproot the controlling identities and emphases, and particularly the controlling idea of identity. Whether identity, for example, is classically or dialectically conceived, it is found in Nietzsche's discourse to be a fiction without the power now in his language to organize and structure a persuasive way of thinking. Nietzsche and those after him are part of a way of thinking that finds radical differences borne nondialectically, primarily through repression, exclusion, or oversight, in all ideas and concepts. The differences are held in mind by the way things are combined in thought and language. Transvaluation is Nietzsche's way of combining ideas and values so as to call those ideas and values into question. It is a process that produces differences without reconciliation or the expectation of resolution. It produces a way of thinking that is controlled by processes of making differences. How this differencing emerges in Nietzsche's discourse helps to form a way of thinking in which differences without substance control conceptual relations.

The antimetaphysical discourse, because it is anti-*metaphysical*, is a metaphysical bearer. All of Nietzsche's leading ideas carry with them a metaphysical and Hebrew-Christian heritage. How the metaphysical heritage is carried and transformed into a discourse that is different enough to be antimetaphysical is one of the major issues of Nietzsche's discourse that continues long after him. This struggle between metaphysical and antimetaphysical ways of thinking is a dominant occurrence in his thinking. If the struggle is confronted metaphysically by lending system, unity, or explanatory resolution to the conflicts in his discourse, Nietzsche's thinking is not confronted on its own transvaluational terms. It can be thought through transvaluationally only by maintaining the struggles and allowing them to yield other thoughts and experiences that strive, differentiate, and develop without resolution into still other struggles. How the tension is maintained and what happens in that process is the issue of thought in this discursive strand. The discursive functions, not a person who thinks, are always the primary loci of power. That discursive quality itself—which transvalues subjectivity—in relation to the power of "subjectivity" and "person" is part of the tension that is to be maintained. Nietzsche's discourse has a quality of subjectivity that uproots itself and moves toward something different.

How does this bearing of metaphysics and its uprooting go on?

1. PASSING THROUGH THE PREJUDICES OF PHILOSOPHERS

Nietzsche is deeply a part of the ideological history that he terms metaphysical. That word *metaphysical* functions for him by naming a broad confederation of thinking and practice that have in common the ascendant ideas of truth, reason, morality, and God. *Beyond Good and Evil* begins with the questions, Who puts the question of truth? and, What wants truth? These questions in their context mean that we need to ask about the will that *seeks* and *wants* truth. In posing these two questions, Nietzsche sets in motion a series of thoughts that are designed to work with and through metaphysical thinking in relation to truth. He is a part of the way of thinking that he is able to see as optional. He wants to pursue a different option, to be molded by a movement of forces that he sees coming together in a new organization of valences, knowledges, and insights. He intends to think his way through his own metaphysical "nature" to a way of thinking that is dimly foreseen by him and that is still obscure in its details.

Truth is an issue of valences, of ordering forces, that give priority and status and thus also give hierarchy and subordination to a group of thoughts, practices, and values. Ignorance and error, for example, are lower in this way of thinking and acting than truth: in the discourse of truth, the powers opposing truth are not conceived as differences on the same plane with truth, but as differences that are lower because they lack the value of truth. Nietzsche notes that *value* means the power, the valence, to evaluate, organize, and rank order.

How do "we" evaluate this will of truth? We meet this will—Nietzsche calls the encounter "a rendezvous . . . of questions" (I.I)[4]—in its power, and the issue is, how are we to encounter it in a power of discourse other than that of the will to truth? To recognize that truth is a valence is a beginning. But that could lead quickly to our wanting to find the truth of truth, a desire that we shall find Nietzsche undergoing frequently, and one that often holds him in the discourse ruled by the will to truth. The opening recognition can lead, however—it has the force to lead us—toward a way of thinking that is not governed by will to truth. *That* move, and not the one toward the truth of truth, is a "risk." If we are not asking about the truth of truth, what are we asking?

Nietzsche's exploratory move is designed to shift the discourse away from traditional, dominating interest in truth and honesty, pervaded as it is with the spirit of seriousness, and to alert us to self-deception in the name of self-honesty. We attempt to think of truth as originating out of its opposite. The traditional idea of an originary basis for truth functions predominantly in this effort. But if the originary basis is not being or a being, if it is nothing that can be thought literally or that has identity and order, then the idea of an originary basis is put into question by the way it is thought. Now it is in combination with absence of identity and order. Nietzsche is not creating an insoluble paradox on his terms; he is devaluing a valence by combining it with counterforces. Thinking the value of the will to truth in this way results in a power situation different from that which accompanies thinking the value of truth within truth's rule. Both the ideas of truth and of originary basis are being thought through to a situation that denies them the power of being and nondiscursive identity. In this reconstituted thinking, truth, being, and identity look like prejudgments in a history of evaluations, or like strong assertions of belief founded in traceable interests and feelings.

Further, a different will is created in the new combination. As this organization operates, it wants to be. Its will to be, its immediate self-affirmation, drives in a direction quite different from the will to truth, which is the desire to be on the part of the truth discourse. Different interests and possibilities emerge. In this changed discourse, one begins to undergo a different thinking. Different attitudes and behaviors emerge as preferable in the changed hierarchy. This risk is underway as the long-lasting stabilities of the other discourse begin to melt away.[5]

The difference from truth that gives focus and estimate in Nietzsche's thinking is "instinct" (I.2–4). At times the concept of instinct proposes an identity for force that is different from the previously ascribed identity, that is, instinct creates normative values different from those that the will to truth creates. Nietzsche then seems to be replacing one faith by another, that is, he affirms the idea that life force is not circumscribed by moral rules or laws. This force is not rational. It "guides" consciousness. It is not regulated by the principles by which we regulate ourselves. It spawns all manner of estimates. It is life and life-giving. It is "untruth." When he thinks this way, Nietzsche is a counter-metaphysics metaphysician. He develops a set of counterproposals that continue to make claims as to what the real and true state of affairs is.

The injection of instinct into the discourse of truth in Nietzsche's manner, however, moves toward an emerging discourse that is not counter-metaphysics, but a way of thinking that is nonmetaphysical. Falseness of judgment is becoming less a problem: the issue is whether a group of evaluations are life-promoting and life-preserving (I.4). Often self-aware fictions that encourage play—fictions that love fictions—put people in touch with a liveliness that had been demoted below the self-unaware fictions of logic or reality-in-itself, a liveliness that now enjoys dominance over "true" judgments. The idea of instinct, which for Nietzsche means energy without truth or a priori law, leads to thinking that the idea of instinct needs to collapse on itself or lead away from itself in some way that prevents a literalization and a consequent metaphysics of instinct energy. As the idea of instinct divests literal claims about being, universal laws, and self-identical reality of their power to convince, it can also function as a deliteralizing force regarding itself. It does not mean to be thought noncontingently. It too is replaceable. The idea of instinct is a force for transformation that has its force as it drives one to think through it to a different idea in a different way of thinking: its power in a hierarchy of ideas transforms the will to truth into a new kind of desire and a different grouping of concepts that we shall discuss.

Nietzsche was always under the sway of the ideas of noncontingency, ahistoricity, and timeless energy. Those ideas exercise a continuing power in his discussion of instinct and body, as well as of will to power and eternal recurrence, as we shall see. But those ideas are continually in question by virtue of the emerging organization of forces in which contingency (discussed as the function of will to power), historicity, (discussed as the genealogical descent fo all ideas, values, and practices), and field-dependent energy (discussed in terms of return and recurrence) have the privilege of challenging their previous masters. While Nietzsche is promising a higher honesty, he is also thinking that philosophy is "personal confession" (I.6) and that judgments are fictions (I.5). Even as one thinks that these two claims are themselves not fictions, Nietzsche turns to the descent of philosophical claims to show contingent plays of forces that generate and define the powers of thought, their efficacy, and that never show references beyond their efficacy and the organization within which they are effective.

We shall see that will and will to power are thought in two ways: as ahistorical energy and as drive that is found only in contingent organizations of forces. In the latter way of thinking, "force" is nothing in itself, but is instead a relational occurrence. When we think in the first context, the instinctive basis of thought means that reasons and rules are founded in an indiscriminate energy that yields *all* differences and opposites. When we think in the second manner, the instinctive basis of thought means that instinct and its will are relational events in a hierarchical, changing order of forces. As the order changes, the instincts change. The life that instincts preserve on the first reading is something like a cosmic force. On the second reading, "life" means *this* life at this time in this history. The second option makes "instinct" and "life" discourse-specific.

The difference in thinking that Nietzsche seeks, in contrast to the "self-development in a cold, pure, divinely unconcerned dialectic" (I.5), is a play of descriptions, evaluations, and senses for energy that experiments with combinations and hierarchies of claims. This different thinking does not have an overwhelming interest in certainty, literal truth, or speculative coherence. At least one side of his thinking is not looking for "truth," but for configurations that move through themselves with the energy that the configurations produce and promote. Not an energy that looks for its own *reflection* by reacting back on itself (not self-protective or dialectical), but a transvaluational one that instinctively moves beyond itself to other transforming configurations. In such thinking, the idea of drive is like a battering ram that breaks apart the wall of certainty, an idea that need not revert back to itself by literalizing or giving itself substantial endurance. Nietzsche avoids the literalizing option often by following out multiple drives, seeing their various and conflicting organizations, and interpreting them as a play of forces rather than as disclosing a reality outside of the given types of life.[6]

If we imagine nature to be deceptive, indifferent, wasteful, without mercy and justice, the effect of this idea may be to displace the inherited, broad notion of nature as an imagined regulative principle. It can incite one to replace that idea of nature with another idea that excites imaginative variations and the inclusion of references to nonregularities, to dislocations, violations of patterns, and processes of dismantling and reconstituting (I.9). Imagining nature in this way does not have to propose a right teaching about nature. It gives, in Nietzsche's instance, a way of thinking that experiences the strength of the human desire to be in accord with "nature," and the strong but unconscious desire to violate "nature" and to be different. The desire to violate "nature," that is, to imagine things according to the interests of the human species, now becomes clearer. This thinking gives an occasion for us to think of our thinking as arbitrarily different from "nature," not as naturally like it. We may now think of "nature" as itself issuing from a desire of the species to be measured, purposeful, certain, and just. The desire that generates "nature" is not founded in "nature." It is rather an insistent interest on the part of the human organization of forces in preserving its human difference in an otherwise unhuman setting. It is an interest in creating our own "nature." This self-creating and self-preserving creature creates "nature" that lacks the distinctions of the human creature, that is, a sense of justice, a knowledge of truth, the ability to worship and to sin, and so forth. "Nature" functions in the service of the human will to distinction, privilege, and domination (I.9). "Nature" appears as a willful projection in the service of human willpower.

In the instance of those philosophers who think back to "the faith of former times," and who, in their desire for those happy certainties of immortality of soul and "the old God," feel mistrust, disbelief, disgust, and scorn for "modern ideas" and "modern reality": what is Nietzsche's suggestion? That one encourage the strength of their disgust, support their energy of refusal, because it is that energy, once increased, that can carry thinking and feeling forward and away, not back to the present holding point, but on and out to thinking with a power that does not yearn for the certainty of another era, for the past plays of energy and force (I.10).

Nietzsche takes a traditional idea, for example, the idea of soul, and notes how it perverted a preceding idea of soul as breath of life, a perversion that develops in a combination of "metaphysical need" and an atomistic persuasion: the ideas of individuality and of deathlessness merge with soul (I.12). He now retains the word, accepts the perversion in its history, and creates transvaluing hypotheses by using such ideas as "mortal soul," "soul as subjective multiplicity," and "soul as social structure of the drives and affects." He works with the submerged idea of a breathlike organization of affect and power, excising from it the later accretions of deathlessness, unity, identity, and ideological certainty. In a movement that conserves the idea of soul with its pervasive sense of life and breath, Nietzsche also transforms the "metaphysical need" for exactness of stance and the fearful need for individual reassurance into an idea that carries its tradition without control by fear of death, drive for certainty, or substantial identity. By this move he understands himself to have a situation, a collection of thought forces, that encourages invention and discovery. Of what? Who knows? Certainly the metaphysical idea is both undercut and thought through to a group of directions and possibilities that, though dimly present, did not have priority in the metaphysical notion. A part of his inherited tradition is maintained, while its hold is loosened, nuanced, let slip. In the play of ideas that accompanies this process, the idea's force wanes, is "forgotten." It no longer has the power to organize other ideas and feelings as it once did. This is not necessarily that kind of forgetfulness by which one does not know that the other idea existed. One can certainly know about it, but it will not have much power in the way it is known about; it is similar, perhaps, to our knowledge of Victorian sexuality.

By pluralizing the idea of will into plays of forces, by showing, for example, that willing is physical sensing, thinking, and affect, that "it" appears always in a hierarchical stance with multiple dimensions and submissions: by thinking that will is no one thing, Nietzsche detaches will from identity and from an association of willing, subject, and essence (I.19). By this thinking Nietzsche makes optional the expectation that will is a state of being. The possibility emerges that willing is a "complex social structure of many souls" (I.19), not primarily the action of a commander or a state of being, but an optional, genealogically descended interplay of control and submission, fluid and without substance or projecting subject.

The order of thinking—Nietzsche compares it to the systematic relation of members of a continent's fauna (I.20)—occurs with the strongest powers arranging and organizing a group of other conceptual forces. Powers establish dominations. These power dominations function through systematic structures characteristic of the particular organization. One is led to think some thoughts, but cannot think others that are natural in a different organization. Remembering unconsciously the originary powers in various settings is more likely than imagining something strange to the established hierarchy of wills, ideas, possibilities, and pariahs. To the thought of order, system, and necessity Nietzsche adds the image of contingent necessity—a fauna on a continent, an interruptible and thoroughly changeable "natural" order. In his discourse the emerging experiences of history, mutation, and relative necessities are added to the metaphysical discourses of order, eternity, and thought, thereby forming a new imbalance among the "animals," a different struggle for ordering rights, a climatic change that weakens the strong and creates the conditions for different ordering powers and a changed species. Specifically, the verbs of temporal forces replace or bypass the nouns and adjectives of eternal variety. Origin and the images of mutation are joined. The chosen verbs, as we shall see in detail, suggest the dominance of impermanence. The ideas of orders now suggest insecurity, possible fear, certainly a desire for expression that is localized in fluid relations and not in subjects. Instead of resemblance and intimacy with nonhistorical and noncontingent founding Orders, orders emerge through processes that resemble only other processes. In this changing mixture the expectation emerges that "owing to the unconscious domination and guidance by similar grammatical functions everything is prepared at the outset for a similar development and sequence of philosophical systems" (I.20). We are able to entertain seriously and with positive affect the likelihood that rules of speech and practices of expression mold all these "inevitabilities" that we find "metaphysically" convincing and obvious. Permanence, in contrast to change, may be rather more the function of grammar than of "reality." The ideas of transcendence, essences outside of historical development, and timeless necessities are in a transvaluational process.

Nietzsche uses the strategy of eliminating certain forceful ideas that have played dominant, discourse-forming roles and that are now able to be thought of as optional, for example, free will. Try to put it out of your head, along with its opposite. One might undergo the possibility that free will is a strategy for thinking of identity as something in itself. This out-putting allows the "device" of free will, with its context of cause, effect, compulsion, in-itself, for-each-other, constraint, and so forth, to appear as strange, unpersuasive. As a device, the free will complex is understandable. But as a truth with metaphysical verity, it now looks awkward and out of place because of its optional context (I.21). It is not strange to want what is lacking, to desire, for example, to be self-caused or positively related to a being that is self-caused, in a discourse of desire for certainty and immortality. But it is strange to be in another discourse that has no such desires and to see people who deeply share these desires when they are known to be no longer inevitable.

"We sail right *over* morality, we crush, we destroy perhaps the remains of our own morality by daring to make our voyage there—but what matter are *we*! Never yet did a *profounder* world of insight reveal itself to daring travelers . . ." (I.23). This leonine statement indicates a primary purpose in Nietzsche's discourse: to go over or bypass a region of language, thought, and practice in an effort to let another region—"a *profounder* world of insight*"—become apparent and effective in spite of the anxiety and self-unsureness (Nietzsche uses the image of seasickness) that accompany the emergence of a new region. By the combined actions of passing over, restructuring, and thinking through a way of life, one is in a position to undergo freedoms and spiritualities different from those possible in the transgressed organization. A different speaking and thinking emerge, not primarily a new subjectivity. Different things come forth and stand out, a different alertness develops. A new discourse threatens to become the space, the scene of life.

Finally, by asking from where do I get the concept of thinking?, Nietzsche raises in a preliminary way the issue of descent: What interests have helped to form this concept of thinking? What kinds of willing yielded the idea of an ego that thinks? What interests have made believable the claim that immediate certainty resides in thinking? From where does the associated insistence on truth come? In this way he displaces a felt certainty with felt uncertainty in the activity of thinking. We are thinking the questions and the issues of descent in a type of activity that one expected to be certain of itself. The dual thought that the state of immediate certainty is replaceable and that immediate certainty is a product of a traceable discourse, this dual thought is a replacement that reorganizes a thinking life and makes optional a felt and fundamental necessity in the previous thinking arrangement (I.16). The arrangements themselves are interpretations. No "one" is doing the interpreting. And the interpretation alters when a displacement, a replacement, or another reorganizing event occurs.

But there is also an important aspect of Nietzsche's thinking that carries forward the metaphysical tradition. He states that the convictions of philosophers are based on personal or perhaps group interests—on specific dislikes, on privileges, distastes, or group leverage—and that we can understand those interests if we see that they are expressions of something much more fundamental, that is, life or the will to power (I.9). If we understand the will to power as life's drive for itself, we look for a flowing, dynamic reality to replace personal and collective will. Our task then is to live according to the energy that is "wasteful beyond measure, indifferent beyond measure, without purposes and consideration, without mercy and justice, fertile and desolate and uncertain at the same time" (I.9). And that task pushes us to agree with Nietzsche's judgment that energy is just that way, as distinct to the way it is said essentially to be in other teachings.

Or, when Nietzsche encourages the strength of disgust and disbelief regarding modern ideas and reality on the part of those who are "trying at bottom to win back something that was formerly an even *securer* possession, ... perhaps the 'immortal soul,' perhaps 'the old God'" (I.10), he appears to be saying that mistrust of those ideas is right, and that by encouraging mistrust one will gain the strength to let go of the old certainties. That strength of conviction on Nietzsche's part, his own joyful certainty that those old ideas are silly when they function as objects of faith—his own strength of belief—asks for agreement or disproof. It invites followers, as well as the enemies that Nietzsche said that he wanted. It is not a doctrine, but it is clearly a position that can be assumed.

"A living thing seeks above all to *discharge* its strength—life itself is *will to power*; self-preservation is only one of the indirect and most frequent *results*" (I.13). *What* does Nietzsche mean? He appears to be talking here about some kind of *what*, and not addressing some power or other that happens to occasion the claim. He speaks of life itself, says that it *is* will to power; he claims that discharge and not self-preservation is its primary characteristic. The claim is opposed specifically to the scientific claim that self-preservation is the dominant instinct of an organic being, and by this opposition Nietzsche makes his claim a candidate for replacing the scientific one. He makes will to power a principle that one should maintain and defend, and the functions of fantasy, imagination, and pluralization fade in the background. The demands of method and systematic relations among principles with the power of explanation control the foreground. They are stated as a metaphysical interpretation.

Nietzsche further contrasts the idea that nature is a law-abiding organism—an idea that emphasizes sameness under law—to his own thought that will to power shows, not the conformities of "nature," but its tyrannies. Will to power, not law, is the continuing necessity of "nature." Will to power is not subject to law. This claim is a frequent one for Nietzsche, and means that will to power exceeds all ordering principles, and to the extent that ordering principles are historical and genealogical, will to power is apparently not historical. Nietzsche is willing to say, "Supposing that [this claim of mine] is only interpretation . . . well, so much the better" (I.22). On his terms, it must be an interpretation. But he appears not to have appropriated the possibility that will to power itself is to be interpreted as genealogical. Nietzsche's direction is clearly away from notions of substance and transcendental essences. Until, however, the will to power is thought of as originative, optional, and only circumstantially necessary, it will tend to have the status of a transcendental energy that explains historical processes. Nietzsche's statement "so much the better" indicates that he wants a process of disagreement in which ultimate laws and forms can be subjected to irony and made apparent as interpretations. His putting will to power in opposition to natural law, however, at best obscures its own dependence on contingent configurations, and at worst suggests that it fills the space of "essential nature" previously filled by law.

He speaks also of the "doctrine of the development of the will to power" as the basis for understanding psychological states (I.23). On the one hand, Nietzsche has in mind that psychologists have feared and repressed anything that looks like will to power and have injected destructive "moral prejudices" as axioms into their research. He also means that will to power is the basis for all psychological development, that it is *the* fundamental drive, and that it is to replace the notion of human nature.

The "prejudices of philosophers" are thus borne forward in the first section of *Beyond Good and Evil* by different interpretations of ideas that are within the metaphysical tradition. The power of explanatory thought is retained, and thoughts are retained that propose that something runs through all orders and hierarchies. But those "prejudices" are also thought in a process that develops a configuration of forces different from those that Nietzsche sees as definitive of metaphysical ways of thinking. Those forces begin to produce affections, concepts, and ways of thinking that function in a nonmetaphysical (as distinct from antimetaphysical) attunement. They begin to create a very different geography of valence and interest. We shall follow first the tensions created by the presence of metaphysical ideas in a process designed to transvalue them, and then we shall see in detail how Nietzsche's discourse develops the transvaluational process in such a way that it undergoes transvaluation.

2. THE TENSIONS OF THE FREE SPIRIT

We shall look at selected paragraphs of section II of *Beyond Good and Evil* first, in subsections noted by "a" (for instance, 1.a), with the Nietzschean emphasis on what happens in the experimental thinking itself, and second, in the "b" subsections, with the emphasis on what is thought and the thought's explanatory power. In both subsections we shall follow the ideas and their combinations in the noted paragraph of Nietzsche's chapter. The two emphases that we shall underscore are always in tension with each other. The first is transvaluational and creates an occasion for overcoming inherited hierarchies of thought and meaning; it undercuts the explanatory and metaphysical meanings in the ideas that it uses. It initiates a different discourse by giving prominence to some of the forces that are subjugated in the tradition (for example, the spirit of irony, contradiction, play without moral purposes, guiltlessness), and by giving power and emphasis to forces that are being released by the tradition in spite of its own interests to the contrary (for example, suspicion, cruel curiosity, historical development without metaphysical purpose, free spiritedness). The second emphasis, which we develop in the "b" subsections, subtly ignores the discursive direction that is emerging in *Beyond Good and Evil* and continues to place weight on the content and identity of such ideas as will to power, the higher type of man, and the model of the artist rather than on their own transvaluational functions. In this second emphasis, Nietzsche speaks as though he were replacing some traditional ideas—such as God, human nature, and reason—with ideas that are better because they are more accurate concerning the realities in question. This tension in Nietzsche's thought between the transvaluational functions of combinations of ideas and the quasi-metaphysical content of the ideas themselves becomes itself an important occurrence for developing the discourse. The tension itself displays the transition-in-process toward a discourse in which, on Nietzsche's terms, metaphysical hierarchies and ways of thinking would have no force. In this tension we see the force of Nietzsche's inheritance and the force of an emerging discourse that is quite different from his inheritance.

1.a *"O SANCTA SIMPLICITAS!"* (II.24)

We humans have made everything around us clear and free and easy. Our falsifications show an inevitability that undercuts and betrays the dominant energy of human order and identity: our flesh and blood are made and invested by our creator. Our creator is a history of morals and principles and values that are designed to simplify and falsify an alien and different chaos—a chaos in the sense that "it" is not of us or by us or for us: "We have contrived to retain our ignorance in order to enjoy an almost inconceivable freedom." This freedom and its attendant ignorance are unconscious parts of human orders. We have sought to be wholly ourselves, to establish our difference in the totally nonhuman setting with an insistent, fierce affirmation of human identity. Our affirmation of *our* difference suppresses the nonhuman energy that empowers the nonhuman differences around us and in us that show only indifference and silence before our interests and wills. We have made rules and laws in order to suppress this violent indifference not only in our knowledges of the world, but in our knowledges of ourselves. We banished or killed or punished those individuals who showed to us that the human was a fragile organization on top of a mindless, flowing energy. We *will* have ignorance, and the cost of that ignorance—the intensity of oppression that it requires, and the justifications and falsehoods, the scheming that must not come to light, the hatred, the stupidity, self-injury, and destruction: these costs constitute a type of joy in surviving as this human difference in the nonhuman clash of forces. We refine our errancy, our difference, by establishments of knowledge, and we refine both the establishments and the knowledges into essential wisdom and quintessential truth. We include and exclude people in this process, repress or destroy contrary urges and interests, raise the stakes to life and death, and experience uniquely human joy in affirming as absolute these embodiments of human anxiety and desire. Our certainties and truths articulate darkly our urge to be—"our ignorance"—and yield for us joyful oppositions between good and evil, God and Satan, creation and destruction. They also embody a primordial terror of life energy, of the nonhuman, the without-order-principle-or-hope. Hence by our principles and hopes we are created to oppress our will to be in willing to be as *we* are. Our way of becoming who we are has invested in it a self-destructiveness that makes spiritual self-consumption and sickness of soul characteristics of the species, a part of the organization, a member of the board. Our simplicities are holy in their loving life. And our holiness is simple in its refusal of its life energy.

By understanding this holy simplicity and affirming the life of *this* understanding, we achieve a distance from the holy and simple discourse that has played a large role in creating the human. Another language and thinking arise from the oppressed energy, and a rearranged hierarchy begins to emerge. It appears to be a different discourse that can make human necessities optional for another kind of life, perhaps a kind of life that is no less falsified, but one made of different life affirmations.

The emerging distance from holy simplicity generates differences from the human. The question for Nietzsche is not whether this distance is good or evil. The distance, rather, generates ways of living and thinking that are not bound to the human creator, to that organization of practices in which life affirmation occurs in the bondage of life-repressive orders. The values of this distance are valences in a play of forces that urge themselves forward and outward in a different mixture, one that gives ascendancy to life affirmation in its lack of humanity. Different plays of energy, different alertnesses, different thinking emerge. The space of life alters. A different force of creation is generated. This distance is thus an affirmation of a growing difference from the human, from "man." It is not only a bridge; it is also an occurrence of transmutation.

1.b "EVEN IF *LANGUAGE*, HERE AS ELSEWHERE, WILL NOT GET OVER ITS AWKWARDNESSES..."

When Nietzsche speaks of overcoming the human heritage of life affirmation through life repression, will to power functions as a principle of continuity. One might well note that this continuity indicates on Nietzsche's terms that his thinking is all-too-human. But even with that recognition, Nietzsche continues to think with a kind of overarching continuity. His thinking did not make will to power a regional necessity except in the external sense that he wanted it treated with suspicion and foresaw a way of living and thinking quite different from his own. He loved his own "error," and also expected this affirmation of will to power to lead beyond itself to a different, "higher" affirmation.

Nietzsche's imagery of higher and lower types of men, by which he details the spiritual inequality among people, strongly suggests a higher order of morality in spite of his consistent denial of that implication. Higher men are free, more sensitive, noble, reckless, subtle, and so forth. Nietzsche frequently thought of a higher order of human reality, a remainder of his tradition with which and against which he thought. His countervailing thought is of transitional states that are not higher or lower on a vertical continuum, but that are different, that break the inherited continua. It is nuance, irony, and violation that mark best the difference among humans. But those differences nevertheless are also characterized in the imagery and value structures of the morality he wanted to overcome.

2.a ". . . GO AWAY. FLEE INTO CONCEALMENT." (II.25–26)

This distance from the older discourse, however, can be lost when a thinker becomes too engaged by opposition. One must beware of defending oneself or inviting martyrdom for truth's sake: "It spoils all the innocence and fine neutrality of your conscience; it makes you headstrong against objections and red rags." By vigorous defense and the hostility of philosophical infighting, the occurrence of the unholy distance is modified back in the direction of repressive life affirmation. It tends to congeal the identity of the specific philosopher, and thus resists the movement of open, free alertness generated by the entrance of this distance. Better to let the spinning go on in the new arrangement, even when it looks crazy to the suppressed orders, than to regain recognized human sanity. "After all," says Nietzsche the comforter, "you know . . . that there might be a more laudable truthfulness in every little question mark that you place after your special words and favorite doctrines (and occasionally after yourselves) than in all the solemn gestures and trumps before accusers and law courts." Letting the distance have its way means choosing "the *good* solitude, the free, playful, light solitude that gives you, too, the right to remain good in some sense." In this way, by giving up the identities of opposition, the vengeance, ascetic ideals, and spirit of seriousness that are an invested part of the other way fade and lose even their indirect power (their valence) for the different thinking and sensing. The thinker is so far removed that the older forces of creation and perseverance cannot be rekindled.

Solitude and distance thus go together. Not particularly the solitude of meditation far from the noisy crowd, but rather a solitude that maintains an emerging distance from the bondages that have spawned our dominant ways of thinking and living. This solitude begets forgetfulness. At least some of the patterns of life lose their domination, that is, they are forgotten in emerging orders, and a different dynamics can develop. Broken connections with the powers of the all-too-human, with what is so natural as to seem to be a law, with the inevitable associations of good sense and laudable intelligence, with what always has been elevated and depressed: the maintenance of this break is part of the discipline Nietzsche advises for those who would think in the emerging discourse.

And one takes help whenever he can find it. Even the cynicism of those who still live in resentment can help the one who thinks in distance from the established discourses of knowledge and truth. Cynics give distance mixed with hostility and perhaps cruelty. By virtue of their cynicism they are inside a process that they do not understand, one that moves toward freedom from their own hostility. They are involved in a human distance that mistrusts itself and holds onto what it also wants to leave behind. "When anyone speaks 'badly'—and not even '*wickedly*'—of man, the lover of knowledge should listen subtly and diligently. . . . For the indignant and whoever perpetually tears and lacerates with his own teeth himself (or as a substitute, the world, or God, or society) may indeed, morally speaking, stand higher [that is, in greater distance from human enslavements] than the laughing and self-satisfied satyr . . ." (II.26). Such listening is not pleasant or satisfying, but it can help as one suffers the transmutations given by distance from our complex networks of life-denying values, habits, and attitudes.[7]

2.b "A SERIOUS WORD"

Although Nietzsche is ironic in this "serious word" to the "most serious," he does speak of our remaining "good in some sense" by this solitude and distance. The struggle of intense opposition makes us "bad." Not totally unlike a monk, the thinker is to avoid the tumult and distractions of the so miserably constituted world. He is to let the movement to something like a higher kingdom, not a kingdom of ends but a place of greater innocence and spiritual health, give meaning to his difference, withdrawal, and sacrifice. This "choice human being," an unholy mendicant, is a seeker, a person of arrogant hospitality for the common, one who is contrasted to the liars of the everyday world.

Certainly the appeal of this and other similar thoughts is deeply rooted in the monastic image as well as in the classical person of wisdom and religious strength. Heraclitus *should* provide the image. But even he is mediated to us here by the masters of religious withdrawal. And deeply within this language is the practice of obedience to a higher power that or who "calls" a few select souls out from the foolish crowd of humanity.

3.a REVERSAL OF PERSPECTIVE (II.32)

When actions had power among people because of the actions' "force of success or failure," not because of their origin or intention, their power was "reactive." The action rebounded on the actor through benefits or losses consequent to the action. Those actions that brought desired things were by someone to be praised or followed—not by a good person, but by a great or effective person. The one who fled in fear and confusion but found the urgently needed water was nonetheless lauded. This reactive force is contrasted to the proactive force of states that originate value. Families of origin and status by birth appear to Nietzsche closely linked with the idea that how an action's descent, that is, from noble or ignoble intentions, constitutes its value. The merit of the intention produced the value of the action.

The "reversal and fundamental shift" from the retroactive organization to the organization of origin is matched in power by the shift now from the organization of origin to the organization of the will to power. Valence does not originate in a lineage of character, intuition, habit, and identity, but in power without intention. Intentions are signs of a more basic energy, and hence all states of mind and identity need further interpretation. Identity, intention, subjectivity: these are signs and symptoms to be thought through by reference to will to power. And will to power is "unintentional." It is not interpreted by reference to its signs. It runs through morality as well as overrunning morality in the self-overcoming of the moral organization, an instance of which is taking place in this thirty-second paragraph.

By interpreting the "moral period" in a descent *from* the premoral time, when reference to either self-knowledge or moral intentions did not play a role in determining what is worthy of praise, *to* an extramoral time when the moral subject is replaced by power without subjectivity, Nietzsche indicates that morality and moral subjectivity are entirely interpretive organizations. He shows that morality developed by means of a reversal and fundamental shift away from a long-standing orientation that had developed neither selfhood nor value by descent. He shows that lineage and descent have their roots, their originating power, in the nonmoral habit of establishing social worth by family history. Slowly the intending, self-knowing subject takes the space of family tree and assumes the position of originator of the value of actions.

The power of descent, however, undergoes a reversal as the moral organization transforms into the will to power orientation: the descent of the moral organization shows the developmental nature of morality itself, and when descent functions as a dominant interpretive reference, one can see the "long secret work" of extramoral power. One can see that power functioning long before morality could be imagined. Morality is a sign of the nonmoral, a force that preceded morality in human history, and intentions are signs of that unintentional force that was manifest in the premoral period. *Descent*, which crafted a reversal of the premoral period (a reactive force of action transforms into proactive aristocratic descent), changes now from a principle of moral authority to an idea that shows a historical development and the optional and replaceable manner of authority. Morality overcomes itself through its depth organization of descent and is discovered as an historically developed interpretation of power.

The lineage of retroactive force can also be seen. In the premoral period an action rebounded to the actor by virtue of its consequences. We are now prepared to understand that this premoral organization continues in the moral era as the power of moral practices to react against the nonmoral energy that empowers them. As the intending agent gains dominance, the absence of intending energy in the agent's *drive* is felt as threat, as enemy, and the agent's intentionality rebounds against its nonagent sources. We will follow this idea more closely below.

The premoral organization thus continues in a transmuted way in the lineage, of moral life, and we are led to expect that the history of both the premoral and the moral periods will be found in Nietzsche's own efforts to think through the interpretation of energy and power as unintentional and extramoral. The negatives, the *un* and the *extra*, carry a lineage that is being overcome. How else could it be, since the reversal taking place in Nietzsche's thinking and the interpretive organization of will to power also mark an era, not an end, not a fulfillment, and not an absolute? "The long secret work" is a process with describable organizations and transmutations. And nothing else. We need not go beyond the history of basic organizations of life to interpret history in a discourse controlled by will to power. In this context, will to power may be thought of as nothing other than one historical development with many others.

3.b "THE DECISIVE VALUE OF AN ACTION LIES PRECISELY IN WHAT IS *UNINTENTIONAL* IN IT."

All rules, practices, and imperatives are found in "periods" of time. They are fundamental interpretations. Morality is as much a contingent organization as ancient Egyptian religion or alchemy were. But the energy that runs through these fundamental interpretations and that is specified as the will to power is not clearly an intrinsically historical process. Nietzsche did not think of his own interpretations as fulfilling an eternal energy. But he did appear to think that will to power was not exclusively a historically developed, powerful interpretation. Is there not a cosmic process being named? Something present to and outside of the interpretive organization? Doesn't will to power pervade all the historical forms of energy? Is it not revealed, for example, in the self-overcoming of morality? And does that not place Nietzsche's idea of the will to power rather strongly in the dominant tradition of Western thought? He disagrees with the particular claim about power and energy in the theistic traditions, but he does think of something timeless found in temporal instances. Will to power is the continuing force throughout the transformation of the human creature, a force that appears to run through all things, whether human or not.

4.a "A DUTY TO SUSPICION" (II.34)

When Nietzsche speaks of duty, we are well advised to be suspicious. Duty to what? Certainly not to ourselves, and the will to power breaches both duties and duty. We are advised in this section to "squint maliciously out of every abyss of suspicion." Nietzsche often thinks of malicious squinting as a sign of resentment and hostility regarding life, but here he uses this embodied suspicion positively. Another transmutation is going on. Hostility against life, which in the instance of this paragraph is taken to characterize bourgeois life, is now turned on the sureness of a world that is lived as though it were simply and literally there. It reverses a fundamental conviction of bourgeois life, and in the reversal a power of suspicion regarding life is turned against itself. This assumption, invested with that seriousness that looks for exactly the way things truly are, characterizes not only bourgeois life but a major part of the intellectual and spiritual life of the age. When we assume the duty of suspicion regarding this standing world, something nondutiful develops: a major difference emerges. Shades of differences blend and flow, truth and appearance lose their opposition, estimate and thinking align. Fantasy, imagination, and world assume kinship. Nietzsche is not making the literal claim that everything is a perspective. He is saying that a product of suspicion in the face of literalism and "realism" is a different kind of world event, one invested with a lightness of flow, an absence of necessity of resentment, ascetic ideals, and bad conscience. Fiction, the opposite of reality in the passing and transmuting discourse, has appeal and possibility. Even the duty of suspicion fades in the emerging interplay of forces as one is carried by thought play more than by judgment, and finds the world in an enjoyment belonging to no one. The world's erroneousness, its deviation from the firm and sure and from metaphysical arrangements, begins to fill the space of "truth." Another order is coming.

4.b "ON THE BASIS OF PERSPECTIVE"

"It is no more than a moral prejudice that truth is worth more than mere appearance.... There would be no life at all if not on the basis of perspective estimates and appearances." While Nietzsche rejects the rightness of literal knowledge, he replaces it with a thorough perspectivalism. The artist is the one who knows how to recognize and use shades and degress of apparentness. The thinker, like the artist, is to create organizations of ideas—perspectives—and to see that "reality" *is* perspective. Nietzsche claims and means that the world is fiction, that is, that truth is fiction. Our task is to think that situation persistently, until we no longer expect literal or objective truths. Nietzsche is making basic epistemological and ontological claims that cannot be conceived thoroughly in the malicious squint of suspicion.

5.a "THINKING IS MERELY A RELATION OF . . . DRIVES TO EACH OTHER" (II.36)

As Nietzsche develops his hypothesis that will to power is primary and primitive force to which all organic functions can be traced, he reaffirms his claim that thinking is a relation among drives and passions that are themselves relationally constituted. The beginning supposition that nothing else is real except "our world of desires and passions" drives us to see that thinking is an articulation of will to power. Just as will to power does not begin in lack or absence but is a continuous process of plenty, of superfluity, thinking for Nietzsche is not necessarily driven by a need-based consumptiveness. It occurs in an overabundance of interests, lineages, and returning energy for moving through and beyond its given moments. Thinking and its energy give profusion. They produce aims and interests rather than being defined by any one or any group of aims and interests, including the will-to-power group. Thinking and its energy produce subjectivities but are not themselves products of subjectivity. They produce rationality and eros-looking-for-fulfillment. Thinking produces ideas, hypotheses, images, experiments, influences, systems, and insight, but it is not defined by the contents that it produces. Thinking is made up of relations among drives, and is not a single thing or a single group of things. Thinking changes with the forces and drives among which "it" plays. In its kinship with will to power, it is no more essentially human than it is essentially anything else. As articulation of will to power, thinking returns to itself rather than being defined by what it yields.

Hence Nietzsche proposes an "experiment" by asking the question whether the idea of will to power sufficiently interprets the material, organic world. What is the purpose of this experiment, which is founded in purposeless energy? To show that a unified will theory explains foundationally all life? It would be a peculiar deception that claimed even to itself no deception at all, but complete theoretical adequacy articulated in literal language—unless the experiment intensified thinking-will, gave renewed power to thinking, and in this process generated a different situation for a new thinking, one probably quite different from this experiment in thought.

By proposing the unified will-to-power hypothesis after facing the duty to be suspicious and thinking ironically about serious searches for truth, Nietzsche suggests that *this* idea of will to power both addresses the monistic, metaphysical interests and carries out the will to power's mode of life: it complicates, multiplies, disjoins, and bifurcates when there are stances of unity and totality. It adds and subtracts in relation to simple ideas and answers. It severs unions and disrupts harmonies. Nietzsche's proposal that an inorganic, goalless, nonrational, nonintentional abundance of energy interprets the force of all organisms, all unities and totalities, urges us to experiment with the thought that totality, unity, and identity cannot tell us enough or even much about life.

This experiment is expressed in a language of explanation, final unity, and univocity of force. But its own force is to put that language into question. Its apparent hope for a true doctrine creates immediate dissatisfaction with that apparent hope. Nietzsche is thinking in the tension that the hypothesis creates. That is a kind of thinking that we shall hear more about.

5.b A DEMAND BY THE CONSCIENCE OF METHOD

Nietzsche had an emerging hypothesis to pursue: if all "reality," however "reality" is understood, is an expression of will to power, we will be able to understand all events as effects of will. If our desires and passions "give" us everything real and we ourselves are creatures of will, we are not necessarily separated from the nonhuman world. Will may be connected with will such that our willing is our fundamental connection with all things—*if* all things or drives are will-like, not because of our process of presenting things to ourselves, but because drive and will are ramifications and developments of something common for all. If will *causes* will, then connections and concretions are all of the same process. And if drive, instinct, and will are basically will to power "as *my* proposition has it," then we "have gained the right to determine *all* efficient force univocally as—*will to power*.... It [this world] would be 'will to power' and nothing else...."

If Nietzsche is not speaking ironically or in some form of double-talk, he believes (he speaks of "our faith") that he should pursue this possibility for explanation in order to develop a dynamic, drive-based interpretation of all things—a rereading of matter and energy that will show the fundamental presence of will to power in everything. Then an account of will to power is an account of the entire world. Nietzsche is suggesting a general theory of instinct and will.

6.a "WHATEVER IS PROFOUND LOVES MASKS" (II. 40)

Why does everything profound love masks? "Owing," says Nietzsche, "to the constantly false, namely *shallow*, interpretation of every word...." This spiritual hiding appears to be a way of letting something take root and grow, as distinct from protecting something shared by a secret community. The individual is not protecting himself. His "sense of shame" undergoes destinies and decisions that are rare, not normal, different, as a god is different even from those who worship him most. A transition is taking place. A new kind of life is coming to be, and perhaps, like an adolescent, this event is not confident in its own body, not ready to be seen or explored, and is inevitably misunderstood because it is so much in process.

Behind the mask—it is the mask that communicates and relates in the commonalities of the age and place—courses are being cut, words are being remade in a forge of rearranged powers, frequent deaths are taking place as the geography of expression and thought shifts, as from a quake. From these transformations new images and ideas emerge, not necessarily well-formed ones, certainly not familiar ones. The thinker may try to avoid using them or being used by them. These people who undergo such events, says Nietzsche, are "inexhaustible in [their] evasion of communication." But the cooking and forging go on behind the mask, even when one has not clearly chosen the mask, when the mask emerges from one's confusion in the midst of a new, undecided event.

Are the ideas of will to power and eternal return part of the mask? Are they hiding something that is still unspeakable for Nietzsche? Or are they like crevice gas after an earthquake? Probably those ideas do hide a coming language that is neither explanatory nor subject-oriented nor poetic in any usual sense. Probably these ideas express a transition from our common descents to a way of thinking that is now both unfinished and uncommon. Probably they hide a shame like "the shame of a god," which is the god's difference among the nondivine. The god's mask is an opposite for the god, an opposite that reflects the divinity in proper disguise. Disguised as opposite, as, say, Eros or Apollo, the god is present but not exposed, innocent by virtue of the mask. This continuing disguised transition is the matter for thinking, and its thinking involves one's allowing courses, directions, and formations to go on without disturbance as a new life forms. Thinking is being alert in and with these transformations, a largely silent process that has begun to yield broadly understandable words, ideas, and images. It is a process whose meaning cannot yet be clear.

6.b "A QUESTIONABLE QUESTION"

The gods might disguise themselves because finite minds cannot grasp or understand them in their divinity. But they *are* gods, not ill-formed things. One can say only so much, as Nietzsche had found, in an environment of German piety and European disgust for life. Nietzsche in fact does propose a way, a discipline that is virtually gnostic, that preserves a special knowledge—the knowledge of a new perspective—and that is both a knowledge of the world and an opponent to the shallowness of the times.

7.a "NEW FRIENDS OF 'TRUTH'" (II.41–43)

Nietzsche's beautiful paragraph on "not remaining stuck" to persons, fatherland, pity, science, one's own detachment, or our virtues speaks of becoming independent. Independent not as a great individual, but as one who preserves and keeps guard over something that is lost by attachment to the best that *we* know. By remaining unstuck, one no longer thinks out of the multiple interests of a person, group, discipline, or established practice (the image is of a prison, an enclave, or a walled space). Rather, one conserves oneself as an area where something unfixed is taking place—that is "the hardest test of independence," as thinking is freed from the best guarantees and commitments of the time.

This unbounded and nonsubjective state of mind gives "a new species" that is not born of the age's best concretions. "Attempters" emerge who follow the temptations, the uncalculated ways, that may lead nowhere or to misfortune. They follow out directions of forces and bits of meaning without fully established assumptions as to what is happening or what should happen. They yield to the temptations that cross the well-marked boundaries and pass on to uncertain terrain. The "truth" of this occurrence is nothing held in common, Nietzsche says, but is rather more like an abyss or a strange nuance. The "truth," that is, is the crossing and the emerging of a different field of balance, pairing, and opposing.

7.b "*MY* JUDGMENT IS *MY* JUDGMENT"

Nietzsche shows that one must detach oneself from the past as it occurs in persons, cultures, and so on, in order to follow out new perspectives and ideas. He speaks of noncommitment as a condition for a radical independence of judgment that is necessary for the creator. He writes as a creative artist who must be free to do the work unique to him. In this freedom he can probe and experiment and possibly bring forth a new way of seeing. He suggests a kind of discipline that promises a new and better knowledge.

8.a "WE FREE SPIRITS" AND "HOW THE PLANT 'MAN' HAS SO FAR GROWN MOST VIGOROUSLY" (II.44)

The freedom born of the emerging differences and distances is itself a transformation of the individual liberty common to the speech of those who affirm the dignity and singularity of the autonomous entity "man." It—freedom—creates the conditions opposite to those commonly thought to enhance happy human survival. In its setting it yields danger and increases the powers of both restraint and audacity. It promotes the art of experiment and devilry. Its home is the ordinary homelessness of foreign ways, practices, and speech. It feels gratitude for those needs and sicknesses that break dependencies and weaken the grip of rules and beliefs. It enjoys the pariah. It cultivates the shadows, the poverty of honor, recognition, and communication, not their established power and richness. This freedom affirms the unofficial. It affirms the hostile and public judgment against itself in order to breed itself from the passion this opposition generates. It affirms the anonymity of its own thinking. This freedom of spirit follows its curiosity without guilt. It wants the unexplored. It tries out its strength with no sense of competition or hope of reward. It meddles, puzzles, plays with arrangements of valences, looks for exclusions, notices silent hatreds, cultivates always an interest in the dark side of each bright cultural light.

The free spirit speaks as Nietzsche has spoken in this grouping of paragraphs. By speaking this way, it cultivates the opposition that it notes has caused "the plant 'man'" to grow vigorously. The growth in this case is toward a way of life and thinking that "man" very likely will not recognize as his own. It is part of the silent work of a constellation of powers that wills its own life without a rebound of guilt, life-suppression, or fear of its difference. If it succeeds, this discourse will involve a way of life that does not fight the energy that charges it and charges through it to other and different organizations. This is a discourse that works to be free of the resentment, asceticism, and bad conscience that have defined man and attacked his vigor. As we think in it, we are in a difference that transforms our dependencies and forms a discourse of difference. As that discourse is thought through, thinking, uncommon in its own descent, begins to occur.

8.b THE FREE SPIRIT AND CREATION

This section brings to a tentative end the grouping of paragraphs that speaks of the formation of the creative free spirit, the artist-philosopher. The artist has been the model, and Nietzsche has given a remarkable account of the artist's freedom that promotes genuine creation in expression and insight. The artist-philosopher is rare. He must undergo extreme rigors of opposition and rejection. He must cultivate the dangers of being an embodiment of what his society fears and judges to be bad or evil. He must work alone in the tradition that both spawns and rejects him. Above all, he must resist the attractions of appealing to the oppressed and outcast, who will distract him and sap his energy. His task is to hear the unique inner voice of an individual molded by the particularity of his gifts and differences.

Through this section we come to see that when Nietzsche speaks of the free spirits, he has in mind the power of creation brought to bear through the work of the remarkably disciplined and gifted persons whose insights and estimates, based in their own creativity, may take us beyond the power of resentment and asceticism that have previously formed us. The few of us able to attempt this new philosophy will look to the sources and disciplines of art, and not to metaphysics, as we learn to think and speak. With this emphasis, the free spirit sounds more like a type of philosopher than a disciplined discursive process that transvalues everything experimentally, including its own ideas and combinations of values.

3. OLD FORCES WITH NEW FORCE

When Nietzsche's writing is experienced in its process of undergoing different arrangements of forces and producing new forces in relation to the forces of traditional arrangements, we appreciate how thoroughly historical his work is in both its tensions and its transitions. What is being transformed is active in his thinking as the traditional metaphysical ideas form Nietzsche's thinking at the same time that they are being deeply changed. We see history at work in those tensions and transitions as we have presented them in the (a) and (b) sections above. The work of history in this case involves a return of a discourse's force upon itself. The return comes out of the traditional reaction that Nietzsche names resentment: a moral, conscious ideological grouping is designed with a deep fear of its own vitality because that vitality, in its lack of unity and identity, threatens the design's own integrity: the life of the moral or ideological design turns against itself in a subtly nuanced group of feelings, attitudes, practices, and ideas. The countermovement is, of course, vital, alive, but it is generated by the organization's desire to impose on its life the restrictions and fears of its particular identity and design. Thus it sickens itself, its vitality is turned against itself. It becomes a self-undercutting force-counterforce that is lived out as suspicion of creativity, domination of contingent states by images of noncontingent states, oppressive insistence on highly restrictive ways of life, comfort in conformity, and so forth. These ways of life build a culture, a loose system of awards, nurturance, punishment, and exclusion. As continuing ways of life they form a "contagion," the creation and propagation of "sickness."

In Nietzsche's thinking, however, the return, which we shall discuss in greater detail as eternal return, is a reversion of the sickness on itself, a kind of self-destruction by the spiritual sickness rather than its propagation. The lion, says Nietzsche in *Thus Spoke Zarathustra*, does not create values. It is the consumptive, destructive image that, in this discourse, has for its telos "higher, rarer, more remote, farther-stretching, more comprehensive states." In this part of his thinking the energy of return, which has been generated in the fears and resentment of traditional morality and religion, remains. But through the reorganization of this thinking the target of returning counterforce is no longer the ensemble's own vitality, its will to power, but is rather its own resentment, fear, hostility, and guilt regarding its will to power.

A powerfully destructive segment of our moral/religious history is present in this aspect of Nietzsche's discourse that turns to itself as self-critique and self-undercutting. This part of his thinking wills its own overcoming. But contrary to a traditional mainstream, that destructive segment is not repressive of its own contingency or its vitality, which is quite other than its own identity. The return now turns on the identities and organization that help to define it; it creates directions that are not controlled by the forces of bad conscience and resentment.

"It may be necessary," Nietzsche says in "We Scholars" of *Beyond Good and Evil* (VI.211), "for the education of a genuine philosopher that he himself has also once stood on all these steps on which his servants, the scientific laborers of philosophy, remain standing—*have to* remain standing. Perhaps he himself must have been . . . almost everything in order to pass through the whole range of human values and value feelings and to be *able* to see with many different eyes and consciences. . . ." We shall look now at some of the values and value-feelings, at some of the traditional valences, that run through his paragraphs on religion in *Beyond Good and Evil*, keeping in mind that these are part of Nietzsche's history, an effective history that works in his thought as his thought works on this history by a powerful and transvaluing return to—a reversion on—the ideas that partially define what he thinks. In this work a transvaluation begins to take place: not primarily a new set of values, but rather a different, exploratory way of evaluating that produces new values.

As we speak of history and transvaluation in Nietzsche's discourse, we continue to find him in a difficult tension. While the *perspective* of a thinking organization, that is, a new type of sovereign individual, is important for him, and while he often speaks in terms of a few courageous *individuals*, the process is also found to be one that people undergo rather than perspectively define. The side of Nietzsche's thought that we shall underscore involves a field of perspectives that is considerably greater than an individual person or group. It involves an organization of forces (of valences, ideas, and practices) that is not personal or individual. It produces types of individuals. The process is a mixture of powers, something like a dynamic organism, that is made of relations and produces relations, only one kind of which is personal and individual. Nietzsche was as clear as his metaphysical predecessors were that human thought is not solely or even primarily the action of a simple individual. Thinking complexes have lives, powers of their own in which people fade in and out. Discourses have lives and energy, and a dominant issue is how those discourses relate to their lives and energy—their will to power, in Nietzsche's account. Individuals contribute to discourses while they are in them and of them. They can add and subtract force. They too are products of force complexes, and they can be part of the complex's return on itself. Nietzsche finds himself privy to an emerging discourse in which describable kinds of life denial are being transformed into types of life affirmation. This new discourse has its positive history as well as its history of oppression. Greek religions, for example, are part of that positive history. Both the positive and the negative forces, however, yield now a way of thinking that is not Greek or neo-Christian, but something different from both.

Historical syntheses and changes are forces within relations of forces, within ensembles that we are calling discourses. They are not conceived on a model of intellectual activity, traditionally understood, but as contingent, productive states of relation of which people are a part. History is a composite of synthesizing processes. It is made up of descents of power relations, which are interpreted by Nietzsche as more like imaginative plays than intellectual systems. *Wissen* (knowledge) and *Gewissen* (conscience) are thought in close association by Nietzsche: knowledge (science) and con-science have been bound together in our history. They composed a productive relation of knowing and morality that has given leverage to individuals as dutiful agents who decide what is true and false, right and wrong, according to selected, established values. Hence Nietzsche's emphasis on plays of forces and descents of power plays, rather than on individuals and persons, is one way in which he finds that his genealogical interpretation of history distances itself from the power complex of knowledge systems and moral systems and those subgroups that are part of them.

The close association of moral and religious systems means that as we think through Nietzsche's discussion of religion in *Beyond Good and Evil*, we are involved in a play of departure and return in our religious/moral history, a process that will produce a different way of knowing and different structures of knowledge. When we discuss eternal return later in this chapter we will be in a position to see that the emergence of this different knowing organism—something after "man"—does not involve us in a higher meaning. It involves us in a process without higher meaning that comes out of the knowing/moral ensemble. The process itself, though continually involving metaphysical ideas, is postmetaphysical, and it is the most powerful dimension in Nietzsche's work.

1. "THE RANGE OF INNER HUMAN EXPERIENCES REACHED SO FAR..."

Although Nietzsche does not often go into historical detail—he is working on the large estimates in which details are read, interpreted, and arranged—the vast range of human development plays a dominant role in his thinking. He speaks often of the effective traces of developments that appear to have been enormous: "These tremendous remnants of what man once was . . . ," "ancient Asia and its protruding little peninsula Europe . . . ," (III.52); "We northerners are undoubtedly descended from barbarian races . . . ," (III.48); "A great ladder of religious cruelty . . ." (III.55). He finds many present practices to be symptoms of ill-recorded or otherwise forgotten social practices: punishments, prohibitions, terrors, privileges, ways of ranking and ordering. The idea of genealogy develops from this sensitivity. The genealogist deals with the primordial dimensions of our ideas and practices, not only by speculating on causes (debtor-creditor relations, for example), but more significantly by looking for the primordial dimension in the present. The primordial is what is usually concealed and is disruptive of the refinements of sensibility that are found to be basically and obscurely related to it, for example, cruelty in relation to religious belief and practices, will to dominance in relation to the saint's appeal. This sense for vast descents and for present, concealed "primitiveness" invested in moral and religious discourses gives him an orientation of distance from the power of moral and religious sincerity and meaning. It allows, for example, the reality-appearance polarity, which once attracted people to images of eternal essences, to attract us now to look at our refinements as surfaces and symptoms of deeper drives. The reality-appearance polarity permits the traditional religious impulses toward the profound and awesome to function in the unmasking of the benevolences and pieties (appearances) that in their disguises express powers that are neither benevolent nor pious. We are on the way to discovering something essential and deep, something unbounded, and we in our lineage are naturally inclined to follow. Even if it is the will to power, its depth and vastness attract us. Once in this profound space, we can fuss over names. Does it love us? Is it indifferent? Is it moral? Is it beyond "God" and morality? But what matter? We are in our Western element, thinking at the deepest levels, made quasi-religious at worst by the very place occupied by our thinking, and at best rekindled in the inspiration and spirituality that can move the most stolid Western intellectual before he knows what is afoot, but moved now in a differing ensemble of forces. How many times has Nietzsche been read with a knowing smile by theists, moralists, and ethicists who recognize where he is taking them: to the profound depths of the searching soul. Nietzsche may be an atheist, but he is in touch with a deep human hunger and with the space to which that hunger leads. He cannot be all bad.

2. WHY ATHEISM TODAY?

The phrase "and we killed him," from *Joyful Wisdom*'s paragraph on the death of God, contains a Judeo-Christian "we." A dominant mood in the religions of the ancient Greeks was gratitude, "an enormous abundance of gratitude" (III.49), in the midst of wars, disease, natural calamities, and cruelty. On Nietzsche's reading this kind of religiousness is celebrated by vitality. There was less oppressive illusion than now in at least some ancient religious practices in the sense that neither morality nor ultimate meaning was expected of the world's and spirit's energy. The power of life was imaged and celebrated. That affirmation is traced in the fears and repressions that invest most of our known religious heritages. Perhaps it is also found in moments of affirmation free of piety, self-sacrifice, and sober concern for meaning and justice. The lives and resurrections of Dionysus, for example, show a close affiliation with the turbulent, driving power of life that is as apparent in orgiastic celebration and conflict as in artistic creation. The crucifixion of the Son of God, however, had a different flavor. It expressed a growing "inversion": "It promised a revaluation of all the values of antiquity" (III.46).

This powerful event carried with it tyrannical revenge against tyrants, a revenge bred by Roman slavery and Hebrew morality. A hard, insistent movement was developing in which an oppressed passion for dominance, a will hardened and dulled by slavery and occupation, combined with a moral God who was born in a repeatedly enslaved culture. This conjunction produced a drive for the death of tyrannical deity and a desire for a god who would love the weaknesses and suffering of the enslaved. The enormous power of this development was partially expressed in the insistence that God died ignobly, sacrificed himself by suffering a criminal's death. The developing, dominant religion turned against the power that produced its own revaluation of classical values. It was an awesome power indeed that overturned and undercut classical civilization, a power that did not shrink from domination and, in the imagery of self-sacrifice, sacrificed nothing of itself, but appropriated other values and practices in a way that would have made Dionysus proud. The enraged suffering of people, however, fashioned the event that produced the death of God and a desire not to know of the tyranny of its own desire.

Like a slave yielding his body and his work to the controlling powers, God yielded his body to the established powers of Jerusalem and Rome. This power of sacrifice becomes one of the organizers of the Christian discourse: sacrifice of the dominant and dominating powers, of freedom, pride, spiritual self-confidence (III.46). God's suicide means that even early Greek gratitude for the world and life as it comes—the affirmation of life without conditions—will be sacrificed. To what? To a self-sacrificing deity. Giving up and giving away became the power motifs. All powers that love themselves—and Nietzsche's observation is that all powers love themselves—must be dethroned. And in their place: the self-loving power of the self-sacrificing God who is served in the self-sacrifice of human souls.

All of this sounds strange if we do not recall the history of Christian piety. Today there remain from that piety the powers of guilt and associated anxieties, the frequent deep conviction that one has no right to be, the desire to please Someone or Something ultimate, the need to be in a supportive and sustaining community, the piety of charity, the conviction that without something timeless and real and person-affirming life could not have the meaning it has for us (III.46). But the power of a self-sacrificing God in the midst of a late classical culture is beyond our experience. The resentment bred of enslavement is not immediately apparent for most Westerners, and God's crucifixion in the modern West cannot mean much more than God's love reaching out to us to show us how to live consonant with his will. Perhaps his will has reverted back to its Hebraic roots through such "northern" leaders as Luther, who "have little talent for religion," back to the expectation that God wants to make us happy on earth when we do his will. That has sacrifice enough in it, but the idea of God's killing himself has receded and inverted to a God who loves the comfort of his people when they sacrifice their lives to him through vows and obedience. God's self-sacrifice has undergone transvaluation. It is no longer the loss of God and the return of God in the ensemble of slave suffering, slave service, and tyrannical demand for self-sacrifice.

The death of God is not a doctrine or a belief for Nietzsche. It is an object of description. He does not particularly like it or trust it. He certainly does not believe *in* it. Its causes are in its origin and in its history of resentment and bad conscience, which, in affirming the power of God's crucifixion and in repressing its own will to power, has slowly destroyed its own originating power arrangements, that is, this God has slowly lost his dominance. The death of God is a symptom of degeneration in a series of events that appear also to have created a possibility that Nietzsche affirms: an ensemble of ideas and practices that is different from "man's," one that is differentiated from the suspicion of life that has marked a sizable part of "man's" story, an ensemble without resentment, bad conscience, or ascetic ideals, one whose event is self-affirming and open to its own passage and transformation, one whose values mean the likelihood of its transformation.

The idea of God's death, founded in the morality of guilt (which we shall consider more carefully) and the power-building/power-denying self-sacrifice of God, occurs in association with the idea that God's suicide culminates in both a historical and a continuing resurrection. The new life of the risen Christ is also a living memory of God's death. Both have force, and the forces interplay with each other. One can affirm on Nietzschean terms that a tradition developed that emphasized a particular kind of love, based on reconciliation and on profound, affective elimination of personal distance made by guilt and inferiority. This tradition developed in the Hebraic and Greek imagery of Christ's life. In that tradition God and lesser divine powers live with enormous force. Nietzsche's interpretation of the death of God depends on the recognition of this tradition, in which the powers of God and the powers of death are thoroughly mixed. This is a mixture that is a part of us, but one that must appear strange in a Homeric or Confucian way of living. God's death occurs in our history as the multiple themes of self-sacrificing and new life play themselves out in the changing patterns. The more strongly this organization affirms itself, the stronger the self-sacrifice becomes, the stronger death-life happens, and the more powerful the forces of transition from the God-ensemble develop.

The traditional pieties consequent to the sacrifice/redemption mix pass on the contagion of God's death in the elevation of such valences as poverty, meekness, humility, acceptance of persecution for God's sake, affirmation of weakness, and so forth. Another kind of power begins to form, equally self-refusing, but strange and attractive, a power that intensifies self-consumption and self-denial to such a degree that a remarkable and appealing power emerges. A different kind of creature from the *"religiöse Wesen"* is forecast in this phenomenon of radical obedience to the self-sacrificing God and of maximized self-hatred. The saint reveals for Nietzsche the life-death mixture in which death, as self-sacrifice, moves toward creative energy without need of redemption.[8]

3. "MASKED EPILEPSY": "A PENITENTIAL SPASM" (III.47)

In Western religious history the saint's power and appeal contribute to the development of the death of God. The discursive function of discussing the saint is "to look away, *to go away*" from the traditional attraction without self-awareness that people have felt regarding the saint. Saints are taken as models, ideal fulfillments, special instances showing the meaning of God's will for human beings. The saint is a conversion: of flesh into spirit, of fault into obedience, of earthly lowness into spiritual height, of vulgarity into purity, of ignorance into wisdom. But in any case, conversion. The power of transvaluation appears now in the costume of finite love for eternal being. First we find the spiritual conversions of saintliness. Then we find more apparent a nonsaintly power that converts piety into a different, nonreligious ensemble. The low and oppressed develop into definitive power that has both religious and developing nonreligious life. The dynamics of will to power occur in religious vestments, and as these vestments are affirmed, the will to power comes out free of vestments. That is the direction of Nietzsche's thinking, and in the process of thinking this way the power of the will-to-power idea has more and more leverage over the organizing power of self-sacrificing love and its death complex. Shall we, Nietzsche asks, look through the clothes—not rags, but the splendid dress of saintly power—and see the denial and hatred, the piety of sacrifice that in sacrifice is turning against itself and revealing a superior force? (III.51).[9]

This force awakens suspicion over such intensity of denial; it awakens a sense of danger regarding the ascetic, because he had not *mere* poverty and humility but an enormous power in his culture that came through his excessive intensity and denial. His rare passion created possibilities, brought people together, made followers, inspired purpose, violence, and disobedience to other authorities. It was an unnatural power, one that broke expectations and seemed violently different and attractive. Even death could be taunted in the saint's procession. The saint's passion for God showed a power other than the self-sacrificing one, a power immediately sensed by the brokers of power, a power to break away, break open, capture, tax, direct, and wage war: the saint's power issuing in movements and away from mystical union, toward the formation of institutions and practices as well as toward something unnameable. This open, formative power was different from the instituted contents of beliefs and practices. It built and tore down and excised energy. Sheer force of life was almost visible—and also a strong hint of transformation to come out of the forces that emerged from the saint's awe-inspiring self-hatred.

In his evaluation of the saint and the death of God Nietzsche "looked away" from Christian evaluations and thought through, instead, another possibility that had come up, "the opposite ideal . . . of the most high-spirited, alive, and world-affirming human being who has not only come to terms and learned to get along with whatever was and is, but who wants to have *what was and is* repeated into all eternity . . ." (III.56). This affirmation of meaning without ultimate meaning, of life in the senseless single "whole" appears to have emerged partially from the conversion of opposites in the saint's lives. The idea of "whole" transvalues "God," carrying both the idea of eternal completion and the absence of completion and meaningful eternity. A double transformation has occurred: first the discourse of self-sacrifice emerging from the force of the saint's wild energy in its cultural occurrences moves toward creative force without self-denial. And second, a transvaluing nonsaintly ideal of world-affirmation and self-affirmation without guilt, hatred, or the experiences of divine suicide in the history of redemption emerges out of the saint's world denial and self-hatred. It is an ideal, in the tradition of ideals that we have come to expect, but it is an ideal that is freer of the history of cruelty and asceticism that produced Western theism, and that Western theism has carried forward (III.55). The ideal is now freer than it could have been without the atheism that issued from the force of God's self-sacrifice. God's death has come in part from the creative force without God that became more apparent through the lives and the impact of the lives of saints. Out of this force the ideal of affirmation with eternal recurrence emerges and becomes effective.[10]

4. "THE PHILOSOPHER AS *WE* UNDERSTAND HIM..."

Nietzsche ends his section on religion in *Beyond Good and Evil* (III.61–62) with series of reflections on the power of functions of religion. It can help strong and independent people, he says, to develop enough force to overcome fear and hostility regarding strength of will, including, of course, religious hostility and bad conscience. Religion can help the strong move toward "higher" consciences and sensibilities and away from mediocrity of aspiration. It helps others to get away from distractions and find solitude for concentration and growth. To others, religion gives occasion for strengthening self-control, for the experiences of self-overcoming that can transform into a loftier way of life than that afforded by religion. And it can make life tolerable by adding ultimate meaning to boredom, senseless toil, and oppression for those who need that sort of thing.

For all the possibilities for growth and self-transcendence in religions, however, Nietzsche observes that their dangers are usually overwhelming. Religious ensembles tend to fixate on their own identities. They tend to preserve every aspect of their experiences: suffering, sickness, hatreds, anxieties, illusions, and so on. Religious self-preservation lets go of very little; hence its power for transformation and the transforming nature of its own beginning are truncated or warped. Theological passions are warped into reflective transcendental claims. Moral intensity is misshapen into concern for maintaining order at all costs. And the deaths, failures, and outlived patterns are kept as parts of meanings, habits, and rituals in a spirit-deadening way. "They have preserved too much of *what ought to perish*" (III.62). Deep transformation and the processes of transvaluation are not affirmed in most instances of religion.

Philosophy as it has been conducted in this section of paragraphs will "make use of religions for [its] project of cultivation and education" (III.61). The religious ideas and values in Nietzsche's thinking, the only partial transformations of religious-metaphysical thinking, have been cast into a process that appropriates them into transformations foreign to their habitual discourses. It is a destructive and creative process that takes place "with the help of religions" (III.61). Those utilized ideas are frequently betrayed, as we have seen, in the interests of being responsive to an emerging way of thinking. The language of Nietzsche's discourse encourages transformation and new forms of life. It discourages self-preservation by obedience on the part of those *willing* to take the risks inherent in departing from the authorities of the passing orientation. It often sides with what is concealed in the established discourses. It builds bonds with the ongoing processes of transformation and transvaluation. Nietzsche's discourse is learning to let go of its own historical conditions by the will to power cultivated in the language. As a philosopher, Nietzsche thinks in the process that designs the perishing, *not* the self-sacrifice, but the transformation of the ideas that are in hostile tension with this transvaluing process.

Hence the remarkable power of his image of the "mocking and aloof" Epicurean God who laughs at the "miscarriage" of Christian energy. The contradiction of a power that once transvalued classical discourse, now struggling with violent seriousness to maintain itself against transvaluation, that is, against death and growth, causes this God to laugh. The energy of the Christian discourse was once an awesome power. But it has now bred mediocrity in the extreme—mere mediocrity without a sense of itself.[11] The philosophers, in league with the released powers issuing from this fearful discourse, can say what Christianity is unable to say. And by saying, by participating in this other raw and developing ensemble, they are a part of a discourse that is free from the now "calamitous kind of arrogance" of a religion that will not let go of itself.

The philosopher is a product of multiple historical processes. He is in a complex genealogy of power relations. He is in no sense above history. He "as we understand him" is a sympathetic part of a movement of thought that is coming through and beyond the discourses of Hebrew/Christian morality, religion, and reflection. This philosopher is a product of Western religion, morality, and metaphysics, but a product that wills the transvaluation that is going on and that lets the producer-parent die.

Indeed, in the new discourse he immediately recognizes this death and speaks of it. In this thinking a new, freer, and more open spirit, the "free spirit," is moved by a will to transformation that informs the processes of thinking and writing. In the tensions and sympathies of these appropriative processes we have found the philosopher's different thinking in our common heritage.

The philosopher himself is a part of a transvaluation of traditional aristocracy. The aristocratic class lived in its own justification and happily sacrificed "untold human beings" for its own benefit.[12] The strength of the philosopher, however, is in his undergoing and going through the differences and oppositions of his history without reducing or distorting those tensions and struggles by such fantasies as "unity," "essence," or "Being." In this discipline and the interplay of forces that make the new thinking, a different kind of thinking being (*Wesen*) begins to emerge. A different image of the thinker is cast and reflected. A different strength takes place that is in the genealogy of an ancient aristocracy, but also deeply changed in relation to it.

Knowing that "life itself is *essentially* [a word that Nietzsche's own paragraph puts in doubt] appropriation, injury, overpowering of what is alien and weaker; suppression, hardness, imposition of one's own forms, incorporation and at least, at its mildest, exploitation": knowing this, the philosopher knows an inevitability of force consuming force in his discourse.[13] This "honesty" about transformation enables him to follow the forecast of a nobility that is itself transformed out of the Western mixture of aristocracy, morality, and religion. He moves toward the discipline of a transforming creature, toward a new discourse, which is arrogant and appropriative, "God-like" in the sense that it accepts it own "value-creating" activity. This discourse knows that it is in and of whatever attracts it, and "everything it knows as part of itself it honors." Self-glorification has emerged from the discourse of self-sacrifice, a self-glorification that gives prominence in its genealogy to images of Homeric nobility and to the arrogance of Homeric poetry. For the philosopher, one of the new noble men, there is "the feeling of fullness, of power that seeks to overflow, the happiness of high tension, the consciousness of wealth that would give and bestow." He is moved by the excess of power that is the life of this discourse grown from the waning, deenergized discourses of fixation and restraint.[14]

Nietzsche is in a surging language, one that remembers Dionysus prominently in its genealogy and is young and vibrant in its oppositions, its partially formed departures and multiple thoughts.[15] Its vitality is for transformation and transvaluation. The philosopher now needs enemies "as drainage ditches for the affects of envy, quarrelsomeness, exuberance" so that he can follow with less distraction from the still-present affects of resentment the developing affects and intentions of creation and refinement—just as he needs such polarities as master-slave, high-low, appearance-reality, honesty-deception so that the wash of history will drain off in the formation of new ways of being. It is, he says, a process of breeding a new species (IX.262), "a philosopher . . . a human being who constantly experiences, sees, hears, suspects, hopes, and dreams *extraordinary* things . . ." (IX.292, emphasis added). "At these turning points of history we behold beside one another, an often mutually involved and entangled, a splendid, manifold, junglelike growth and upward striving, a kind of *tropical* tempo in the competition to grow . . ." (IX.262).

A type of positive repression takes place in this breeding process. The calm assurance of preestablished order and the congruent serenity of wise thinking is forgotten in a "positive force of repression" that replaces continuities with disconnections.[16] Forward movement and vitality create lapses or spaces of opportunity where once there had been traditional kinships, associations, and reflective connections. Instead of the insistent, slow-moving, often chanting memory of religions, morality, and their accompanying thoughts, the philosopher's discourse now moves forward, out, and away from the holding patterns, putting old ideas into changed contexts, rhythms, and styles. It creates a body of forgetfulness that eliminates the tissues of repeated hostility and fear. In resentment, the call out and forward by things, the appeal of things in uncertainty and indefiniteness arouses hostile suspicion, cautious offense, withheld interest. This holding and insisting state is itself vengeful regarding life and produces attraction to inferiority, inability to love freely what is beautiful, and suspicion of those who have forgotten the connections of resentment. In this state one looks intuitively for fault and such "weaknesses" as contradiction and inconsistency: that is one way to remember hostility. One wants to measure wrongs and rights, to distribute things in the restrained measurements of good and bad, of tables and categories and beliefs, with alertness for possible deviations and rebellion. The measure of the same in this discourse is fearful hostility to the creative momentum of the will to power. "All instincts that do not discharge themselves outwardly turn inward—that is what I call the internalization of man . . . that is the origin of bad conscience" (*Genealogy*, pp. 84–85). This "pain" remembers itself through punishment, repression, and sacrifice as well as through metaphysical ordering and measuring. This pain may be transformed, however, into "a bait for life" (IX.262) in the forward momentum of an unleashed discourse, one that has learned how to forget repressive connections, and thus how to remember the will to power. Then the idea of universe, for example, is dispersed into multiple orders, and the ideal of an organic whole falls out of the discourse's momentum. Then differences are not resolved or given synthesis by the philosopher, but are multiplied. For a time, at least, proliferation replaces synthetic measurement by preestablished categories.

4. A DISCOURSE OVERCOMING ITSELF

Is not the function of these two ideas, will to power and eternal return, in Nietzsche's discourse to provide resolution and synthesis? We have seen that they give synthesizing order in the "junglelike growth" of genealogies, descriptions, and ideas that tumble through Nietzsche's thinking. They offer a basis of sameness and a whole-giving image for all things.

We shall look first at will to power with two questions in mind: How does Nietzsche describe will to power? How does his account of will to power function in his thinking?

Nietzsche was disciplined in his interpretation of the world. He wanted to show that will to power better explains the appearance of things, that is, it better explains *things* than other, competing ideas, such as that of a creator-subject. "Our knowledge has become scientific [viz. disciplined] to the extent that it is able to employ number and measurement. The attempt should be made to see whether a scientific order of values could be constructed simply on a numerical and quantitative scale of force. All other 'values' are prejudices, naivetes, and misunderstandings. They are everywhere reducible to this numerical and quantitative scale."[17] Nietzsche adopts the scientific approach, which he understands, as we have seen, to be governed by number and measurement. He measures phenomena by a quantitative scale. Further, "force is to be found in quantity. Mechanistic theory can therefore only *describe* processes, not explain them" (*Will to Power*, p. 660). The quantitative scale is a scale of force. He intends to describe degrees of force, not entities that have degrees of force attached to them, and by this process of description he will have interpreted all things by reference to degrees or amounts of force and the interplay of these forces.

The relations and plays among forces are different from the forces themselves, of course: "We cannot help feeling that mere quantitative differences are something fundamentally distinct from quantity, namely that they are *qualities* which can no longer be reduced to one another" (*Will to Power*, p. 565). *Quality*, then, refers to the differences-in-play of quantities of force. Nietzsche's discipline is not to single out forces, see them in a totality, and describe the totality of a sum total of its constituents. The qualities of force relations are not reducible to the constituent parts, and Nietzsche proposes as the subject of his discipline descriptions of qualities, of the interplays of forces. We have used such interchangeable terms for these interplays as *organizations, ensembles, hierarchies*, and *fields*.

Will to power has reference to interplays, not to some preexisting essence of each quantum. On Nietzsche's terms there are no quanta outside ensembles: they are relationally conceived. So his science of number and measurement is a description of qualities of force produced as the interplay of various factors of force. By not reducing quality to quantity he in effect claims that quantities are "real," that is, are effective only as nameable elements in some ensemble. They are contributing elements, and presumably they have independence of *this* ensemble only to the extent that they occur in other ensembles. And the quality of *this* ensemble could be a contributing factor, that is, a quantity of force, in another ensemble that has a different quality.

Instead of quanta having a trans-ensemble nature, they are distinguishable only by virtue of their different effects in ensembles. Differences of force in a complex play of forces, not a common nature, is their "identity" (*Will to Power*, p. 1062).

How, then, are we to read "force," if not as an essence that is present in all ensembles? The idea of force is the organizing principle of the discourse that is emerging from traditional patterns of thought. Will to power names the quality of the ensemble that is expressed in the transforming, transvaluing discourse that Nietzsche joins in its early stages of development. His "measuring" account of force articulates the quality of will to power that empowers, arranges, and distributes this discourse. Modern science, which we have found, according to Nietzsche, to be in the genealogy of resentment, ascetic ideals, and bad conscience, is articulated in a transformation toward an ensemble whose estimates and hierarchies multiply unities and disassemble categorial totalities. It produces a *Wesen* of difference that is called nobility in *Beyond Good and Evil*, and, finally, this transformation of science foresees a *Wesen* that is beyond (over) the ensemble of man.

When Nietzsche says in *Will to Power* that "this world is the will to power and nothing else! and you yourselves are also this will to power—and nothing besides," he is holding the world in his "mirror":

> And do you know what "the world" is to me? Shall I show it to you in my mirror? This world: a monster of energy without beginning, without end ... enclosed by "nothingness" as by a boundary ... a sea of forces flowing and rushing together, eternally changing, eternally flooding back ... blessing itself as

that which must recur eternally, as a becoming that knows no satiety, no disgust, no weariness: this is my Dionysian world of eternally self-creating, the eternally self-destroying . . . my "*Beyond Good and Evil*," without goal, unless the joy of the circle is itself a goal. . . .

The differentiating element in this "world," its quality, is will to power combined with eternal return. Both a group of metaphysical claims and a countervalence to such claims occur in the paragraph. It contains claims making up a nihilism from a metaphysical point of view. But when the paragraph is read as subject to its own claims, those claims are known as supported by nothing other than the energy of this "picture," this ensemble. *Its* energy is not to be taken as a part of something beyond it and universal. *It* is a self-reflection, not of Nietzsche particularly, but of a powerful grouping that in desiring to be itself has no desire for foundations outside itself. In willing to be itself, the discourse wills the will to power. In willing the will to power, it wills an image of a discourse supported solely by its own interplays, the genealogies of those interplays, and the other interplays that they forecast.

The energy of this discourse, as a qualitative interplay of forces, has its validity in its effective organizing power. "The will is a creator" (*Thus Spoke Zarathustra*, "Of Redemption"). The will to power originates in a full interplay of forces, not, for example, from a lack of energy or a need for relation. Its characteristics are ebullience, fullness, overflow. It frees its participating forces from that repression of will that has characterized its predecessors: "Willing liberates: that is the true doctrine of will and freedom . . ." (*Zarathustra*, "On the Blissful Isles"). It gives out forces for creation and self-enjoyment. It has been fed by the forces that gained strength through opposition and repression, as we have seen—not the affections of enslavement, but the hardness and sense of life bred by struggle with the preceding controlling powers. In its youthful energy it profuses, rephrases, appropriates, expands, bypasses. Its profligacy is in its affirmation of its energy to be whenever and however it occurs. Hence its satisfaction happens in self-affirmation, not in the fulfillment of unfinished goals. Intensity, not teleology, is its hallmark.

But Nietzsche has also claimed that the destruction of past traditions occurred because of their violations and fears regarding their will to power. We have discussed these ideas in detail, and *The Genealogy of Morals* has reference to the will to power in the entire sweep of human history. He did not think that it is limited to the emerging discourse. Will to power is used as an explanatory concept for the movement of its entire history, and particularly as an explanation for the decline and degeneration of its closest "relative." Like any other discourse of absolutes, Nietzsche's discourse makes its central idea, its dominant force, the force that dominates other forces in its discursive appropriation of them. It gives focus, unifying power, and it sets in motion an undercutting movement. This relation of metaphysical claims and antimetaphysical effects sets the direction of thought for a significant current of reflection running through the twentieth century. We are familiar with the undercutting effect: it is transvaluing metaphysical ideas by putting them in play with equally forceful ideas about movement without ultimate meaning.

One way that this undercutting functions is through the observation that will to power has an oscillating rhythm. As the quality of a limited, forceful interplay (that is, as the quality of a discourse), will to power is not an essence that unfolds inherent meanings or an inherent identity as it develops into an historically extensive process. In its discourse it not only interprets itself as a nonsubject without essential identity; it oscillates in the interplays of forces; by this oscillation it creates zones of identity in which one or another group of forces makes hierarchies that exclude some identities, and that themselves have a limited number of possibilities for identities. These groupings play themselves out, and particularly in the regrouping and transitional phases the loss of the dominant identities accompanies the manifest power of transformation. There is no center, no anchoring ballast. Centers of will power are identities. Will to power shows itself particularly as the centers fade out, lose their magnetism. Will to power is manifest in its movement without center. The concept of the will to power functions in this rhythm of identity formation and identity decline as an ability to give identity and focus in Nietzsche's discourse. On its own terms, this idea is expected to lose its centering ability, to be overwhelmed. It is a part of an oscillation, like the movement of a circle that in its movement changes the smaller ensembles of movement within its circumference.

Nietzsche often speaks of a sense of rightness or honesty that accompanies the individual who undergoes ego sacrifice or identity sacrifice in a process of affirming will to power. A satisfaction peculiar for the ego traces the movement from energy with center to the power of energy without center. In language that transvalues Christian sacrifice in the images of crucifixion and resurrection, Nietzsche finds that ego loss without retention of desire for ego gain has pleasure in returning to a source that is without identity or subject interest. His own happy movement in the course of *Thus Spoke Zarathustra* to the image of the last man who is still all-too-human, and beyond to a state that is not a man-state, is also a movement in the power of the idea of will to power toward an anticipated ensemble that is beyond the will-to-power ensemble.

When this movement through dominant identities is denied by the forces of those identities, the reconstituting trajectory of the movement is diverted. The regressive force against destruction-creation is a return, certainly, but now a return not to the quality of energy without center, but to the identity, to the particular magnetic center. This kind of return, observes Nietzsche, particularly in the course of *The Genealogy of Morals*, weakens or sickens the self-identifying complex. The oscillation continues as the repressive energy of the identity's struggle for its endurance represses the identity's energy in order to control or stop the power toward transvaluation and redesign. The turning now occurs as the internal weakening—the "sickness"—weakens the power of repression and strengthens, through pressure and forceful concentration, what is repressed. The repressed, with its increased energy, turns out from the identity center, perhaps at first extravagant in its emerging liberation, and turns toward its own constitution and recentering.

If the center of the emerging identity ensemble affirms its own generative process and does not identify itself and its valence by reference to endurance and universal validity, and *if* it centrally affirms a decentering momentum, then the oscillation of its power will not mean blind repression, self-sickening, and return of energy through regression. It will move "gaily" in its own self-transformations and, *by that kind of movement*, create the conditions for its successors.

If Nietzsche's thinking is successful, it will give the conditions for successive thinking in the process by which it effects its own overcoming and undercutting. That effectiveness is in the function of its ideas—in how they encourage their own transvaluation. If one follows those ideas for a time, the process of self-overcoming will develop. If one thinks these ideas metaphysically without the antimetaphysical forces and the consequent tensions that constitute self-overcoming, one is in a discourse different from Nietzsche's. The transformations that might go on are more likely repetitions of those that led to Nietzsche's discourse. At least they are different from the images and visions that they spawn by virtue of the absence of the metaphysical/antimetaphysical tension. They will not develop in the strain of forces or in the affirmation of the will to power that center and decenter Nietzsche's inheritance. The discipline of Nietzsche's discourse and its transvaluation involve the maintenance of its tensions until its metaphysical predecessors and its own "all-too-human" struggle transform into a different creature that knows all parties in the struggle as an aging or dead paternity. And if one participates knowingly in the transformative process, one will be in it with a sense of difference and perhaps of pleasure that are not characteristic of most other modern discourses (cf. *Zarathustra*, "The Intoxicated Song").

In "The Intoxicated Song" Zarathustra says that "joy wants itself, wants eternity, wants recurrence, wants everything eternally the same." This "deep eternity" *is* recurrence. Nietzsche often describes eternal return as the return of each pain, sorrow, injustice, and so on, and in those statements he emphasizes that the effect of the idea of eternal return is to transvalue the ideas of final telos and ultimate meaning by the force of another idea (eternal return) and image (time as an enclosed, revolving wheel). He is thinking through the idea of existence without meaning or aim. There is not even a finale of nothingness. Eternity. No completion. And in this thought he finds existence and the world affirmed (he sometimes says *redeemed*) in their own occurrences.

Their own occurrences are return, oscillation, eternal return; and the effect of affirming these occurrences is to reach out discursively for power (an important phrase in *Will to Power*, see p. 675). Reaching out for power is in contrast to reaction and reversion. The move out eliminates the sickening process that is in its own ancestry. Thought metaphysically, the claim is that the foundation of all existence is now affirmed in a group of values that have a dimension of noncontingent validity because they are appropriate to the transhistorical nature of the will to power. But when the idea is thought in terms of its discursive effect, it releases the discourse from alignments of self-protection with self-affirmation. Returning returns. No identity controls the process. Identity control is itself transvalued. And the discourse is free for its multiple, struggling orders. No meaning rules over them. There are surging powers in a quality of energy that affirms them all in their lives. Out of this affirmation—out of this quality, the will to power—the orders are affirmed strongly so that they move beyond themselves in the power not of reversion but of affirmation. If the discourse works, the power of negation peculiar to traditional Western metaphysical thought is transvalued into a different quality of forces. Then the idea of will to power is itself transvalued into something different that Nietzsche's discourse could not, true to itself, imagine.

The language of this account indicates that Nietzsche's struggle has been partially surpassed. Or have we assumed an Olympian distance as though the struggle of metaphysics were not in our thinking while we embody metaphysics in a self-blinding gaze? Have the tensions of Nietzsche's discourse produced options that are at least freer of *his* suffering, options that have broken through the process of transvaluation that he underwent and furthered? Has the language of this chapter in this book presented a written tableau as though free of death, strife, and replaceability? Have we encountered Nietzsche's discourse in a reduction by commentary? Or are we too working on a genealogy that has produced a return to Nietzsche in a state transmuted enough to appear to be of him, but is not his at all?

3

The De-struction of Being and Time

We have found emerging in Nietzsche's discourse relations of words and concepts that in their conflictual order develop self-transforming processes. This is not a *mere* transformation in which continuing stabilities are modified within parameters that themselves remain largely unchanged; rather, it is a process in which the basic possibilities for thinking change. We have found that this changing, this transforming is governed by emergent differences and interplays among words and things and not primarily by Nietzsche's individual, leonine effort to overcome and overturn traditional ideas. The traditional ideas themselves, in their defining organizations, are transmuted in the discourse. They are beginning to occur differently, we saw, in a process that they no longer govern. That process has begun to suggest ideas and differentiating principles different from those that traditionally governed the ideas that Nietzsche used and that used Nietzsche. We have followed an internal, discursive process that moves through and beyond Nietzsche's own organizing and transitional ideas. Our attention has thus been focused on the discourse itself and its self-differentiating conflicts as it gathers and plays out the ideas that move toward remarkably different groupings, remarkably different occurrences. It is not personal perspective, we saw, but different thinking in the discourse in which persons might take a part. This thinking is not so much oppositional as it is generative through the conflict of powers. Its frequent opposing and critical forays had the discursive function of breaking up or loosening traditional hierarchies, reversing stable relations, or contorting inherited orders into possibilities for different ordering. When these functions succeeded, they cleared the way for different hierarchies that issue in different thinking. The dominant oppositions and pairings are displaced and replaced by others.

We shall now follow the development of one strand in the post-Nietzschean discourse in Heidegger's *Being and Time*. How does the difference between metaphysical and nonmetaphysical thinking unfold in *Being and Time*? How does this conflict function in this book?

Being and Time is significant, first, in bringing the traditional issues of ontology together with the new phenomenological way of thinking. In spite of its new way of speaking, it was understandable within traditional metaphysics—not as a foundational epistemological treatise, but as a major encounter with the question of Being. *Being and Time* also broadened the scope of phenomenology as it was developing at that time, and brought to its center the ontological issues that its exponents had thought were beyond the range of interest and responsible thought. Temporality is the bridging concept. Both traditional metaphysics and post-Kantian critical and dialectical philosophy had questions of time and history at the core of their thinking. *Being and Time* made temporality the interpretive idea for the "cardinal" question of the meaning of Being, eliminated the dominance of an epistemological orientation, transformed the ideas of subjectivity and transcendence, and posed once more the issues of history and interpretation.

But *Being and Time* has had a major influence on discourses that are as severely nonmetaphysical as they are nonphenomenological, several of which we shall consider in later chapters. They are not so much opposed to metaphysics and phenomenology (partly because of the influence of *Being and Time*) as they are merely different from them. How this book helped to develop ways of thinking and speaking that have largely eliminated in their languages the two major types of philosophical thinking that it brought together is the question this chapter will address.

In this chapter we shall follow parts of *Being and Time* and see how the book's language and thinking realign words and thoughts out of its own tradition so that something different from Heidegger's intentions in the book begins to develop. We are following a discourse in formation through the power of what Heidegger calls de-struction, which is his way of cutting through formulations to their basic issues and questions in preparation for re-posing those issues and questions within the scope of Dasein's being. Something more happens, however. Dasein itself becomes subject to the process of de-struction, the process that was designed to elevate Dasein as the central arbitrating occurrence for this essay. Dasein is the disclosure of our essential preoccupation and resistance regarding the question of

Being, and as such it locates and anticipates all ontological thought. But it turns out that Dasein is in part constituted by the structures that are to be de-structured. It finds itself in this developing discourse on a slide to the periphery. The way of thinking in which Dasein seems to function as a unitary center is learning to place unitary centers in question. Its own self-showing in this language undercuts the way it is conceived and spoken. *Being and Time* is itself a phenomenon of Dasein's de-struction. In bringing together the extraordinary power of traditional ontology and contemporary phenomenology, it develops a way of thinking that departs from them both and initiates a different way of being, one that promises to leave Dasein to its passing era. Human being as such begins to fall into question through *Being and Time*'s discourse.

1. THE DISCIPLINE OF THE QUESTION

The question of *Being and Time* is the meaning of Being. It is not a question about meaning intrinsic to Being, if Being is understood as an entity outside of history and time. From beginning to end, this essay intends to pursue the *question* of the meaning of Being, and by that pursuit to recast the prepositional objects (of the *meaning*, of *Being*).[18] If Being as well as meaning are rethought as questions, then questions, not "Being" or "meaning," will set the thinking course. And if the questions are asked radically enough, if their provisional intent is kept firmly in mind and if neither explanation nor representational thinking that look for reasons take control: if questioning originates a thinking without either certainty in advance or the expectation of certainty, then the *question* of Being will guide the language and ideas regarding Being.[19]

The question of Being resides in a history, the complex history of Western metaphysical thinking.[20] And this history has produced the being that is the primary subject matter of Heidegger's discourse: Dasein. Dasein is the occurrence of the question of Being as metaphysics's creature. We do not have the occurrence of a transcendent Being that is manifest in determinant conditions, in this case called Dasein, but the occurrence of the history of multiple strands that are focused more or less dimly on the issue of Being and that constitute the "there," the place of meaning for this issue. The issue of Being, the question of Being, the language of Being—the entirety of the Being question—and as we shall see, Being: all are in and of this history. The historical being termed Dasein is constituted by this history and shows what this history means in its structures and possibilities.

Dasein—human being—is a being of languages, practices, the indelible memories of traditions, the relative memories of regions and societies; it carries deep cultural currents, surface conflicts and possibilities. From its inception prior to traceable memory, and through its traceable development in all phases of Western culture, human being (*the* being of Western civilization) has harbored the issue of Being. The issue of Being has taken multiple forms: in Homeric poetry, in Greek drama, in the heroic paradigms of human life, in the practice of Greek medicine, in early Greek thinkers, and in Socrates's perplexity over Being ("We who once believed we understood [the expression 'being'] . . ."). How the issue was specifically experienced is always controversial, given our distance from the early languages and minds, but that it formed the philosophical and spiritual heritages that yielded human being is clear for the author of *Being and Time*. Dasein is the being whose being is in question. That claim by Heidegger is a claim about our common histories and our common abilities for speech and thought. We are mortal beings for whom Being is to have meaning, and this destiny reaches as far back as do our commonalities and abilities to live as we do and as who we are in common.

Heidegger's descriptions of the "structure of Dasein" are descriptions of how this historical creature is. As a historical entity, its *is* is made in major part by the question of Being. Without the question of Being, Dasein would not exist. Some things could well be there, and non-Daseins may well occur on the earth, looking the way we look, perhaps, but not the same creature: creatures formed, rather, by radically different discourses, living out different *Wesens*. Heidegger's descriptions are thus a part of the history of Being. They are conceived in that history, in Dasein's discourse, and they are moved by the question of the meaning of Being.

But currents other than metaphysical ones are also at work. In the legacy of Hegel, Marx, Kierkegaard, and Nietzsche, metaphysical thought has become optional. We have seen the transformation of metaphysical ideas and thinking take place in *Beyond Good and Evil*. One could do similar studies in other post-Hegelians and find similar transformations: the way of thinking that established value, truth, and so on undergoes transformations that mark the boundaries and the possibilities of the traditional issues and make them optional. The emergence of transformative ways of thinking, reversals of hierarchies and enfranchisements of disenfranchised parts of the metaphysical discourse—all of these offered radical possibilities for thinking that had been virtually unimagined. Metaphysical thinking can continue and perhaps yield other, very different transformations. But it is now marked as optional, as regional, as contingent. It cannot realize the absolute, or circumscribe the truth or dream of perfection and completion, or define reality in a power of exclusive right, except in its own domain in which it establishes its own right. If it is true to its own multiple occurrences, however, it cannot produce conviction without knowing that its time is marked by other thinking that has placed it in a genealogy without privilege, placed it in a historical era. In the discursive strand we are considering, this "placing" is carried out by the increasing power of the idea of difference through transvaluation and through the de-struction that takes place in *Being and Time*. Heidegger's thinking is provisional.[21] It is conceived in recognition of the question of Being and in the associated recognition that traditional metaphysical thinking represents answers elicited by that question, although those answers fully recognize the question or still it. The question is part of Dasein, and both Dasein and the question are frequently muted by the answers. But the answers have as *their* meaning the question of Being, not Being outside of questions. They bear the question, and do not exist without it. Dasein is a being built out of forgetfulness, as well as out of the issue of the meaning of Being and its many constructions. Forgetting and meaning are also in Heidegger's own thinking in *Being and Time*. He attempts to hold them in the forefront of his awareness—to let both forgetting and meaning regarding Being be apparent—by maintaining the *question* of Being. He finds his access to human being in the question that is formed in human being and human development, in its history, language, and daily life.[22]

The idea of temporality develops and holds in awareness the question of Being in *Being and Time*. We shall note in detail that Heidegger at times speaks of Being in relation to time in a way that appears to be metaphysical and to resolve a metaphysical issue. But the dominant power of the essay is in linking Dasein, as a historical being for whom Being is in question, with the idea of the temporality of Being. This thinking could be seen as a reversal of Hegel. Does it not create a whole thought in which the whole is not and cannot be absolute? Does it not de-structure the idea of subjectivity in its account of finite human being? But the essay has a different cut. Standing Hegel on his head is not the primary aim of this reversal of metaphysical thinking. Rather, the essay attempts to articulate the question of Being with alertness to its history by showing that the structure of the question, the structure that makes the question, is of time, and that this structural whole is finite. Analogical thinking is blocked, made unconvincing. Representational thinking is challenged and threatened. Nontemporal grounds for explaining temporality are folded into their historical matrix and given their own time. The question of meaning itself is housed totally in a historical and threatened being.

A discipline of the question develops that elicits alertness for its own finiteness, and this disciplined alertness continues to yield a de-struction that is like the transvaluation that we saw function in Nietzsche's discourse. The differences from Nietzsche are at times extreme, as we shall see, but they have this commonality: metaphysical ways of thinking are being thought through and different ways of thinking continue to emerge and develop in the de-structuring process. For Heidegger, the region of this development is dominated by the priority of the *question* of being, and if we find the discipline of the question compromised at times in *Being and Time*, we shall also find the essay undercutting its own compromises and turning its seeming solutions for metaphysical problems into yet more radical questions by failing on its own grounds to make part of its language and conceptuality believable. It undercuts its metaphysical claims and language by the question that it develops and elaborates even while its elaborations are at times metaphysical. The overcoming of metaphysical thinking in *Being and Time* occurs as a way of thinking and speaking develops through de-struction that calls into question its own metaphysical attachments. By its destructive process it maintains the question of Being.

2. "... IF OUR DASEIN IS TO BE STIRRED BY THE QUESTION OF BEING."[23]

Heidegger says in his Preface to the Seventh Edition of *Being and Time* that the essay would have to be rewritten before it could be continued. But its way—its language and subject matter, its manner of thinking through the issues, *and*, presumably, its inadequacy—*its* way is still a necessary one "if our Dasein is to be stirred by the question of Being." What is necessary about its way if it had become unsatisfactory for Heidegger during the twenty-five years between its publication and the time he wrote this prefatory remark?

Apparently human being needs to be moved by the question of Being. Moving the reader or the author is not the point. *Dasein* must be stirred, that is, the being whose being is in question is to be stirred by the question of Being. Dasein is the temporal, historical, and mortal organization where Being is apparent. That organization is to be moved by raising a question—the question of Being—that has not been playing an effective role in its particular ways of existing. Our commonality, our Dasein, is to be modified, affected, by this question. The writing of *Being and Time*, in which Heidegger brought that question into the open field of explicit understanding, into the living world of reading and thinking humans, is designed to put that field of commonality in question by the question. The book is not primarily addressed to single, reading subjects. It is an address from and to Dasein: from a history and to a history by the being that was produced by that history and lives out that history. It is designed to be a discursive event, to change—stir—a discourse by the question of Being.

Assuming that *Being and Time* were successful in its intention, that it stirred Dasein, that it were a discursive event that changed discourse by its question, why would it be unsatisfactory? For Heidegger, this discussion and questioning of Being was self-limited. It began and ended, and was not to be continued. It had succeeded in stirring Dasein by the question of Being, but once successful, it ended at the beginning of another kind of language and thinking that emerged from it. In its effect it became part of a development, but it was also finished as a vocabulary and procedure. We shall see that its effort was to make optional and unsatisfying its own way of thinking and speaking, and that that result followed from stirring Dasein by the question of Being. When the question of Being gained power in contemporary Dasein, different ways of thinking and speaking began to develop.

3. HOW THE QUESTION STIRS

Heidegger states at the beginning of *Being and Time* that we must bring back to expression the question of Being.[24] The situation that necessitates our recalling the question is termed oblivion (*Vergessenheit*): the question is in a forgotten state, and Dasein is oblivious to it. When the question regains expression, Dasein itself will have been modified by the emergence of focused attention in relation to the forgetfulness: in remembering the question of Being, Dasein is modified by an issue, a question, that is a major part of its own continuing life. It is changed as a way of thinking and speaking as the question that has empowered a significant part of its thinking and speaking is rethought and respoken. Heidegger does not say that forgetfulness and oblivion regarding the question of Being are obliterated. Forgetfulness is a major formative aspect of Dasein. The formations of forgetfulness are now brought into association with the recollection of what was forgotten. The effect of this juxtaposition is to mark and limit forgetfulness. One of the de-structuring effects of bringing back the question of Being occurs in its interaction with the structures and patterns that were formed as Dasein pursued forgetfulness of the question that moved it to forget. The question of Being puts in question Dasein's language, formed as it is in forgetfulness, regarding both itself and Being. The speaking and thinking that emerge when this question is brought to life and given governance over thought are different from those of Dasein's forgetfulness.

Perplexities related to Being form the entrée for Heidegger (1). As the most universal concept in Western metaphysics, Being is taken as both indefinable and as self-evident.[25] He shows that Being has been thought to pervade everything, and that it is taken as widely understood. But in the history of metaphysical thinking, Being in fact is always a problem (that is, an inadequately appropriated question) surrounded by a thicket of only partially developed ideas and assumptions. The perplexities, misunderstanding, and frightfulness regarding Being, not a line of thinking that is to be advanced, provide an opening to this question that has shadowed Western thinking. The question of Being involves the inherited ideas about Being, and its history shows the relations of ideas that have indirectly manifested the question. The important focus for *Being and Time* is not what has been said about Being, however. It is rather the issue's elusiveness and unthought quality that are definitive of our history. Pervasive confusion regarding the question of Being has had defining power for our existence in common, for Dasein. The question of Being is hidden by conclusions and resolutions that claim universality, and by definitions that miss or lose the question. The question of Being is unresolvable by the ideas seeking to resolve it in Dasein's history. The unresolved quality of the question of Being and Dasein's search for a definitive center are, as we shall see, connected.

The question of Being initiates search (2). If Being were "known" without question, if Dasein had an intimate relation with Being beyond question and doubt, a very different process would have developed and something would have emerged other than Dasein. Dasein "knows," is constitutionally familiar with, the question of Being, but not with Being as such. What Dasein "knows" is "revealed," Heidegger says, in its search. And further, Being-as-questioned is also revealed in the search. How the search goes on gives definition and specificity to Being: the theoretical procedures and results of the search are founded in the question of Being and in its indirect manifestations. We can see that Being will be interpreted and explicitly thought through Dasein's pretheoretical and inexplicit question of Being and that "pretheoretical and inexplicit" refer to historical processes in a historically constituted, discursive organization.

The question of Being is formulated as the question of the meaning of Being. That is, Heidegger's point of departure is metaphysical. We are already involved in an understanding of the meaning of Being, and "from this [understanding] grows the explicit question of the meaning of Being and the tendency toward its concept" (2). The meaning of Being, this metaphysical issue arising out of a metaphysical understanding, will be the transitional organization through and beyond which the essay will think. When we know what Being means, we will have thought through the metaphysical issue, and we will be in a position to see how the question of Being leads beyond thinking the meaning of Being. So instead of tracing the concept of Being to an origin in a being and instead of tracing beings back to an originating being, Heidegger finds his access in the state of being that he calls Dasein. "An exemplary being," he says (2).

Dasein is exemplary because it *is in relation* to Being: it is formed in and constituted by the question of Being and by vague meanings for Being; everything in its occurrence, all beings, are related to the question of Being. Dasein is thus always an understanding of Being, not as a subject that constitutes a world, but as a "meeting" of all things nameable, relatable, knowable (4). How things happen together, the way interactions can take place, how theories and knowledges can develop and fall into crisis: the dynamic structure of being-in-the-world is an ongoing issue of Being among all beings. Heidegger indicates that the formed relations of sciences, the transmission of our disciplines, the formations of beliefs are interpretations of beings that have as their continuous basis the question and the interpretations of Being (3). "The question of Being thus aims at an *a priori* condition of the possibility not only of the sciences which investigate beings of such and such a type—and are thereby already involved in an understanding of Being . . ." (3). When we clarify the meaning of Being we clarify the question of Being that infuses all our histories' formulations and investigations. Dasein is the region of things-in-relation that is the question of Being in operation. As historical, Dasein marks the limits for Western thinking as well as for *Being and Time*. The historical wholeness of Dasein, not a part of it or something that is outside of it or only at the beginning of it, is the "foundation" for inquiry. All of the questions and all of the answers originate in the existence, the living constitution, of Dasein. "Dasein is a being that does not simply occur among other beings. . . . In its Being this being is concerned *about* its very Being. Thus it is constitutive of the Being of Dasein to have, in its very Being, a relation of Being to this being. . . . It is proper to this being that it be disclosed to itself with and through its Being" (4).

When this clarification of the meaning of Being occurs, Dasein explicitly understands its language, thinking, and practices in the question of Being. It finds that the meaning of Being in the question of Being is its own meaning, which has moved it and enabled it throughout its existence.[26] With this account of the meaning of Being and the question of Being, Heidegger intends to push metaphysical thinking to its fundamental existence, to its meaning. The effect is to de-structure this way of thinking by showing that it has missed its own origin, and that when its origin—the question of the meaning of Being—is thought through as temporality in the context of finitude, the conceptuality and language of Being change, and hence, we shall see, Dasein changes.[27] We shall see also that the priority of Dasein for this study de-structures the inherited ideas of reason and subjectivity when Dasein is interpreted as foundation and as being-in-the-world. It is neither reason nor subject. But it is the connectedness of all beings; it transcends parts and totalities, and it is alert. In its occurrence understanding and interpretation take place.

The "problematic" of *Being and Time* is thus *in* the history of metaphysics. By basing his entire essay on the question of Being, Heidegger intends to place himself squarely in the history of metaphysics and ontology.[28] Human being is historically constituted, and by intensifying the history of the question and meaning of Being Heidegger turns to Dasein as a basis for his thinking rather than to abstractions that forget their own historical essence.[29] "Dasein," he said, "grows into a customary interpretation of itself and grows up in that interpretation" (6). Not simply the individual person, but Dasein grows or is grown by all manner of arrangements and hierarchies—that is, by interpretations—and these historical structures define Dasein and accompany it "constantly."

Not only does tradition "ensnare" Dasein in ways of thinking and relating that hide its "closest" experience and question. *Being and Time* is, has to be, part of the ensnarement (6). De-structuring is Heidegger's way of thinking through the "problematic" that obscures Dasein's originary experience. The experience, which is the questionableness of Being—Being-in-question—is carried in Dasein, although suppressed and sublimated in the traditional issues of Being that promise some form of traditional "resolution."[30] If our language can begin to respond to the questionableness of Being, it can, perhaps, begin to recover what the tradition has carried and covered over. Heidegger speaks of "loosening" the hold of traditional ideas, of "dissolving" the traditional concealments. If the limits and possibilities of dominant ways of thinking can be shown by an account that works with them in relation to their obscure, experiential grounding, then those limits and possibilities can be "demarcated," in this instance demarcated by what gives rise to them and is hidden by them. This is a strategy to break the hold of metaphysical thinking both in the tradition and in *Being and Time*. *Being and Time* is to break the hold of metaphysical thinking that grips its own conceptuality.[31] If the structure of relations, assumptions, associations, and images can be loosened in the essay, then perhaps another kind of experience that is in the language and thinking and behind or under the dominant structures may be more apparent. Perhaps it will shine forth like a phenomenon and illumine Dasein's forgetfulness.[32] Heidegger's strategy is to show how metaphysical judgments have hidden the temporality of Being, and how thinking and temporality are connected in human being as it has come to be. We shall see this strategy at work as we consider the metaphysics of the phenomenon, the language of the "whole" in *Being and Time*, and the problem of meaning.

4. THE FORMULATION OF THE QUESTION OF BEING

(A) DE-STRUCTURING THE FOUNDATION

"The de-struction of the history of ontology essentially belongs to the formulation of the question of Being and is possible solely within such a formulation" (6). The history of ontology, with its way of forming the question of Being and its consequent loss of interpretive contact with the experiences of time that accompany that question, is a defining part of Dasein. Being comes to thought and expression in a space or place ("*Da*") that is thoroughly conflicted in the question of Being. Although essays after *Being and Time* will explore in extensive detail how Being is lost in the historical formulations of its question, *Being and Time* makes the temporality of Dasein the dominant focus. The temporality of Being is historical, but in *Being and Time* the details of its history are subordinated to the structures of temporal occurrences. We shall note a continuing tension between history and temporality in this essay, a tension that will lead to the de-structuring of the idea of meaning.

Heidegger's account of temporality as the meaning of Dasein's being shows that in Dasein's history temporality has been dissociated from Being. This book is conceived in the ontological tradition that it is designed to de-structure. Only by working in and through its own history will de-structuring take place: Dasein is de-structured as the history of ontology is de-structured both in thought and cultural practice. This task will be carried out through a process of formulation that de-forms its own conceptual and attitudinal bases. When this is done, the detailed work of rereading the work of the formulators of the Western tradition can be carried out in the way of thinking that comes out of the de-structuring situation.[33] Heidegger obviously does not intend a reduction to nontemporal or pretemporal essences. He is following an understanding that is constitutive of the formulating being and that is lived out in such temporal activities as thinking, speaking, and relating.[34] As we shall see, both formulating and de-structuring the question of Being occur in existing networks or ensembles of words, ideas, and practices, and do not have essences or existence outside of the networks. As de-structuring goes on, the networks shift and alter, and different possibilities come to be. The question of Being and its formulations are in living interactions. They are "understood" in and as ways of thinking, speaking, and living. The formulation of this question takes account of how things are together, how the ensembles take place. Our formulations are interpretations of the ensembles that we live, and these interpretations also express the ensembles that constitute our common being. The question of Being is at the heart of Dasein's own occurrence. It pervades its life and thought. To ask about it is to express it. But if it can be formulated in such a way that it begins to de-structure its own history, it might transmute into a different question and initiate a way of existing that is not like Dasein. Heidegger takes the initial steps of de-structuring the question of Being in the way he asks and develops the question in light of the idea of temporality.

Dasein is thus in the world metaphysically. Its theories and interpretations are founded in this world. But the question of Being carries with it suppressed elements, such as time, care, and finitude, that readjust language, thinking, and existing when those elements come to the fore. *Being and Time* is a process that takes part in the readjustment as it thinks through the metaphysics that is inevitable for it. This thinking through realigns some of the priorities and dominances among things and theories as it reconsiders time as a buried part of Dasein's understanding of Being.[35]

Since Dasein's temporal structure and not the detailed history of interpretation is the access for *Being and Time* to the question of Being, the structures of Dasein that are ignored or suppressed in Dasein's activities and relations will be the bases for beginning the de-structuring process. The essay addresses the question, What are the elements of Dasein's occurrences that are forgotten in its occurrences? As the forgotten elements are given priority in the book's language, those ways of thinking that suppressed them are changed and a different way of thinking and speaking begins to develop.

Since Dasein is a historical being, and since its defining elements are historically originated, Heidegger can give a descriptive account of structures of Dasein without a specific history of those structures, and develop in a preliminary way the claim that what is *necessary* for Dasein is historical and finite. The continuous mortality of Dasein invests the necessities of its being. The book is designed to think this thought, not prove it or show why a rational man has to think it. It is a way of thinking, one organized by finite temporality, that is foreign to our dominant traditions.[36] *Being and Time* is conceived as an essay by a Dasein about Dasein.

Dasein is "ensnared in a tradition which it more or less explicitly grasps." And ontological understanding is most particularly held by the snare (6). Ensnarement is fundamental for both Dasein's language and its process of developing beyond its traditional language and self-interpretation. In this sense, ensnarement qualifies all the existential constituents of Dasein and all ontological claims of the essay.[37] Given the claim that Dasein is ensnared in its being not only by everyday involvements but by tradition, we can maintain Dasein's priority in *Being and Time* only by keeping in view the primary importance of the essential forgetfulness in Dasein of *the* question of the essay. Dasein is ensnared in forgetfulness. Heidegger, in an effort to keep this forgetfulness in mind, turns under the traditional dominances in order to let the suppressed question of Being and its meaning emerge. But Heidegger's language, his activity of turning under the traditional dominances, is always affected by the forgetfulness that he wants to bring out. He does not speak from a transcendent stance, but from within the developing and changing history. His language is part of the tradition's transmissions, although it functions in a de-structuring manner. He says, for example, that our traditions have thoroughly overlooked Dasein's "foundation" in temporality. What happens to the foundation in this book? This central word moves the reader, as we shall see, to the inevitability of the dissolution of Dasein. *Foundation* is a central term for Heidegger that loses "foundational" overtones before Dasein's description is complete. The word itself is de-structured through its function in *Being and Time*.[38]

(B) FOUNDATION AND PHENOMENON

As long as "foundation" is paired with "presence," language carries the expectation that things *are* in their presence, and "presence" suggests stability now. Foundation then means stability of presence, something that is the same now, that is, always now, that is, forever. Something the same, coming to presence now, seems to generate reality as present, as the now: the now seems to be the temporal moment of the same's occurrence. The dominating issue then is, what is the nature of the foundation? Once we determine that, we will know what is now always. Foundation beyond time as the guarantee of the now overwhelms the process of time, and the question of Being then is a question of timeless nature that temporal creatures struggle to understand. Kant made the question of temporal constitution foundational by his discussion of imagination and structure, a tentative move away from the Aristotelian dominance of thought by the idea of *ousia* and now-presence. But Kant also wanted a timeless foundation, and could not see that in moving away from Aristotle he was activating a pre-Aristotelian thought of Being-in-question, of foundation without stability, of foundation, perhaps, without temporal transcendence. A return to the *question* of Being, however, began to emerge after Kant with the recognition of the possibility that the foundation of knowledge is temporally enacted. Could Being, as foundation, also be of time? Could the idea of the founded now obscure Dasein's moving question? In the dominance of the now, could Dasein have forgotten the question of Being? Could this word *foundation*, so rich in presence and timelessness, give us a way back to the Dasein-initiating experience of Being without foundation?

The phenomenological method of investigation (7) is Heidegger's way of approaching Dasein in the midst of the renewed question of Being. Not reduction or argument or dialectic, but a different *legein*, a different way of speaking and investigating that intends to approach the issue of foundation without the traditionally and metaphysically informed idea of reason. Instead of determining Being by definition, he approaches Dasein in a way designed to maintain the *question* of Being. The first step is to see if an approach can be used that does not repeat the traditional interpretations of Being that are built into the expected language of approach and method. Heidegger uses, rather, the phenomenological approach of finding both the access and the method that are "demanded by the things themselves."

Things themselves carry histories and cultural meanings. They are referential in the networks of their occurrences to all manner of other things, bearing complex pasts and fields of possibilities. They happen in associations and configurations, in horizons of uncertain futures, with passing, fading, and highlighting going on in their infinitely complex moments. They are always in contexts of signification that define them and what they can be. Although Heidegger at this point, in the seventh section of *Being and Time*, does not mention the temporality of phenomena, we note that in recalling the question of Being he has in mind the self-presenting, past-bearing, future-occurring way of things themselves. That phrase "things themselves," presence-oriented though it appears, in fact forecasts in this essay the destabilizing occurrence of future and past that uproot the fixity of presence in Dasein's inheritance. The metaphysical idea of presence is being de-structured as Heidegger rethinks both "foundation" and "phenomenon" in the horizons of time. That horizon disengages the triunity of presence, foundation, and thing.

As a part of the living world—the discourse—in which the inquiry takes place, "things themselves" are also uncovered and accessible through their own ways of being, not primarily as "objects," but as living, active parts of the world in which questions and inquiries arise always in referential schemes. One does not have to create access to them or for them. One has to find the approach that responds to their access and answers their claims, their ways of timing, spacing, relating: their being. The self-given accessibility of things means that one need not deny their history or the history of Dasein while approaching them in a contested freedom from the metaphysical emphasis on presence. Their history is in and of their self-presencing. Things are both metaphysical and nonmetaphysical in their history. The history of Dasein is in play in this de-structuring move, and that history, with its dominant metaphysical current and its nonmetaphysical undercurrent, is allowed to interplay with the temporality and history of "things themselves" through the essay's phenomenological method. That method, in the description of the *Da*, the place of Being's occurrence, will allow the question of Being to articulate itself: Dasein will place itself in question as it describes itself and finds itself through its investigation to be in question. *This* being-in-question is the occurrence of the question of Being. Heidegger's phenomenological approach to Dasein is designed to allow the question of Being to guide the inquiry, to be articulated in the inquiry, and to call the reliable steadiness of the inquiry into question. The fulfillment of this design is the de-struction of *Being and Time* itself, whose own adequacy as an approach to Being is fully in question by its end. The question of Being de-structures this essay's own metaphysical pretensions to a continuing descriptive adequacy: the question will not allow *Being and Time* to be a "foundational" essay, as we shall see in greater detail.[39]

Heidegger's discussion of "phenomenon" is based on the Greek *phainesthai*, the middle voice of *phaino* (7.a). The middle voice is lost to modern languages, and we resort to reflexive formations, such as "what shows itself." The reflexive structure, however, relies on pronouns and nouns in a fashion that distracts from and probably distorts what the middle voice could say with one verb form. We lack the voice to say conveniently, "the occurrence of self-showing." We say, "showing itself from itself." The middle voice mutes the "it" and does not need the reflective "self." It consequently could say an occurrence that was neither active nor passive, nor even necessarily reflexive.[40] Bringing to daylight, that is, daylighting or brightening, seems to be meant in *phainesthai*. Phenomena are occurrences, manifestings, that in their coming to be do not indicate initiating action or reception of action. Phenomena are beings, *ta onta*, that in being manifest and palpable indicate a middle-voice process that we can best express as self-showing, that is, a process of coming to light without action in the midst of all kinds of action. "Beings show themselves from themselves," although we need to hear the middle-voice alternative in this reflexive phrasing.

Heidegger's phenomenology thus speaks of things that are self-showing without agency in their occurrence qua self-showing. The logos of beings is not to be taken as the structure of constituting agency. Neither a who nor a what is intended when he speaks of self-showing. The "founding" process of coming to light is middle voiced, and its structures, its logos, are not finally accessible to literal or figurative language. How are we to "address" phenomena in light of their accessibility in the middle voice? Speaking may let something come to light. *Logos*, taken in its meaning of speech (*apophansis*), is self-showing (*apophainesthai*) as it is spoken about (7.b). Words let something be seen in self-showing occurrences. The *phainesthai* occurs as something is spoken about and shown. The speaker, says Heidegger, is a medium, while the speaking " 'lets us see,' from itself, *apo* . . . , what is being talked about" (7.b). Two kinds of things happen: as *apophansis*, speaking shows what is spoken of; as *apophainesthai*, speaking shows itself coming to light as its own occurrence, an occurrence keyed by the *apophainesthai* of the addressed. Heidegger is proposing in his phenomenology a way of speaking that is alert to both functions. If *apophansis* is taken without *apophainesthai*—if the showing activity of speaking is taken without the middle-voice process of self-showing—speaking will be interpreted as making present, or as "presencing." But if both functions are held together, speaking will be interpreted as addressing not only *what* is shown, but as showing itself with the self-showing of what is shown. The middle-voice function is not primarily one of representing or designating; it shows out of itself. The *what* that is shown is not central or peripheral. The atomic imagery behind "central" and "peripheral" is dropped. What is shown is in self-showing. And since self-showing is not a what or who or an action, the present time as a determinant does not now dominate the concept. Further, since self-showing is not agency-centered and cannot be thought of as constitution or synthesis, its communication cannot be adequately conceived in terms of literal or figurative language.

How to speak otherwise is a continuing issue for Heidegger. Since he has posed the issue not in terms of power but rather in terms of release, opening up, and disclosing, a primary emphasis on domination, submission, and transvaluation is foreign to his way of speaking. "De-struction," although involving a release of subordinated and subjected ways of thinking, puts emphasis on release of words and ideas that are not power oriented. There is also considerable conflict among terms and ideas in *Being and Time* as they are changed by its different and changing discourse. But what is to be let seen, through the descriptions and conflicts, is a submerged aspect of Dasein—its self-disclosive, world-related openness—that will reorient Dasein around the self-disclosure of Being. In this preparatory essay Heidegger's language takes a step toward overcoming the ignorance of Dasein's own coverup, Dasein's not knowing that it has developed itself by putting derived aspects of its being in front of something else that it is but can hardly speak of. Its *"pseudesthai,"* its "being false," needs to come out into the open (7.b). That coming out of being false into the open, into the *phainesthai* of its being, might yield the significantly different way of speaking and thinking that *Being and Time* forecasts. Consequently, the kind of language that Heidegger requires in the essay is one that maintains the question of Being and puts in question everything that is unquestioned or not really in question in Dasein's tradition. If he can put in question the literal and symbolic certainties of a tradition by another description that can be taken as literally accurate about Dasein, and if he can also develop that account in the question of Being which the Dasein analysis cannot resolve or adequately answer in any literal terms, then he will have maintained the question of Being. He will have developed a discourse in which that question de-structures the essay's own seeming certainty. The book will be a "medium" that shows something other than the totality of its contents, and other than what it speaks directly about. A remarkable combination of *phainesthai* and *pseudesthai* would occur.

If *Being and Time* is successful in holding together *apophansis* and *apophainesthai*, its literal, descriptive claims will be offset by a process that it embodies, that it "says," with and beyond its literal accounts. This process lets self-showing be seen in and through what is described. In that way, the essay will hold in question its descriptions, interpretations, judgments, and syntheses. Their adequacy and manner of speech will not circumscribe or justify their own occurrence. Their active voice will not be sufficient for their own self-evidence. The *apophainesthai* of the discourse will be in the questionableness of its fully developed and established speech. The question of Being will thereby be allowed and seen in a discourse that shows in detail how Dasein manifests itself.

The question of Being thus shifts the meaning of "founding" and "foundation." In this context, causation language clearly misleads. The ideas of agency, extratemporal process, and substance are being set aside.[41] "Standing" in question, which we shall find associated with "exsistence," rather than present endurance, is the "foundation" of Dasein, and this understanding has begun to undercut the constructive use of "foundation." The concept of foundation in relation to Dasein is moving toward an interpretation of Being without foundation by virtue of its use in the context of Dasein's question of Being.

When Heidegger makes the expression "to the things themselves" the motto of his phenomenology, he has no objects in mind. That phrase in his context means "*apophainesthai ta phainomena*": "to *let* what shows itself be seen from itself, just as it shows itself from itself" (7.c). The *let* is affiliated with "shows itself from itself" and with "how." *How* things show themselves will be *let* seen. That means that the discourse itself, by making the *how* of self-disclosures its guiding principle, will develop an intrinsic understanding of its own middle voice: an understanding of Being as self-disclosiveness, is being developed in the texture of this discourse. Coming to light, rather than apparent objects, guides this understanding. When descriptions of things coming to light and the self-disclosure of the discourse itself are held together in the essay's speaking and thinking, Heidegger's phenomenology will have achieved its preliminary goal. He will have shown that by paying attention primarily to how things show themselves, and by casting that descriptive effort in the question of Being, language becomes alert to: (1) the covering up of the question of Being that is pervasive in how things show themselves, and (2) the pervasiveness of the uncovering self-disclosure of the discourse. This language participates in the coverup, and also recognizes it. Being thematically guides this discourse as the pervasive commonality of all beings. It is let be as question in Dasein's covering up and self-disclosing. The discourse as a process gives space and thematic effectiveness to Being in its middle voice, lets Being be the phenomenon of this *apophainesthai*, this speaking situation that speaks itself as other things are spoken of.

The interpretive work of *Being and Time* is a field of conflict between metaphysical thinking and the disclosure of Being. The interpretation is carried out as ontology, cast now in the question of Being, not in the presence, atemporality, or definability of Being. The ontological orientation carried with it an emphasis on structure: Heidegger's Dasein-analysis is thus a description of the "basic *structures*" of Dasein's self-disclosure. These basic structures cast the question of Being as the question of the *meaning* of Being. On the other hand, Heidegger, in treating the question of Being as the issue of the meaning of Being, is showing how Being has been concealed-revealed in Dasein's way of being: a historical, developmental investigation that shows how the meaning of Being has been a concealing factor for human being. The analysis shows this concealment in the way that the context of meaningfulness shifts from propositional and systematic language to a language of existential insufficiency, mortality, and disclosure without substantive basis. Nevertheless, *this* investigation is also a part of that history; it is moved by the issue of meaning in relation to Being. It names the meaning of Being and pursues the question of meaning at the same time that it transforms that question.[42] By giving an account of the meaning of Being, Heidegger will have shown how Dasein has been constituted, how it has come to be as it is in the context of its history with Being. As a part of the discourse that de-structures metaphysical thinking, the essay takes as its focus the determination of the meaning of Being, conceived in response to the concealment of Being by metaphysical language and thought.

As an investigation of the meaning of Being, however, the essay itself is conceived in a language of structure, whole/part, immanence/transcendence, meaning/non-meaning—a language that becomes doubtful as the concealment and self-disclosure of Being become apparent in this discourse. In *Being and Time* Being is conceived as "transcendence pure and simple" because Dasein lacks a language for it. Its "transcendence" offsets all of its determinations. As language and thinking begin to appropriate the concealment of Being in Dasein, the "transcendence" of Being will look less and less like transcendence. Being's "transcendence" will be overcome as the question of Being is recalled and as the discourse itself is disclosive of Being in Being's middle-voiced concealment. This disclosure will make phenomenological ontology and its focus on "the cardinal problem, the question of the meaning of Being in general" (7.c), a part of a passing era.[43] The occurrence of this phenomenological discourse makes obsolete its own method and problematic. In order to see more clearly how this self-overturning occurs, we look next at how the idea of the whole of Dasein functions in the book.

5. THE WHOLE OF DASEIN

(A) INTERPRETING THE PRIMORDIAL QUESTION PRIMORDIALLY

When Heidegger begins his discussion of Dasein and temporality, he has already identified being-in-the-world as Dasein's "primordial and constantly *whole* structure," given a detailed structural account of how it is constituted, and "centered" that account in disclosiveness. He has shown that Dasein's everyday, factual way of existing and its pervasive common structures are united not in selfhood or subjectivity, but in "care." Dasein is a "structural whole." He understands himself to have "delineated in a unified way" Dasein's totality and to have established Dasein as "a primordially unified phenomenon" (39). Care is common for all of Dasein's disclosures. It shows Dasein from itself; it occurs as Dasein's middle voice. This self-showing is evident in Dasein's essential unease in its being. Dasein shows itself and is primordially alert regarding its being in its lack of a securing foundation and in the insufficiency of its presence. In its unity it lacks certainty of Being, and in this lack it finds its being.

Insufficiency and unity are emerging, as we expect, in close association in this description, and "unity's" traditional alignment with a whole identity that is timeless is fading.

Care is Dasein's "understanding" of its being (39). Dasein is, but without sufficiency of Being. *Its* unity, *its* being, is one of "difference" from Being.[44] There is a basic alertness constitutive of Dasein, one that "knows" Being as both forecast and not fully present. The partialness of Dasein, its nonpresence, its "difference,".is understood in Dasein's middle voice. Dasein's unity is in the *question* of Being. Care as the whole of Dasein names this living state of alert incompleteness.[45]

"What then do we mean by the primordiality of an ontological interpretation?" (45). This question initiates an elaboration of Dasein as a whole, now in the context of temporality. The "constitution" of Dasein's existence leaves as a puzzle the meaning of Being because in Dasein's history Being is not the same as Dasein's occurrence. Yet we are "looking for the answer to the question of the meaning of Being as such." We look because the *issue* of Being is in the texture of our existence. And further, an understanding of Being in general also "belongs to the constitution of Dasein." Not, of course, an understanding that is founded in Being as such; not one founded in a creative action that produced beings out of Being; not an understanding that in some fashion depends on Being as something outside of Dasein's history. But one that is founded in Being-not-there. The "not-there" is part of the "there" of Dasein. This "not-there" is to be understood temporally, and that means historically. The nonpresence of Being *means* that Being as Dasein's *question* has no meaning, no status or reality or "being" except in Dasein's history.

Further, this understanding of Being that is constitutive of Dasein will provide the missing unity of Dasein and Being.[46] We will find that the unity exists in Dasein's history and that the historical manifestation of this unity exhausts its occurrence. But before this primordial interpretation is possible, Dasein's potentiality to be in accord with its being must develop so that its thinking and speaking will be based on its own occurrence and not on the self-forgetfulness of everyday life.[47] As we shall see, in authenticity the wholeness of Dasein comes to life; that is, Dasein then comes into accord with its history, its temporal constitution; and, owning itself historically, it is prepared to let go of the transhistorical, transtemporal hopes and hypotheses that are a part of itself. As a mortal, historical whole, Dasein can let its metaphysical part fade away. It is ready to remember its forgetfulness, and by remembering, to overcome the control of that part of itself that has submerged its alertness vis-à-vis its being in multiple, self-forgetful concerns.

The primordiality of this interpretation involves an existential achievement by the historically constituted Dasein, an achievement of a way of caring that makes apparent the unity of Dasein in its care. How it lives out its temporality is basic for how it speaks and thinks in its temporality.[48] More to the point: the historically constituted unity of Dasein needs to be appropriated before it can interpret itself on the basis of *its* being. As it comes to terms with itself in its full mortality, its own occurrence becomes evident and wholly apparent to itself.[49]

What does "wholly apparent" mean in this essay? The de-structuring of *whole* as well as of *foundation* (or *basis*) is taking place at the same time that these words anchor this part of Heidegger's discourse. "Whole," "primordial," and "basis" are being so arranged with "death" and the phrase "being-toward-death" that dissolution of the *central*, constitutive being, of Dasein, is providing the interpretive key for "whole." The words that could well be the hallmarks of substantive presence and an emphasis on the "now" of temporal sequence are functioning in a context by which they express no-whole-there even as they speak of completion and identity. It is not that something is missing; it is rather that the entire structure shows that nonidentity—not something, neither subject nor object, but nonidentity—is at work in the question of Being. The dissolution of substantive identity occurs in the "wholeness" of human being. The absence of Being in the question of Being and the "completion" of Dasein in being-toward-death complement each other in the language of *Being and Time*.

Heidegger develops this thought partly by interrelating the structures of *Being and Time* as tightly as possible. The book's schematic and systematic style is well noted. The key "existentials" of everydayness, state-of-mind, understanding, and discourse provide schematic points of reference throughout the book. Heidegger shows the totality and wholeness of Dasein by recapitulating the self-forgetfulness of Dasein in his discussion of Dasein's self-showing as care. He recapitulates the structures of care in the structures of temporality. And through it all he shows that the meaning of Being provides the webbing for the intricate pattern. But always, at every point, at all the junctures, and at the end of all the recapitulations, what is not present—"something" standing out from the whole—disturbs the *completeness* of the scheme that gives definition to the wholeness of Dasein. The very issue of wholeness, for example, is outside of everyday life, as Heidegger points out at the end of his discussion of Dasein in its everyday way of being. And we come to see that if we are to think of temporality appropriately in terms of the missing and the outstanding, we have to release ourselves to Dasein's own continual release from Being and allow Dasein's "inmost potentiality of being," its ability not to be (50). The "outstanding," far from being a "what," means something like an "arrival of a departure." This continual departure of Being, of what people have sought and spoken of and died for, can be "heard" and allowed as Dasein releases itself for its own occurrence: free of substance, never a completed identity, question-plagued, and, with the steady departure of its longed-for resolutions, fully there.[50]

Thrown as it is into the immanence of total strangeness and nonidentity, Dasein's own occurrence, its own disclosure, involves constitutively the possibility of its own demise. When it is in full accord with itself, it, in its sense of wholeness and appropriateness, is radically fragmentary in its being. The "wholeness" of its being shows that Being is not wholly there at all. Heidegger is not saying, of course, that Being "is" somewhere else or that Being *is* at all. The history of Being, however, has promised a different completeness. It has been associated with staying presence, deathlessness, and eternity. That "Being" is not "there" except as question. And the question—such living associations as life-death, being-dying, really here–really not able to be here—the question shows Dasein *itself*. The tighter the interpretation of Dasein is drawn, the more Dasein stands out in the mortal arrival-departure of what preoccupies it: Being. The "there" of Being is question, not analogy, substantive participation, or kinship through identity or origin. Although Heidegger's language suggests at times that perhaps Being, as pure transcendence, is like a mysterious Other, lost always in Dasein's differentiation and way of being but strangely and indirectly present, the movement of the essay is in another direction. Being is not to be taken as metaphysical identity in any sense. It is to be kept in the orientation of the *question* of Being, that is, it is to be interpreted historically as what is outstanding—as what arrives departing—in Dasein's coming to be as it is. Dasein has taken solace in supposing Being to be "there" in some sense—as absolutely Other, an indefinable ground, Being analogous to being, absolute subject, pure spirit, pure matter. These ideas have carried a sense of presence and radical difference from finite being, and in this metaphysical difference the question of Being, though skewed, has been carried. But for Heidegger, all such ideas resolve the question of Being and forget Being in the resolution. Being is outstanding for Dasein as question, and that question has guided Dasein in becoming as it is.

When Dasein is free and open in its questionableness and mortality and is alert to its many and usual ways of covering over its finite wholeness, it "reaches" its "primordial truth" (60). Released from the habituating forgetfulness of its own being, it is "free for its world." It lets things be as they are in the world, an orientation opposite to projecting onto things its ways of hiding from itself. Free for itself, Dasein frees things to be as they are. Release is Dasein's primordial truth. The claim is that as Dasein has been released to be as it is through the question of Being, it releases finite beings to be as they are. The unity presupposed by this claim is articulated in the term *being-in-the-world*. Heidegger has shown that there is no separation of Dasein from world. Dasein is world-relation. The human world is founded—comes to be—in the historical development of the question of Being. Being able not to be is "in" all things. The world means: How are we to be? Who are we to be? Is there any meaning of Being? What does it mean to be? The middle voice of the human world is the question of Being, and releasing things in their "primordial truth," in how they are, involves hearing always the question in the midst of all the determinations, significances, and myriad possibilities and necessities. The horizon is always there, indefinite and disclosive.

The release of Dasein is thus a release in a development that lacks an introduction and a conclusion. In that sense, Dasein's history is not like a narrative, but more like a lyric: utterly there, shining, unified, and nothing else but its expression and the history of its expression. Dasein does not found the world as a subject founds a place to live. And the world does not found Dasein as a continuing reality might be said to be the foundation for a mortal thing. Dasein and world are, as Heidegger frequently says, equiprimordial. Dasein's primordial truth is thrown disclosure. Qua disclosure, *there*. Qua thrown, wholly temporal and historical.

The open resolve of Dasein "reaches certainty . . . only in the anticipation of death" (61). With this claim Heidegger has moved toward de-structuring certainty in relation to wholeness, and a language of question has begun to recast the idea of Being.

(B) EXISTENTIAL STRUCTURES AND HISTORICITY

The idea of continuity plays a strong role in *Being and Time*. The existential wholeness of Dasein is a principle of continuity. If Dasein is not the same forever, it is the same yesterday, today, and tomorrow. The idea of discontinuity that has played a crucial role in forming the strand of post-Nietzschean and post-Heideggerian discourse out of which we are speaking is not foreign to *Being and Time*. Heidegger separates Dasein from the constancy (*Selbständigkeit*) of a substantial entity (61) and weaves that separation into the texture of his discourse. He uses the language of constancy—he de-structures it—as he speaks of the constant certainty of mortality. As Dasein opens to its deathliness by anticipating it, one kind of certainty is dissolved: Dasein's "indefiniteness" reveals itself "completely." That certainty, characteristic of metaphysical discourses and based in the discursive authority of substantial identity, is dissolved in a way of thinking in which existential anxiety overrides self-certainty (61). The de-structuring project means that what is destructured—that is, traditional ideas and beliefs—plays a definitive role in the discourse that proceeds to realign the ideas and beliefs and the practices that arise from them. Our traditional insistence on linear continuity, for example, that we find in institutional emphasis on the same practices or on the same words or on rituals that pass "down" the same authority through the same vessels or instruments or through sacramental touching—that power-insistence functions in *Being and Time* in Heidegger's way of dealing with existential structures. Existence is the carrier of the sameness that makes linear continuity possible. The discipline of history and its unifying methods are based on Dasein's existential characteristic of historicity. And the sameness of existential structures gives Heidegger hope for a definitive interpretation of Dasein's continuing sameness throughout its history. The primary difference raised in *Being and Time* is the ontological difference between Being and beings, and that difference is susceptible to the metaphysical interpretation that thinks of Being as different from beings because it "is" outside of Dasein's ontological limits. One might say that Dasein's existential structure, which defines its limits and possibilities, defines the temporal and historical field that Being transcends or exceeds and in which Being is manifest. Dasein's constancy, in that case, would be taken as differentiating it from the unrestrictedness of Being. Then one would expect disclosure, not *Selbständigkeit* or subjectivity, to be Dasein's opening to Being: *Being and Time* would then be a footnote in a metaphysical tradition. It would not suggest a nonmetaphysical discourse, but would be an essay in that metaphysical tradition that attempts to modify the dominance of the ideas of substance and reason. Traditional mysticism could then be taken as one of *Being and Time*'s links with the metaphysical tradition.

Although that interpretation is viable if one stays within metaphysical language and thought and applies them to *Being and Time*, the book has been effective in developing quite a different strand of discourse. Both Dasein's existential formation and ontological difference are historical occurrences, just as Being, outside of its question, is a historical forecast or speculation. We shall look now at Dasein's historicity in this nonmetaphysical way of thinking, and think of Dasein's historical unity as Heidegger's way of coming to difference without reference to substantial identity or to a specific denial of it. His de-structuring of "unity," "identity," "timelessness," and so on, clears the way for a discourse without affirmation or denial of metaphysical thinking. That way of thinking is not completed or clearly anticipated by the author of *Being and Time*, but it is foreseeable as the de-structuring process realigns words and thoughts and sets in motion ways of thinking that become possible as de-structuring goes on. Our task now is to see what happens when "the fundamental structures of Dasein [are] conceived 'temporally' with regard to their possible totality, unity, and development and as modes of temporalizing of temporality" (61).

If Heidegger had thought of the existential structures of Dasein in terms of activity, as if they were structures of a constituting state of being, their activity or the activity in which they were found would have been *the* issue for his thinking. Activity and disclosure would have been closely associated. He sets aside the idea of activity, however, in favor of the possibility that disclosure is neither active nor passive. As he shows particularly in his account of being-in-the-world, that polarity will not do for setting the space, the limits, for a description of how things are together with Dasein. We have noted that the dominance of the active and passive voices in our speaking makes difficult any other options in our thinking. One of Heidegger's tactics in *Being and Time* for enabling our thinking of existential structures as disclosive but not as constituting or receptive states, is to conceive of human being as "thrown." He brings together the metaphysically suggestive idea that human being is thrown, as distinct to its having a sense of its origin and purpose, with the words *null* and *history*. His now familiar phrasing is that Dasein is "the possibility of the *im*possibility of its existence." Dasein's being is potentially "the absolute nothingness of Dasein" (62). As the *ground* of its own death, Dasein finds itself as though thrown—not as severed from an absent origin or as related by infinite difference to a mysterious source. Dasein finds itself "the null ground of its death" (62), which means that the only trace of nontemporal primordiality is mere nothing. The metaphor of "thrown" harbors no trace of a thrower or of an origin other than Dasein's own history. Dasein seems to be fully and completely—wholly—its own thrownness. Nothing else is traced in it. So Heidegger speaks of nothingness, not of absence, and of historicality, not of origin. And as we have already seen, Dasein's thrownness is the arrival-departure of Being. It occurs as the *question* of Being without the presence of Being.

"Temporality" occurs as nothing and as existence. When Dasein is "transparent to itself" in its "indefiniteness" and "wholeness," it is free for its temporality (62). Then it "clears away every concealment of the fact that [it] is left to itself" (62). It is prepared to know that historical relations reveal only history, that its history makes up its being, and that its "structures" are historical. The question of Being, forming a peculiar center in Dasein's history, will have its meaning in that history. Being, indeed, has been indicated in Dasein's deathliness.

The idea of disclosure links death and history. One way of thinking them together is to see disclosure—coming to light, being in the open—as an immaterial and nonhuman event. Human being is disclosive, not through its own agency, but through something quite different from agency. As disclosive, human being might be taken to be in another, nonhuman realm or region. This metaphysical option suggests that substance, identity, and subjectivity are not primordial links with Being. Being is disclosiveness, and the difference between human agency and disclosure as such is like the difference between the human and the absolute, whatever "absolute" might mean. Die though we may, disclosiveness goes on, serenely perhaps, or at least untroubled, free, and beyond the care that shows it obliquely to humans. That way of thinking, however, leaves out the historicity of both death and disclosure. It suggests that disclosiveness *almost* has a status outside of history—*almost*, because "status" is in time and disclosiveness leaks outside of time. In some metaphorical sense we need to say that disclosiveness both *is* and goes beyond "is" to timelessness.

Heidegger, on the other hand, says that when Dasein is free and open with its own mortality, is ready for its thrownness, and anticipates its dissolution, it is able to raise the question of Being and to notice when the question is forgotten. Itself in question, Dasein understands the question of Being. By making authenticity a turning toward Being and by linking mortality, temporality, and historicity, Heidegger places in question a transcendental attitude toward disclosure, one that Heidegger also shared ambivalently. Let us look at this ambivalence.

By free and open appropriation of its finiteness, Dasein has aligned itself with those discourses that hold in doubt final certainties, unquestioned truth, and positive dispositions toward absolutes. This is not an epistemological stance, not a skepticism, but a way of being with one's being. It is like a basic attitude that is open to and in touch with feelings as well as ideas, one that experiences itself through its relations with things and people. It finds that open resolve with dying and death, with the occurrences of becoming (that is, with its middle voice)—that the acceptance without reserve or compromise of dying and death—produces a way of existing in which both the question of Being and forgetfulness of that question are apparent. One is able to see that they have been covered over by structures of meaning characteristic of most of our culture and society. After his analysis of authenticity and Dasein's owning of its deathliness, Heidegger pursues a "still more primordial" interpretation of Dasein in an investigation into the conditions of authenticity. This next step, though it presupposes Dasein's free and open resolve, is more primordial in that it aims to show how authenticity is possible, what its meaning is. The next step deals with temporality and historicity, one consequence of which is to make it doubtful that the continuing "structures" of Dasein and their disclosiveness can reveal anything more than the history of the question of Being.

An ambivalence runs through this part of Heidegger's discussion. Authentic existence, free and open resolve with mortality, brings to light a basic understanding in Dasein: that its being is finite, always ending, never complete in its stasis or existence. Its "completion" can be spoken of with justification only ironically, as its cessation. When one is able to bring together this fundamental understanding and an explicit interpretation of human being and Being, the metaphysical orientation around time and timelessness begins to crumble. Now the temporal occurrence, *Geschehen* (72), of Dasein plays a role explicitly in relation to history in this section. Heidegger is not suggesting that one interpretation, or even one group of interpretations, necessarily follows from authenticity. He is saying rather that authentic existence is a major affect in how one thinks and speaks. In that case, the occurrence of temporality "grounds" this thinking and speaking, no matter how varied or different the thinking and speaking may be in various circumstances. Dasein's existential, temporal understanding runs through them and gives them a unifying basis. Temporality in the sense of temporal occurrence is both in and outside of the interpretive histories. It is like a transcendental state that founds historical occurrences.

Indeed, Heidegger emphasizes that temporality is the ontological condition of historicity.[51] It is also the condition for the inevitability of history, that is, of historicity, and of the historical being of Dasein. *But* the historical being of Dasein is temporality. Historicity and temporality are equiprimordial, says Heidegger, and that means that these basic existential structures are themselves historical (73). Now Dasein's existential state, which appeared earlier to function as a transcendental foundation, is thoroughly historical. Put transcendentally, the condition for the possibility of historical occurrences is the occurrence (*Geschehen*) of temporality. But the condition for the possibility of temporality is historical development.

The tension in *Being and Time* on the one hand has influenced the development of existential-transcendental thinking in which Dasein's structures of existence are taken as enjoying a transcendental status. For example, temporality, taken as a transhistorical basis for history, explains history ontologically by reference to Dasein's being. Dasein's being in its transcendental status is definitive of Dasein in all cases. On the other hand, if Dasein's historicity is emphasized, the transcendental motivation is undercut. History via mortality seeps as it were into all the existential connections and shows that Dasein's accomplishment of authenticity is an existential accord solely in Dasein's historical constitution. To be in this disposition also means to experience all positions, all stances and understandings, in Dasein's mortality. Not only will authentic sensibility continually pass over into everyday insensitivity; the conditions for authenticity also are experienced as finite and mortal. "The essential constitution of historicity" (74) names *historical* inevitability, and a human being who enters this developing interpretation is close to the idea that inevitabilities are regional and subject to description in their development and demise. Dasein's mortality means not only that it happens always in its deathliness; it means too that the being of Dasein is a historical development, and can pass away or over into something that is not at all as Dasein is. In this way of thinking, Being occurs as thrown question, as a living situation in which exists a creature that reflects on itself in terms of Being.

Heidegger's ambivalence in relation to temporality and historicity in *Being and Time* de-structures the transcendental-metaphysical strand that runs through the essay. The transcendental term *equiprimordiality*, for example, associated with *structure, fundamental, condition for the possibility, essential constitution*, and so on, is itself conditioned by such terms as *finite, historical, mortal*. That association effects a turn away from the transcendental turn. The effect of the essay leads toward thinking the history of Dasein as the history of Being. In that case, outside of this history there is neither Dasein nor Being. The question of Being, which has played a primary, constitutive role in Dasein, holds in question Being as such. Being is not Dasein, but it is found thrown as question in Dasein's history, without meaning except in that history. Its claim to transcendence dissolves in the *nicht* of Dasein's occurrences. And dissolving, its question perpetually begins again.

Heidegger's account of the unity of Dasein and his emphasis on the whole of Dasein's being has developed a way of thinking in which the whole of Dasein's being is like a fragment. It is the "place" of the question of Being, and it is constituted historically by that question. Yet "only the being 'between' birth and death presents the whole for which we are looking" (72). This stretch of life is pervaded by the "null," by not-being, by indefinite possibility, by the constituent mood of anxiety, by thrownness and historicity without nonhistorical transcendence. The Sartrean term *seepage* or the postmodern *inscription* is appropriate in this context. Nonbeing seeps through the existence of Dasein. Nonbeing inscribes the unity and wholeness of its ontological discourse.

As the association of Being, unity, wholeness, transcendence, and deathlessness is de-structured, the discourse itself tends away from those words. "Temporality" has begun to displace the anchoring and continuing functions of "Being." Nonunity, nonbeing without dialectic, the "spaces" in which fragments occur, the occurrence of differences without resolution, occurrences without substance: these kinds of words and issues emerge through the discourse of *Being and Time*. The linguistic, historical being, Dasein, is taking a turn that Heidegger could not really anticipate. History, temporal development, differences without *a* unity to integrate them all—such issues are emerging out of the question of Being and are leaving behind the language of transcendence, ontological structures, the unity of Being, and foundation. The *difference* between Being and beings becomes dominant. Being and beings move slowly toward the periphery of historical discourse. Dasein is changing "primordially."

6. HISTORICITY

(A) POSING THE ISSUE OF HISTORICITY

The issue of historicity, of the ontological basis for historical occurrences, is set in the context of Heidegger's preoccupation with Dasein's finite unity. Only after that unity is demarcated, named, and explicated in terms of care, temporality, and mortality does Heidegger turn to the way the unity of Dasein is shown in historical processes. Just as he has shown how all of Dasein's ways of being in the world manifest the mortality of Dasein's occurrence, he will now show how all historical happenings manifest Dasein's historicity. He will found historical realities and possibilities in Dasein's being. But just as Dasein's finite being destabilized the configuration of foundation, ground, Being, and unity, historicity will further destabilize the idea of transcendental unity, will eliminate subject-object pairing in thinking about history, and will recast the question of history into a nonlinear conception of historical happening. *Historicity* functions as an elaboration of mortal temporality, and only when Dasein has come to a free and open relation with its own deathliness is it prepared to reinterpret history and historicity with primary reference to its own being. Authenticity, Heidegger shows, is Dasein's opening to its essentially historical being.[52]

Dasein is not essentially a subjective occurrence. Its middle-voiced happening—its being its own phenomenon—and its being essentially world-relational rather than a subject that relates to the world, mean that the activity and structures of subjectivity are utterly misleading when one begins to think about human being and the meaning of Being. Heidegger uses "disclosure" to de-structure the dominance of subject terms for interpreting human being and Being—hence his beginning of his discussion of phenomenological method with the middle voice of *phainesthai* and *pseudesthai*. Neither showing nor concealing is active or passive. Authentic Dasein yields to its disclosure, its self-showing, in its unprotected and bare deathliness. A thorough concealing continues in traditional and everyday ways. Dasein's open, nonresisting acceptance of its being makes clear that concealing goes on, that it *is* a concealing occurrence, and that concealing need not be the basis for interpretative thinking. When historicity and deathliness come together in Dasein's resolved openness with its being, the dominance of the subject has already been de-structured. The question of unity is clearly not a question of unity of subjectivity. And any idea of history and historicity that cover over Dasein's deathliness, thrown fragmentariness, the question of Being, or the deep and structural sense of its own instability—such ideas will not attract authentic Dasein.

If history is not interpreted against a backdrop of subjectivity or of objective reality, how it is to be thought out? How is Dasein's finite middle voice to be rendered into active interpretation and thinking? What happens to Dasein-the-foundation in this process, which appears relentless in its de-structuring of inherited patterns of thought?

Heidegger's intention of grounding historical occurrences and their study in Dasein leads him to formulations taken from transcendental phenomenology. He replaces talk of consciousness with discussions of understanding, interpretation, and state of mind, and casts his discussion outside of the problematic of consciousness. But he establishes the unity of Dasein in the transcendental terms of ontological conditions for the possibility of ontic states.[53] Historicity, which is "basically a more concrete development of temporality," consequently functions in this discussion as the steady structure that grounds "the endless multiplicity of possibilities" for historical occurrences (74). Heidegger is convinced that without an ontological structure, particular occurrences would lack ordered identity. So he emphasizes the transcendental-like structures. The historical status of historicity itself is uncertain in this way of posing the problem. Historicity can be taken to be transhistorical in the sense that it grounds all temporal events, or it can be taken to be thoroughly historical, that is, itself generated in a developing process. If historicity, belonging as it does to the being of Dasein, makes history possible, then it would appear to be transhistorical. If historicity is itself historical, then it would be a finite structure and a process characterized by birth and death. Heidegger probably means both of these possibilities at different times. Regardless of his intentions, the struggle that takes place in the context of deathliness and finitude between the transhistorical and the historical elements in his language moves this discourse toward a way of thinking in which history is seen as the way all necessary conditions occur, so that the question of history is posed in exclusive reference to history itself and not in reference to the conditions for the possibility of history. Histories become their own conditions. This way of thinking, however, becomes viable in the context of Heidegger's thought only when the issue of unity and conditions is de-structured. This begins in *Being and Time*, but the book was not written in the full impact of that process.

Historicity, as we shall see in the following section, is conceived in nonlinear terms, and whether Dasein has a specific, developmental beginning—a birth into history—is not a primary concern. Finitude and historicity are not to be conceived in a quasi-explanatory context—for example, that Dasein did in fact have a beginning in a natural or world-historical process. Doubtlessly it did. But Dasein's historicity is already assumed by the concern reflected in that claim. We are not looking for origins or originary developments. We are attempting to pose the issue of historicity in terms of Dasein's self-disclosure as a temporal, finite being. The account needs to begin in Dasein's appropriation of its thrown mortality: it needs to begin with an effort to think from and toward its appropriation of self-showing, without explanation, and without many traditional guides for speaking and thinking. If Dasein can hold itself in its mortality and in the question of the meaning of Being, perhaps the transcendentally oriented language will discover something that it cannot handle. Perhaps the awkwardness of finding through the metaphysical and phenomenological traditions something that is covered over by them will make possible a different and less encumbered way of speaking and thinking.

(B) THE MIDDLE VOICE OF TIME AND HISTORY

Heidegger uses the expression "temporality temporalizes" in showing how Dasein's being relates to everyday experiences and schemes of time (cf. 75, 78, 80). He wants to show that Dasein's understanding of its being is embedded in the casual, everyday manner of experiencing time. He further wants to show that care and Dasein's essential caring for its being in its being are indicated even by everyday life, in which one could not care less for ontological issues. Our interest, however, is in Heidegger's use of an expression that recalls the middle voice.

Temporality temporalizes: that is one way to interpret Dasein's historicity.[54] Dasein's "stretch" between birth and death, the occurrence of "primordial temporality," reveals the whole of Dasein and its "constancy and steadiness" (75). Dasein is its historical constancy, and is the basis for the particular constants that we find in history and everyday life. Heidegger looks for a way to say that something unfolds out of itself and throughout the human world without indicating dialectical development or objective "world-historical processes." The "foundation" of temporal occurrences is itself an occurrence, and "time is neither objectively present nor in the subject nor in the object, neither 'inside' nor 'outside,' it is 'prior' to every subjectivity or objectivity, *because it presents the condition of the very possibility of this 'prior'*" (80, emphasis added). Time as the condition for temporal subjectivity and objectivity is neither active nor passive. It does not simply reflect back on itself; it temporalizes. Temporality shows temporality as it occurs.

When the fundamental condition for all subjective and objective temporal relations is thought out in this middle-voiced way, subjectivity falls away in relation to "condition." Temporality does not occur as subjectivity or subjects occur, nor does it receive action. Temporal "there" takes place. Everyday time emerges and develops. Birth and death stretch out together in a finite process that in its self-showing does not allow reduction. Dasein is its own occurring. In this process of coming to be and ceasing to be, always, as not subjective and not objective but in a middle voice, Dasein's being is in question. As time "times," meanings both show time and cover it (*phainesthai* and *pseudesthai* happen together). History takes place not as a story or a complicated world-historical procession, but as Dasein "times" out. Dasein is not "in" history by being historical; it is historical in its self-showing. Since it is self-showing in the birth-death stretch, it is more radically historical than can be conveyed by an evolutionary, developmental idea. Every objective explanation expresses Dasein's concern for its being, shows Dasein as care in the process of birth and dying, and fades in its promise of certainty as Dasein experientially recalls its being. In its middle voice, all of Dasein's certainties fade out. Such fading is one more instance of temporality temporalizing.

When one holds in mind Heidegger's insistence on a unity of structures and a unified process of temporality with this middle voice aspect of his thinking, the discourse-developing tension in *Being and Time* is clear. As temporality is thought through, it becomes clear that Dasein's historicity means that no objective or subjective stance for Dasein as such can withstand the fading-out process. Dasein is not an occurrence that begins in time. It care-fully "times," and therefore can tell itself of real, objective origin. Its occurrence ex-sists in the sense that timing stands out (*ecstasis* is Heidegger's term) from all factual standing. Dasein's constancy is ex-standing: the middle voice will not be absorbed into the active or passive voices that provide continuity by stances, connections, and receptions. Dasein begins to appear as historicity in the strong sense that historical explanations of it fall short and conceal its finitude—its originating and dying time. The constancy promised by Heidegger's transcendental, phenomenological language has been turned into a radically finite event by a middle voice in the midst of an otherwise objective description of human occurrence.

(C) WHAT HAPPENS TO HISTORY?

There are two emphases in the way Heidegger thinks of history in *Being and Time*. They may well be complementary, although either's dominance of the other will lead to considerably different ways of thinking.

The first emphasis thinks of Dasein as having come to be and as mortal. It combines this thought with the question of the meaning of Being. Dasein is not only the "stretch between birth and death" in its thrownness; Dasein is also a history that manifests beginning without metahistorical meaning or grounding. Meaning occurs *in* Dasein's history, and finds no transhistorical reverberation. The "stretch" of the individual is like Dasein itself, the finite stretch between birth and death. Always aborning, always dying, always witness to beginning and end, Dasein is its own basis for believing that as a way of being it is subject to beginning and ending. Not only is history as such consequently finite (since history is the stretch of Dasein's being), but historical segments have only Dasein as their continuing ground. For Heidegger the transcendental thinker, Dasein is the condition for the possibility of history and histories. For Heidegger the de-structionist of transcendental thinking, Dasein does not mean its own continuing. It is a passing away that has no preestablished directedness toward some type of eternity or toward long endurance.

Within this emphasis, the question of Being looks like a defining aspect of Dasein's being. The history of this question completes and exhausts its meaning. If Being is desubstantialized by making it the questionableness of the question, Being, and not only the meaning of Being, is thought as finite. Being is then taken to be the question of Dasein's finitude. It is "beyond" any grasp, formulation, or way of life. It is the ground of Dasein's thinking and doing. It is the strange, fading, and revealing basis of being-in-the-world. But it does not appear to be outside the occurrence of its own history. In *Being and Time* Heidegger does not think of Being as intrinsically historical; Dasein is intrinsically historical. The possibility that Being itself is historical as the question of Dasein's historical being, however, is not far removed from the essay's way of thinking; it often seems to be only one de-structuring step away.

The second emphasis sets aside the imagery of beginning and end.

Historicity becomes the dominant word. It names the way finite Dasein shows itself. This approach asks us to recast the issue of history as the question of how Dasein shows itself, of how temporality temporalizes. We begin to forget the problems of relative versus nonrelative grounding as we appropriate our own finite temporality. This part of Heidegger's de-structuring process thinks outside of the context of universal-particular and relative-absolute, although his opposing terms *ontic-ontological* and *existentielle-existential*, as well as his overriding concern for unity and ontological continuity, are in tension with historicity as middle-voiced, nonnormative occurrence.

Within this second emphasis one can easily think of Being as a self-showing, self-concealing mystery that is not circumscribed by Dasein's linear procession. Temporality is like a mysterious emission of Being, and the problem is to learn to think of emission or the *schicht* of *Geschichte* in substance-free language. The history of Being is how it is lived out in its arriving-withdrawing. Does Dasein highlight, as it were, Being's withdrawal? Its self-showing? Does it live as though Being were not there at all? Does it learn to hear Being's occurrence in its own historicity? Its question arises from its mystery, its continual escape from meaning and from the temporality that reveals it. Dasein's historicity is the occurrence of Being's questionableness in existence. And Being's difference from Dasein, which is shown through Dasein's own mortal, fragmentlike quality, is able continually to incite existential doubt and wonder; Being's withdrawal is hinted at in the absence of meaning and the existential incompleteness that pervade Dasein's meaning and undermine all momentary fulfillment.

The difference of Being is essentially shrouded in Dasein. Dasein's own self-showing, its difference from subjectivity and objectivity, shows nothing exactly; certainly not something other. But it does show a dimension of ocurrence that escapes our grammars, words, and syntax. Thinking in acceptance of such mystery partakes of the mystical in the sense that the thinker is in touch with, is in the hearing of, unsayable, unspecifiable difference that occurs in the ground of Dasein's own occurrence. Meditative discipline, attitudes similar to reverence, and the affections of noninterference and noninsistence are appropriate.

Within both of these emphases, difference pervades relations of similarity, continuity, and contiguity. Whether thought in terms of the finiteness of history as such or of Dasein's occurrence as historicity, our thinking Being and time together in this essay shows that beings in their definitive relations are "gapped" by nothing definitive or sayable. Heidegger thinks of this difference as that between Being and beings: in the "is," Being happens in a strange intimacy or closeness with Dasein that disrupts continuity in mortal "timing." *Being and Time* leaves the reader (and Heidegger too) with the question of how to think out mortal "timing," and the question holds multiple possibilities for ways of thinking that emerge from and leave behind the de-structuring that has gone on in *Being and Time*. Is human history to be thought in reference to its gaps and fissures that make intelligible in terms of self-defining historical regions and demarcated spans of time the indwelling absence of definition and identity? Is thoughtful speaking to take place by plays of differences that disrupt totalities of meaning and the sense of grammatical connections? Is the acceptance of finite temporality to be developed by studies of ways in which our languages remember and forget temporality temporalizing? Such projects assume the de-struction of Dasein as it is thought in association with transcendental grounding, and indicate that at least an initial phase of the de-structuring process worked: the unity of Dasein turns out to be unthinkable in terms of a unitary continuity for differences. That "unity" appears rather to be *phainesthai* and *pseudesthai* at once, that is, no unity at all. That is not what Heidegger intended. But it is what his discourse accomplished.

(D) THE STRIFE OF THE QUESTION OF BEING

In the penultimate paragraph of *Being and Time* Heidegger says that "we must look for a way to illuminate the fundamental ontological question, and follow it." In the margin of his copy of *Being and Time* he noted the words "a way" and wrote "not 'the' sole way."[55] The essay is the result of his intention to pursue the question of Being by "the understanding of Being that belongs to existing Dasein." He has tried to show how Dasein's understanding of Being is articulated in formative, traditional ideas about Being. At best, such a study will have instigated a "strife in relation to the interpretation of Being." This strife for which the essay has served as preparation will bring out the question of Being.[56] Once initiated, the strife takes priority over the way Heidegger presents his investigations, that is, he has started a process that he suspects will not be controlled by *Being and Time* and probably will not support his own way of developing its question. He is in a question that is not his, one that he knows to have made possible his own work and the continuing work of the book that he has brought to a close. But he is not sure how this possibility for raising the question of Being is to be interpreted. At the conclusion of his investigation of Dasein as the "place" of this question, he asks, "How is the disclosive understanding of Being belonging to Dasein possible at all?" By "going back to the primordial constitution of the being of Dasein that understands Being," he has initiated strife around the question of Being. That strife puts his work in question and articulates both the question of Being and an understanding of Being to which Heidegger knows that he has not done justice. Should it happen that the strife of this question were also its Logos, its gathering, then we would expect Heidegger's discourse to have initiated a process of investigating and questioning that goes far beyond the constraints of his triggering analysis. The strife would be disclosive of a discursive history that produced a dominant way of being—Dasein—that has as its future continuing strife. Should the strife end, Dasein would no longer exist. By initiating this process, *Being and Time* has anticipated its own demise and been true to its own unresolved conflicts. Both nonresolution and conflict will continue in this discursive strand in the dominance of difference.

4

Recurrences without Representation

Transvaluation and de-struction have been two of the controlling words in the previous chapters. By following the transvaluing and destructuring process in *Beyond Good and Evil* and *Being and Time*, we have found in the discourses of these books an interplay of the books' ideas with their own discursive shifts of meaning and significance. We have seen the possibility develop out of these changes and processes for a way of thinking in which difference has much greater valence in relation to the idea of identity than it had in the philosophical lineage of these two books. We have noted subtle changes in linguistic organization and hierarchies. As these changes have developed in *Beyond Good and Evil* and *Being and Time*, both essays have become unsatisfactory on their own terms. Nietzsche's ambivalence regarding metaphysical thinking and Heidegger's inadequate language regarding the question of Being have become apparent because of the effect of the noted discursive changes in each of those books. Each philosopher intended to develop the leading ideas found in each book. But neither could know or intend what began to develop in the power of discourse that emerged with their projects. A language of difference rather than of identity began to form. The continuity of this language with its history has been clear. But continuity has emerged through the processes of transvaluation and de-struction, continuity developed less by relations of similarity or analogy than by departure, de-formation, reversal, upturning, return to suppressed or forgotten emphases: transgressing rather than conforming, finding the cuts and tears in operative orders and organizations—faulting—and thinking with priority given to the sublimated or outcast ideas in the metaphysical tradition. These discursive elements have formed part of the initiation of the language of difference, not contemplative or ritual events of union, not rhetorical harmony, not desires for appropriateness on the part of aspects of a whole cosmos, not longing for union with another, not disciplined obedience to special authorities or texts, not experiences of sameness pervasive in differences. In the decline of the effectiveness of the idea of identity in these two essays, a different discursive experience of difference has developed.

We saw, for example, that Heidegger's understanding of disclosure and existence is not within the power of subject-object polarity. Although authentic existence seems at times to be an accomplishment of identity, the occurrence of authentic existence, we found, is not an occurrence of identity. It occurs as Dasein's openness with its own being in the question of Being. No one does the opening. It is allowed, and in this language the idea of subject is sublimated in a discourse of Being that gives emphasis to question and difference. Heidegger's idea of opening out, of unlocking, has displaced the idea of activity by a subject or by subjectivity. The issue is not whether there is identity or whether similarities exist. It is how identity or difference govern other words, an issue of their relative discursive power. As difference gains power, for example, completion, origin, and status are conceived increasingly in terms of cessation, boundary-with-no-identity, nonbeing, and occurrences without sub-stance.

Throughout *Beyond Good and Evil* and *Being and Time* we found uncertainty regarding metaphysical thinking. Sometimes the language was that of opposition—antimetaphysics—and of metaphysical counterclaims. At other times *non*metaphysical language developed—not anti, but a language broken away from and different from metaphysical thinking. The transformation of metaphysical thinking and the de-struction of metaphysics, however, were not finished in these books. The books are processes that are thoroughly involved with what is being transformed or de-structured. In Foucault's thinking, however, there is less ambiguity in relation to metaphysical thinking. He comes after *Beyond Good and Evil* and *Being and Time*; these discourses have had effect, have led beyond themselves, and have contributed to a situation in which the priority of identity does not rule the discourse. Foucault's work comprises a sustained effort to think through difference, to let difference have its sway. It is a way of thinking in which the desire or longing for ultimate meaning, timeless order, or metaphysical truth do not occur. The strife foreseen at the end of *Being and Time* comes into a style and thought of difference that turns this strife into a discourse-forming power. In its power, a nonmetaphysical thinking develops.

Nietzsche's work influenced Foucault's ideas of power, genealogy, memory, and event. But more significantly, it developed a direction of thought in which one is naturally attuned to "exhaustion, excess, the limit, and transgression—a strained and unyielding form of these irrevocable movements which consume and consummate us."[57] The tensions in Nietzsche's thinking, his struggle to think by reference to power developments and descents instead of truth, and his ways of achieving freedom in relation to traditional authorities both in philosophy and in daily life: these tensions, moods, and styles of thinking, with their irony, aphoristic breakage of reflective certainty, their nomadic mood and discursive infighting, created an atmosphere that nourished Foucault's thinking far more than any group of truth claims on Nietzsche's part. The divisions, discontinuities, and differences that are found in Nietzsche's thinking helped to make the discursive space for Foucault's work.

The effect of Heidegger's work is no less powerful, but it is less evident in Foucault's writing. Being, in Heidegger's language, is found in self-communicating events in our dominant traditions. It is thought by Heidegger in its difference from beings, not as identity or as a being, not as reason, will, consciousness, an unconscious, not as reposed perfection, teleological energy, or a principle of order. Scission, hiding, forgetting, fracture, historicity, and death have been the words that aid Heidegger's thinking through the *question* of Being. Its question, not its presence, gave birth to Western philosophy. The question, the issue of Being, can pass away just as it has spawned the dominant discourses of our history. This question and its threatening power have made our traditions those in which searches for certainty, senses of mystery and limit, preoccupation with presence and absence dominate. The question of Being has generated emphasis on the coming to be and passing away of things, the limited identities of beings, the puzzle of life-with-death. It has been lived out through ideas of "reality" that have forgotten the question that developed and moved them. The question in its primordial, traditional disturbance has often been changed into an idea about primordial, moving presence—a something—that is the *Wesen* or essence of all other presences and that supplies meaning to their fragmentary existences. Heidegger's work recalls the question behind and through the texts and practices that have formed us, given us the boundaries of our thinking, created the unconscious topography that makes us as we are.[58] Derrida's phrase, the undecidability of texts—emphasis on *that* dimension of discursive occurrence rather than attention to a sum total of influences and meanings—indicates an important part of Heidegger's legacy. This emphasis on undecidability, on multiple, often contradictory, simultaneous histories and possibilities, and the departure of what Foucault calls the consolations and familiar murmurings of metaphysics follow from Heidegger's way of posing the question of Being and thinking through that question.

Foucault is not tempted by the schematism or the language of *Being and Time*. He is much more attracted by "the invention of acategorial thought" and "an ontology . . . [in which] differences would resolve of their own accord."[59] Although Foucault does not often think in direct reference to Heidegger, Heidegger's emphasis on *Riss* (tear) and the tearing effect that goes on in his own thinking is repeated in Foucault's attention to difference in his own non-Heideggerian thinking. We have seen that one of the characteristics of Heidegger's discourse is to lead to non-Heideggerian ways of thinking in the wake of its own de-structuring. The question of Being as Heidegger follows it does not lead to a still more developed idea of Being. It leads to thinking without Being or with Being-in-difference, a thinking in which metaphysical styles, ideas, and issues have lost much of their power. We saw this effect in the discursive function of difference, developed in terms of question and de-struction in *Being and Time*. Its power is not in what is literally repeatable in reportorial knowledge. Its effect occurs as one thinks in the discourse itself and undergoes the question and de-structuring that are in it. Both transvaluing and de-structuring are "understood" through their happening. They can be observed, but if the observing discourse is not in the processes of transvaluing or destructuring, those "thoughts" will be in another discourse with another effect. Foucault's thinking has been effected in these processes. He works in a language of difference that has been formed in the work of Nietzsche's and Heidegger's thinking and in other thinking similar in effect to theirs. In their effects he does not attempt to recodify for this time their thoughts. Repetition moves to a different plane of thought, in which Nietzsche's and Heidegger's effects are repeated in the effective power of difference and of the hierarchical changes in concepts that go on in their wake. Through the differences of his thinking, Foucault, like Nietzsche and Heidegger, attempts to speak of what is unspeakable in tables of categories and images of unity, although we shall find him much less involved than Nietzsche and Heidegger in metaphysical thinking. *Their* transvaluing and de-structuring need not be repeated. He thinks in differences made through their discourses.

Foucault does not ask primarily about texts, unless "texts" be taken in a broad sense to include the texture of a given society, institution, or practice. His language of difference is not primarily about language or writing. When we use the word *discourse* in the context of Foucault's work, we have in mind a complex interplay of speaking, doing, and knowing. Historical-social interactions are always prominent in his ideas. As we follow the idea of difference in his work we are dealing with relations among things, among bodies, words, rules, professions, principles, buildings, habits, ways of perceiving, stating and asking. These relations and manners are at once established and porous. As in a cloud chamber, a change of contextual volume or velocity alters the configurations and the ways the configurations can form. His own work, of course, is also in a configuration, and the play of difference in his work provides a focus for thinking in a language that welcomes its own power configurations and fragility. That play has developed, cloudlike, as difference has gained discursive power, and Foucault's work furthers this power as it follows discourse-forming alignments of power. We continue to think in the language at hand, with it and through it, in such a way that the language of difference functions through our claims and recognitions. A process we shall call differencing is the effect. In the differencing, understanding takes place.

1. VARIATIONS ON DELEUZIAN THEMES: THINKING WITHOUT REPRESENTING

Platonism has divided and separated things in order to find the "pure models" on the basis of which one is able to distinguish pure realities from copies.[60] Foucault retains the dividing and separating, but he finds models in a language of difference. Platonism is reversed and subverted by making, in the absence of sameness, "delicate sorting operations" on the basis of differences. The emphasis is on images of surfaces and borders under the jurisdiction of difference rather than images of heights and depths in the domain of identity. As the sorting out of differences goes on without Models, the Identical, or the Same, "irony rises and subverts; humor falls and perverts" (p. 168). The phrase "incorporeal materiality" collects a significant part of Foucault's subversions and perversions. As we work on the meaning and function of this phrase, we have in mind the questions: How do irony and humor "speak" of difference without the dominance of identity? And in what sense does incorporeal materiality name occurrences without Unity and Reality? We shall move toward the idea of repetition of differences as we look at this peculiar term, incorporeal materiality.

In discourses without ideas of Model, Idea, or Same, we find instead bodies, that is, organizations or "materialities," that have had specific functions and specific surfaces that differentiate discrete bodies in their various external relations. We may speak of bodies of knowledge, as

Foucault does, of bodies of desire, institutional bodies, professional bodies, and so on.[61] The metaphor of body indicates singular kinds of organizations that, as kinds, resemble and diverge from one another in varying degrees. Their simulations are found as surface plays, not in deep interiors or transcendent models, through the powers and languages that constitute their functions, limitations, alliances, and conflicts, not through will or energy that has deep or transcendent identity. Instead of something *sub* that *stances* the organizations, we find "phantasms" that have desires, interests, repeated qualities and characteristics, but nothing primordial about them. Phantasms are plays of surface relations, matters of moment, identity, and power; they are differences coming from plays of differences, differences with growing and passing similarities: they are simulacra.

In and through the play of singularities—things, bodies—that reduce to nothing but that persist for a time in their interplays, we look for words to speak of how the interplays occur, of the connections among things. *Phantasms* is one option: "Phantasms must be allowed to function at the limit of bodies; against bodies, because they stick to bodies and protrude from them, but also because they touch them, cut them, break into sections, regionalize them, and multiple their surfaces; and equally outside of bodies, because they function between bodies according to laws of proximity, torsion, and variable distance—laws of which they remain ignorant."[62] So the corpse, for example, into which knives cut and that showed the lesions and growths that had been hidden behind tissues, the knives that cut them, and the hands that moved the knives function out of the "phantasms" or the incorporeal materiality of a changing body of beliefs and practices. This changing body produced the modern medical body that housed and defined both sickness and health. This incorporeal materiality was a grid made up of ordered knowledges. It was a surface that produced the research hospital; it had kinship with the eighteenth-century style of family life, with the disinherited poor, the centralizing needs of emerging governments, a crumbling theology, and the transformation of seventeenth-century beliefs about rationality into empirical perception with a suspicion of inferential connection.[63] The surface imagery, which coupled with insubstantial powers (phantasms), with "bodies" that are on a surface of other bodies, speaks simultaneously of differences and organizational identity. The elaboration of surface by such words as *limit, against, stick, protrude, touch, cut, break,* and *multiply* speaks of things that are in external differentiation by virtue of differentials or powers that have only movements and moments.

Phantastical movement is elaborated by "mime," not by the orders of a king or lord or master of the house. The series of "liberated simulacra . . .

mimes itself" (p. 171). It does not copy something that is original or basic for it. "Scenes that refer to each other," or mimes that create by—no longer do we say by illusion; illusion in relation to what?—by movements that mean themselves in relation to other movements and that create scenes that are not representative in relation to something else, but that are self-presenting. Just so. The setting in this theater, the chair on the dais, the series of lights, the empty lighted space—the stage organization—are continually displaced by a series of interpenetrating movements and patterns that create a different exterior in the displaced space of the stage, not an inwardness, but a powerful external difference, a specific locus of intensity that draws away from the staging and projects out of the staging its own limits and organizations as mute communication, as phantasm against the incorporeal material of staging (or, to say the same thing, as incorporeal material fringing through the phantasm of staging). The mime is an extrinsic event of imagery and energy that is played out on a stage space that it crowds and pushes while the stage space sets and limits it.

Out of this distance from metaphysics, seen in one instance in the imagery of mime and external space, Foucault speaks ironically of Deleuze's "metaphysical treatise." We followed the language of Heidegger as he reshaped the idea of Being, gave it strange and different discourses, and differentiated it from its metaphysical history. Foucault has little interest in reshaping or denouncing metaphysics, or in countermanding metaphysical thinking. He does pause long enough in his (and Deleuze's) different images and hierarchies to observe that Deleuze can at least use the word *being* to speak of "extra-being"—of the "phantasms, idols, and simulacra" that are the incorporeal things with which metaphysics deals. This report from a nonmetaphysical discourse does not find metaphysics "doomed to illusion." Metaphysics could be *doomed* to illusion only from its own position that thinks of Reality as the benchmark for recognizing illusion. If that thinking still had the benchmark but could no longer speak with conviction about Reality, it could feel doomed. Or it could speak of the doomed from its Reality-centered stance. In Foucault's discourse, metaphysics has been "haunted" by illusion and has "feared" the simulacrum, the likeness that is not a copy of something originary. He is observing that likeness without sub-stance and surface without depth have been in metaphysics all along, but there as rejected, feared, hunted down, and outcast. In contrast to Derrida who considers metaphysics so successful in its elimination of its rejected aspects that only traces of eradication remain, Foucault says that illusion "is the product of a particular metaphysics that designated the separation between the simulacrum on the one side and the original and perfect copy on the other" (pp. 170–71). In this case Foucault is outside of metaphysics and is returning to metaphysical thinking in the rule of elements that metaphysical discourses have carried, but have scourged and imprisoned and treated as though they were not on the metaphysical surface. Deleuze's is a "joyous metaphysics," one that is "freed from its original profundity as well as from a supreme being, but also one that can conceive of the phantasm in its plays of surfaces without the aid of models . . ." (p. 171).[64] In a discourse of Reality and One Good, Deleuze's would be an "epidermic play of perversity." In Foucault's discourse, however, instead of perversity we find in Deleuze's thinking an increase in "compassion for reality," for the intensities that form topologies of similarity and conflict (p. 168). The intensities are "meta" in relation to bodies, and they are like illusions rather than like dense bodies.[65] The absence of Reality and Purity in this thinking is no loss. There is in the imagery of mime, for example, a process of dissolving the orders of thought and desire that produced "the philosophy of representation." Those orders are networks, as we shall see, that utilize ideas of an "original, the first time, resemblance, initiation, faithfulness" (p. 172).[66] Without a primordial interior, the space of mime "gives rise to a mutual resonance," a surface play in which the hierarchies of primary, untouched purity, originary source, or fundamental likeness are erased.

Event is the word of choice for the intangible interplay of bodies on surfaces without depth. "Stitched causality," says Foucault. "As bodies collide, mingle, and suffer, they create events on their surfaces, events that are without thickness, mixture, or passion . . ." (p. 173). Their collisions and other surface contacts form successions and associations, all manner of linkage. They do not build something substantive or inherently like something else. They build, rather, continuing approximations and departures.[67] To say as Foucault does, repeating Deleuze, that accounts of events are metaphysical is to say that event-thinking turns traditional metaphysical intentions and desires on their heads. He weaves between Deleuze's observations that bodies are external to events and his own observation that bodies are events, while he shows that in either case "*meta*physics" occurs for Deleuze in a way of thinking that keeps the "extreme point of singularity" always in view, a point where there is perpetual dissolution, separation, ending, and returning—continuous dying—as meanings form on the surfaces of colliding bodies.[68] The events of dying function for Foucault (and Deleuze) as they did for Heidegger: they give voice to contingency and difference and allow affirmation on a line of radical differentiation (life—death, this—that, I—not—I). This line of difference connotes the dying away and contingent return of identities. Affirmation in this language occurs in moods of positivity on this line without hope or desire for sub-stance, for movement toward or around something ultimate, or for a final triumph of identity over difference without identity. Meanings perish and repeat on the meaningless surface contacts among things. Meanings do not penetrate to a center. They do not represent something beyond their reach and in whose standing likeness they occur. They refer to themselves only. They perish and repeat in a play that gives delight to Deleuze—a delight that delights Foucault in this discourse of surface, resonance, and mime.[69] Foucault writes about Deleuze's metaphysical de-struction with no hint of nostalgia for depth-mystery or centered identity, with no sense of despair after the de-struction of world, self, and God, with no desire to hope for their return. His discourse recognizes metaphysics like a young man who looks at an old print of his great-grandfather and recognizes his own transformed likeness through distant kinship. Foucault's peace and lack of agitation in the presence of metaphysical thinking also differentiate him from Nietzsche and Heidegger. His discussion of Deleuze is after metaphysics.[70]

The concept of event as Foucault appropriates it is an "affirmation of disjunction" (p. 177). An event, that is, an initiating occurrence with meaning (for example, using a scientific technique, publishing a text, conceiving an idea, a battle, a policy), may have resonance and reverberation, "not in the heart of man," says Foucault, "but above his head, beyond the clash of weapons, in fate and desire" (p. 177). Events resound in the formations that follow in their wake, such as the death of God resounding in Nietzsche's discourse, and Nietzsche's discourse resounding in discourses that came in the wake of his writings, such as the fates and desires that emerged out of Nietzsche's and Heidegger's writings far in excess of what they could have intended; Foucault's own pleasure in Deleuze—a fate in Nietzsche's and Heidegger's lineage; Deleuze's "metaphysics of the incorporeal event" (p. 176)—a fate in the transformation of metaphysics; affirmation of the limits of the power of the idea of identity—a complex desire in a discourse "above the heads" of those who speak and feel within it. These things are fates in the sense that they follow out of events that resound in them, just as these things are themselves events that may have further resonances.

These events are not originary in the sense that they give primordial meaning, have primal significance, or stand outside of their own meaning. Their location has no privilege. They have resonances, and they are repeated in resonance. By resonance they continue to function with no other stance or presence. "The event is that which is invariably lacking in the series of the phantasm—its absence indicates its repetition devoid of any grounding in an original . . ." (p. 177). The event resounds in repetition, which for Deleuze is its "extra-being," for Foucault, its lack of being. It merely is as resounding, as phantasm. Its repetition disguises nothing. Nothing is dissimulated. It recurs when repetition occurs. Its teleology forms in a series of repetitions with accretions, subtractions, modulations. There is no event-nub that is supplemented or spun out. It is something that happened and that is carried on like a repeated phantasm in other happenings.[71] It is like an infinitive—for instance, to think—that is repeated in its lack of substance in multiple ways.[72]

The "indefinite multiplicity" (p. 178) of events indicates discursive processes, that is, series of meanings and practices that are not synthesized subjectively, but are rather cast together through sequences, contiguities, dissensions, mergers, and so forth. They are "repetitions without models" (p. 179). Thinking is one type of discursive repetition, a series of phantasmal events in which the thought-things are discursive reverberations of events in their indefinite multiplicity. The mime, as an analogy for thinking, is silent communication coming out of a large number of possibilities. It is both highly studied—crafted—and also remarkably incomplete in its definiteness. It arises in silence, communicates with a silent backdrop, and lapses into silence. Fissures of indefinitiveness pervade the communicative event. The mime affirms rather than resists the fissures in its miming. It produces and releases in a way that simultaneously emphasizes and effaces the mimist. A quality of discourse reverberates through the miming. Thinking that affirms its own quality of discursive event is like that. Rather than a subject-object disjunction or an absolute subject-object, an $I = I$, repeating movements with resonances of other movements in new formations constitute the process of thinking. "The thought-phantasm does not search for truth, but repeats thought" (p. 179). As an event, this kind of thinking repeats phantasms and affirms this repetition. It does not attempt to establish commonality, but lets reverberations of events resound in its own setting. It "displaces" the difference that it thinks in *its* place, gives a variant surface of enactment, and in Foucault's thinking it lets go of interest in generality and universality. Meaning is generated without the restrictions of universality or desire for *the* truth. The infinitive quality of indefinite multiplicity has sway in the arrangements of words and desires.[73]

In such an arrangement, global resemblances do not occur. Thinking does not represent things in structures taken to be universal. Things-to-be-represented occur in that thinking that has pared things down to just-so identities, that is, to phantasms that refuse their phantasmal multiplicity. The discourse of resemblance and its drive to represent identities with accurate likenesses do not function now. "Let us pervert good sense and allow thought to play outside the ordered table of resemblances; then it will appear as the vertical dimension of intensities, because intensity, well before its gradation by representation, is in itself pure difference: difference that displaces and repeats itself, that contracts and expands; a singular point that constricts and slackens the indefinite repetitions in an acute event. One must give rise to thought as intensive irregularity—disintegration of the subject" (p. 183). Thought becomes, in Deleuze's word, nomadic, a singular, processing, relational discursive event of intensity, one that takes shape out of the interplay of discursive forces. Each event displaces and differentiates the others. Interpretation, expulsion, transmutation: in a word, differentiation names the events' occurrence. In a Nietzschian reverberation, Deleuze and Foucault find plays of forces an appropriate metaphor for many events. These intensities do not re-present. They resound, repeat, reform, return play for play. They are "intense irregularities" (p. 183) that disembody and disintegrate as they focus and formulate. So a scale of differences rather than a grid of similarity allows us to think about discursive relations without eliminating their intense irregularities for the purposes of understanding.[74]

One intention in Foucault's discourse is to release difference from its "subjugation by the idea of being. Being is paired with the idea of sameness that pervades differences. In their subjection, this sameness gives differences their relation and modality. When they are ordered in terms of categories, their categoriality expresses their commonality. Being pervades their order and is expressed in tables of categories that bestow on differences knowability and relational stance. Differences then cannot be thought as real except by reference to the categories that distribute them, call them to order, and organize them. Categories express being and "suppress the anarchy of difference, divide differences into zones, delimit their rights, and prescribe their task of specification with respect to individual beings" (p. 186).

"Difference can only be liberated through the invention of an acategorial thought" (p. 186). This invention is a way of thinking governed by difference. Identity, for example, is conceived as the repetition of differences. Thinking itself is thought as differencing and repeating. Things are repetitive expressions. As the expressions change, things change, transform, transmute.[75] The invention is a suppression of categories, an elevation of repetition, and a process in which familiar things and possibilities undergo thorough change. Thinking and thought are now different from thinking and the thought ruled by being, identity, and category.

What happens when this invention of acategorial thinking begins to operate? Categories have established those bodies of knowledges by which we have lived and structured our society. We have advanced by changing or reorganizing the categories. With them we distinguish the true and the false, the good and the bad. "No sooner do we abandon their organizing principle than we face the magma of stupidity" (p. 188). Within the discourse of categorial thinking, the loss of categorial thinking promises anarchy, boundless monotony, and cultural darkness, as well as the deterioration of professional superstructures that have given us the means of survival. There are reports, however, from this other thinking: "We find the sudden illumination of multiplicity itself—with nothing at its center, as its highest point, or beyond it—a flickering of light that travels even faster than the eyes and successively lights up the moving labels and captive snapshots that refer each other to eternity, without even saying anything" (p. 189). The categorial stance that promises catastrophe if it should pass away is felt as an "inertia of equivalences." Discourses, preferences, hierarchies, solutions, and affirmations do not, in fact, die with the passage of the categorial stance. Rather, they gain lightness. Things brighten, stand out in their difference. The life of words and action—of events—reverberates with vitality. Things that have been suppressed, almost missing and always hedged in by suspicion, begin to play and resound in their repetitive, changing series. Intelligence sharpens on a new stone, and the "shock of difference" (p. 190) transforms into a vitality awakened from a fearful trance. A different mime. A different play. New life.[76]

The experimentations and variations within a rule of difference have unseated the repeated association of unity and being. *Being and Time*, for example, treats the history of metaphysics as dominated by a *single* issue: Being. This emphasis on singularity both repeats the metaphysical emphasis and describes an era that is passing. *Being and Time*, by taking part in the passage of that of which it speaks, is transitional for the language of difference. Foucault, on the other hand, does not find any single idea or rule to define the history of his and Deleuze's thinking. The singularity of being, which changed from a substance to a historical inevitability in Heidegger's writing, is itself in a multiplicity of repetitions, images, and changes. Fates are multiple, not contained by a channel or by a larger synthesizing factor such as Being or Becoming or History—or by Difference thought as a unity of ends and pieces. No unity is maintained in Foucault's (or Deleuze's) accounts of processes, unities, continuities, rules, and regulations. As we shall see in greater detail, fissure, the uncodeable or noncategorial, occurs with the rigors, necessities, and inevitabilities of our particular setting.

We turn now to the phrase "line of transgression" as an elaboration of the idea of the recurrence of differences. We are involved in a way of thinking in which—through which—differences multiply when identities, steadfast rules, and accomplishments are thought. Categories are accounted in such a way that they are both recognized as categorial functions and as acategorially fissured. Foucault's is an effort to think in such a way that, in thinking, we undergo recurrences without representations and necessities without Necessity.[77]

2. THE LINE OF RECURRENCE: TRANSGRESSION

Foucault uses Deleuze's use of recurrence to speak of relation and identity without the traditional power of the ideas of unity and being. Nietzsche's image of time as an endlessly repeating circle is too suggestive of unity even in its transvaluing function. Instead, Foucault develops the image of a line, not like a taut string or the course of an arrow, but perhaps closer to a border of an experience or a line at the future of the present, or the line into which one continually moves as one walks forward: a line of difference suffused with repetitions and departures, a line that divides and cuts without action, one without indivisible units; a line that happens as differencing and along whose trajectory there are recurrences, but one on which "the analogous, the similar, and the identical never return" (p. 194). As recurring, things do not return to something that has patterned them or that is primordial for them. In that sense, recurrences are "singular differences" (p. 194). Instead of saying that something recurs, such as being or law or becoming, or instead of saying that nothing recurs, Foucault says that differences recur. The line, the fissure, happens. It has no curvature promising completion, not even the meaningless completion of Nietzsche's transvaluing circle. The line happens as fissure, not as definite demarcation, but as a splintering, yielding line of repetition, recurrence, and disappearance. It marks necessities by chance, unities by bifurcation, identities by multiplicities. It gives to any singular voice—to any univocity—antiphony and cacophony, and it makes any singularity an ascending or fading echo that is repeatable, but not recapturable or re-presentable. This consequence of Nietzsche's "intolerable thought" of eternal return is the "empty sign" of formless differencing (p. 195).[78]

The frequently recurring image of the line in Foucault's spatial imagery is part of his effort to bring to further expression the language of difference without the powerful emotions of good sense that have constituted part of the holding power of metaphysical discourses.[79] The positive feelings in those orders that have defined value, soundness, rightness, and goodness also carry aversion or fear regarding whatever falls outside the orders or is heavily suppressed within them. By combining line imagery with "transgression" Foucault is able to speak of the transgressive dimension of identities and orders without universalizing transgression or difference. He is able to dislodge those affective powers of metaphysical discourses that rely on the dominance of ordered identity for interpreting and judging things. As one thinks within the language of transgression and the imagery of lines, the affiliation of ordered soundness with stability, survival, and affirmation does not occur. There is neither a dialectical movement with the interest of continually reestablishing the same through differences, nor a sense of life and life-affirmation built around "same" or "identity." Limit does not mean negation, denial, or constitution. Foucault's is an experiment with the idea of difference that forms without centering identity. Metaphysical good sense does not develop or have holding power in this formation. A different group of feelings and thoughts develop. In the domain of difference identities repeat and resound differently, and within it people feel differently.

The marginality of philosophy provides one setting for Foucault's language of difference. Philosophy has not ended, Foucault says, in contrast to Heidegger. It has become culturally marginal. The language that was natural to philosophy as it spoke of final and ultimate things and as it spoke from the center of cultural life and meaning can only be repeated awkwardly now on the margin of human endeavor. The marginal state of philosophy provides marginality for thinking, not originary identity. It gives possibility for thought-in-difference, outside of power centers, mainstreams, and major loci of confidence and status.[80] Philosophy may regain "its speech and find itself again only in the marginal region which borders its limits" (p. 41). It can speak from its situation by the distance of metalanguage or "in the thickness of words" that begin to articulate thoughts that lack traditional clarifications and elaborations. Philosophy is "dispersed" among the variations of these alternatives, "disarrayed" among, on the one hand, metalanguages and, on the other, dense, probing experiments. These distances and separations give philosophy its speech—line it out, as it were, by setting the lines, the pauses, and the breaks that define a contemporary rhythm (p. 41). That marginality can carry with it the inherited fears of being on the border, at the limit, characteristic of centrist consciousness. It can seem vaguely better to speak as one spoke at another time, confident of belonging to a cosmic order. How are we to speak philosophically when our possibility for thinking philosophically is in dispersion, disarray, marginality?

One might begin to think in the experience of the limits of the language of thought: the philosopher is aware that "he does not inhabit the whole of his language like a secret and perfectly fluent god. Next to himself he discovers the existence of another language that also speaks and that he is unable to dominate, one that strives, fails, and falls silent and that he cannot manipulate, the language that he spoke at one time and that has now separated itself from him, now gravitating in a space increasingly silent" (pp. 41–42). Such a language beyond the philosopher's language could be nontraditional philosophical speech. Or the body's nonphilosophical communications. Or experiences outside the power of reflective speech or outside the purview of the integrated and integrating subject.[81] The previous powers of thought and speech have "hollowed out a void in which a multiplicity of speaking subjects are joined and severed, combined and excluded" (p. 42). The identity of the traditional knowledges in association with changing cultural circumstances has engendered a multiplicity of unordered exclusions, and "void" rather than images of "totality" or "unity" names their topography. The contemporary philosophers' situation involves a breakdown of philosophical and subjective unities as the traditional, discursive identities have become optional in a space that they no longer define and that have ways of speech foreign to them. It is a space of dispersion, not simply of disagreement, but a space without unifying sovereignty or a defining identity. In these dispersed strands, as one thinks with them and in them, their separations and dissatisfactions dominate. Relation is as often intrusion and collusion as coherence or recognition. In the dispersion words are born in differences, without traditional understanding or a reasonably predictable future. A totality is not apparent. Thinking begins again, in the resonance of repeatable but weakened and by-passed formulas and ideas, and in a discourse formed of breakdown, dissolution, and marginality. Thought is not only not in the center. It has no center.

Foucault picks Bataille's work as an occasion for speaking of the subject's disappearance from the space of thought. Bataille is an author of "constant movement to different levels of speech," of "systematic disengagement from the 'I' who has begun to speak," an author who "shifts in the distance separating a speaker from his words," a master of "inner detachment from the assumed sovereignty of thought and writing," a person Foucault finds disciplined enough to stay with the shifting and differencing that occur on the margins where thought can take place. He measures "the extremity" of the subject's disappearance and finds an opening for thinking and speaking where the subject used to be, at a vacant spot, which at one time was a center, but is now a fissure where energy collects and disperses things namelessly.[82] This dispersal without the unification provided by a transcending identity generates communication in violation of philosophical traditions, not out of resentment, but in languages that develop from the dispersal. The differences of identities are not traversed, for example, by a sameness of Subjectivity, which promotes universal knowledge by thorough self-knowledge. They cannot be overcome by inference based on the essential sameness of grids and orders or by perceptions that recapitulate external structures through re-presented systems of likeness, but the differences can be interrogated. One "gropes" in uncertainty, probes the differences, touches the limits, penetrates strange areas; and discourses develop in these processes.[83]

Recurrence, or repeating without totality or an originary foundation, constitutes a line of difference. This limit does not demarcate the beginning of another organization or type of being, or the ending of this identity. The line of difference running through recurrences marks the absence of definite demarcation: "The narrow, black line which no perception can divulge . . ."

The line metaphor produces for Foucault a differencing process. *If* he were in a metaphysical discourse, he might use the line to speak of a fundamental absence, an abyss, that disrupts a world of continuous meaning and law-abiding relations. In this instance, the line would produce counteraction within the discourse by denying the substantive nature of ultimate reality and by asserting that ultimate reality cannot be thought. But the meaning of "absence," "abyss," and "line" would still be correlated with ultimate reality. It would constitute a claim about ultimate reality. The line, however, functions differently in Foucault's discourse. It names difference without reference to ultimate reality. It does not show ultimacy breaking through the contingencies of meanings and laws. It merely transgresses. It marks the mere absence of categorial relations, substantive presence, and continuity. In his essays the line happens discursively as connections form by arbitrary reversals—by standing Christian mysticism on its head, as he does in "Preface To Transgression," for example, and finding a point of departure for thinking of mystical experiences by reference to flesh, silence, absence, loss, and fissure, a procedure by which he finds meaning, connection, and intelligence through arbitrary moves rather than through religious meanings or a continuous causal chain. Acausal connection, he calls it.

The line also functions through the mood and thought of Blanchot's term *contestation*. In *contestation*, instead of a *principle* of negation, both Foucault and Blanchot find "affirmation that affirms nothing, a radical break of transitivity." He affirms, but at the limit of his affirmation there is nothing further, neither a negative nor a positive ground, neither a fundamental principle of negation nor a series of dialectical moves based on the universal power of negativity. The line also functions as groups of categories are used without themselves being ordered by a totalizing categorial system—a procedure we have encountered under the name of acategorial thinking: categories order each other in a repetitive interplay. The interplays—the various related orders—change, transform, and transmute. Those changes are themselves ordered and interpreted by plays of categories that in their ordering and interpreting processes change and transform. Categories do not control their interplays and do not capture the transformations. The language we are presently using, for example, orders and interprets with the power of *difference, change, transform*, and *transmute*. As these words and their orders function and make differences, they forecast, on their own terms, their own cloudlike mergers and meltings that cross or eliminate their own borders and yield other formations. The line runs silently through this discourse.

One symptom of the line's transgressive function is dissatisfaction. Its power functions by eliminating or mitigating thoughts and affections that cluster around positive and negative ultimates. It violates the satisfactions—usually they are unconsciously and deeply embedded in the discourse—that accompany a sense of ultimacy. Even if the affirmed, *fundamental* order is beyond our reach, even if it is experienced only through the hope that its mystery will become visible, there is in most discourses a satisfaction that occurs through reference to something ultimate. The reference feels right, often a person feels true, in the right direction, meaningful when he or she experiences things in a context ordered by something ultimate or by a sense of ultimacy. One might feel that stretch of being that is beyond comprehension—the mystery of being. Or one might feel deeply, deeply grounded in one's thinking; one has escaped the arbitrariness of mere formations and formulations. One has a sense of ultimate order, of final beauty, perhaps of Law that controls principles, rules, and criteria. Those powerful senses and affections are disappointed in the function of the line metaphor. The reader is dissatisfied at the borders where he or she is accustomed to feeling continuity, even if the continuity is a neutral one of mystery or a threatening one of Negativity or Negation. In this discourse a mere difference occurs, a little lapse, like a final breath; it shows nothing and hides nothing, and leaves one thinking, "Is this all?" The discourses of ultimacy carry disappointment with this "Is this all?" "There must be more" is often the border statement.[84] Foucault's language, focused around the line imagery, expresses no disappointment, no sense of loss. "The radical break of transitivity" that is meant by the line carries with it feelings of life in "a constantly affirmed world," a world in which origin lacks the exactness of fact or category, one without promises of a final homeland or a defining center (pp. 36–37).[85]

Foucault's accounts of origins of institutions and practices in the mere confluence of events are experiments toward finding knowledges and ways to speak that are not finally centered in anything. The transgressive difference expressed in the image of the line is put to work in the genealogical approach to practices and institutions. The thinker's peripheral space provides a "place" of attention to the descents, the reverberations, a place for thoughts and habits that create identities by steady repetition without a center. In his lack of an enduring center, the thinker can know the line of repetition that both limits and constantly de-centers the identities that are made by repetition. Nietzsche's idea of eternal return has been put to work in a new sphere where orders are transgressed by the processes that give order. The line of transgression continues to return in the repetitions that momentarily overcome dispersion and random display. The idea of limit without Being means in Foucault's discourse that we are able to follow developments and rules for developments—the orders of discourses—by their lines of formation and deformation without totalizing or centralizing them. We are able to trace these lines and come to know the history of things by reference to their limits and multifarious possibilities without "monotonous finality" (p. 137). Our tracing work also lacks finality, and as a discourse it is as arbitrary and fateful as any organization that is transgressed by the repeating line of no order.

3. GENEALOGY

The image of the line and its functions repeats several modern experiences. We have noted the peripheral and de-centered place of philosophical thinking in our time. Dispersions have been formative in many other areas of modern life. A unitary cosmos, for example, that functioned in rational inferences and provided the texture for moving from surface symptoms to unseen causes in medical practice, has been replaced by the regional unity of the body in medical science. Direct observation of lesions, for example, does not need a functioning belief in a rationally structured cosmos. A rule-governed region—the body—suffices.[86] Further, the idea of "man" as a unitary subject of knowledge has been replaced in literature, linguistics, and economics by ideas of separate, historical fields.[87] Modern sciences look for truths, not Truth. Histories of morals have frequently replaced Moral Truth in ethical discourses.[88] Such dispersions have de-structured the power of "unity" for language, and replaced an intuitive emphasis on unity with multiple fields, regions, and powers that perpetuate de-centering and dispersion. Genealogy as Foucault conceives it is a way of following the emergence of orders with their rules and practices and with their various functioning axioms. As genealogy is carried out, it develops its own idea of origin and unity. It does not need a functioning idea of primordial origin or unitary development. Genealogy is a way of allowing differences, discontinuities, and the priority of exteriority and spatial imagery while one finds and comes to know ordered regions of human life. The image of the line moves through the genealogical approach as an image of transgression as well as of linkage. Genealogy is a discipline for knowing repetitions and resonances of power: a way of knowing that is organized by the transgressed idea of power.[89] Transgressed power as we shall see means a mélange of ruling powers without overarching unitary, categorial rule. One issue of genealogy is how to follow the repetitions of power formations without turning *emergence* into *origin*. The idea of event is designed to confront this issue.[90]

The genealogist finds, analyzes, and follows the effects of events. Events are singular occurrences of networks of power that have organizing or de-structuring effects through repetition. They erupt in destabilizing ways, such as the publication of *Lady Chatterley's Lover*, the use of the atomic bomb, the formation of the idea of the death of God, or the development of the computer. They disperse dominant subjects, as, for example, Descartes' idea of the *cogito* scattered biblical and ecclesiastical authority for thinking. Events modify hierarchies of value, change dominant directions for thinking or feeling. Nietzsche's thinking, for example, modified the scholarly values that had formed out of the practices of scribes and advocates. Nietzsche's transvaluations of metaphysics and the values in discourses of transcendent Reality in *Beyond Good and Evil*, as well as Heidegger's de-struction of metaphysical thinking in *Being and Time*, are events on Foucault's terms, just as Plato's discourse on Forms or Aristotle's on activity are events. The effects of events—events take effect—are networks of powers and things that take shape in reverberations and repetitions, and that range from the overtones and arrangements of subtle and tiny details of speech and action to the formation of leading institutions, concepts, tones, and styles.[91] Events give rise to institutional change, to the emergence of new institutions and the fading of others. But they do not have built into them inevitable meaning or teleology. Their reverberating effects link things, but those effects also contribute to fundamental changes that leave an event—the development of the bow and arrow, for example—in an anticipation whose memory or its ramifications—for example, advanced projectiles—becomes its repetition.

"Homogeneous but discontinuous series" is one phrase Foucault uses to speak of events in repetition.[92] We have seen how the idea of event disrupts the idea of categorial relations among events. The discontinuities of series are found not only among the crisscrossing sections; discontinuity characterizes the particular series itself. "Homogeneity" refers to patterns of repetitions and reverberations within a series under the hegemony of certain powers. Rather than think of a series as a sequence of instants each of which is self-same and immediate to itself, Foucault says that discontinuity characterizes even the smallest occurring aspects: the image of the transgressing line dominates also as he thinks of the particulars in a series.

He is experimenting with a way of thinking in which any notion of atom-subject, temporal instant, or self-same identity is de-structured by discontinuity. No occurrence totally mediates itself to itself; nothing underlies or pervades the occurrence as a substantive or dialectical same. Chance as well as regularity pervades: "Discontinuity strikes and pervades the smallest units." Both individual things and the rules and procedures that link them and give them discursive identity and predictability occur with external and internal discontinuity. They are always mutable, seamed with nothing at all.

The term *networks* names homogeneous and discontinuous series. Series of repetitions are discursive things that are "stitched" together by various incorporeal forces—ideas, habits, grammars, customary association, professional status, priorities of some knowledges over others, accepted sufferings and comforts. Networks emerge from events, for instance, from the mingling of old assumptions about healing and the new practice of collecting the poor to avoid mass contagion, to form a new group of institutions and practices such as the mental hospital or medical teaching by the procedure of rounding. Events occur in networks, for instance, in the systems of punishment, social exclusion, and healing. Through it all there are mingling regional necessities of connection, collisions, transversing continuities, separation, repetitions of kinships, meanings, identities; and laws and principles emerge through networks and events. The perimeters of the networks alter through accumulations of piecemeal shifts and emergences of unimagined possibilities. The clarity of an origin or the necessity of a connection are functions of a discourse that insists on its own repetitious imprint as it understands itself, its history, and its future without regard for its chance emergence or the vacancies that traverse its regularities.[93] In Foucault's discourse, peripheral as it is, one is alert to the chance beginnings of centers of power and interpretation, and one is also free of the intuitive censorship of those countervailing thoughts and dispositions that would decenter them down to their least dominated detail.

The genealogical option for developing knowledge from the periphery of Western philosophy consequently pays attention to "the vicissitudes of history" and "cultivates the details and accidents that accompany every beginning" (p. 144). The points of interest are "jolts," "surprises," "unsteady victories," "unpalatable defeats," and these kinds of things are the bases "for all beginnings, atavisms, and heredities" (pp. 144–45).[94] The defining word for a network of accidents, intersections, chance events, and affiliations is *descent*. The genealogist identifies and follows descents as they are inscribed in the texts of books, manuscripts, institutions, and ways of life. He or she identifies the traits, "the subtle, singular, and subindividual marks that might possibly intersect in [sediments of ideas] to form a network . . ." (p. 145). Rather than search out resemblances, the genealogist "sorts out different traits" and details the network in which they function and by which they exist.

Genealogical study follows dispersions. One brings accidents into focus, the intrusions of unexpected elements, surprising reversals, mutations that generate regional continuities, deviations that disrupt established practices.[95] By genealogy a heritage becomes apparent in its "heterogeneous layers" as well as in its resemblances and continuities. In this kind of study neither the ideas of resemblance and similarity nor the idea of unity control the approach or prescribe the structures of meaning and connection. Instead, power arbitrates discourse. The plays of dominations are repeated in human inheritances, and the idea of plays of dominations establishes the discursive space of discontinuity and periphery in this language.

Foucault's genealogical work effects differences. Like Nietzsche's discourse, Foucault's disturbs and fragments what is traditionally considered to be unchanging or unified (p. 147). But in contrast to Nietzsche's, Foucault's discourse is not internally characterized by strife with metaphysics. Power has no ontological overtones, for example. The image of line and the idea of external connection replace Nietzsche's quasi-metaphysical ideal of the eternal return of the same. The idea of difference has overridden the idea of identity in this discourse that develops on a periphery that emerged in part through the effects of Nietzsche's discourse. It proceeds by breaking established power alignments. It substitutes, displaces, disguises, and reverses by its own divisions and distributions: its effort is to introduce discontinuity into our formative language.[96]

In its effectiveness, genealogy is a "curative science" (p. 156). Foucault makes the descriptive claim that the European sense of identity is weak and confused. Nietzsche had claimed that the will to power sickens its dominant expressions in the West, some of the symptoms of which are self-destructive pieties and mores, disturbed self-consciousness, and institutionalized cruelty in the name of creative services. Without appealing to the will to power, Foucault finds that the principles of unity have lost much of their force, that the centers of confidence and identity available to us are parodies of the formative power they once had. Forces of synthesis have also dissipated as heterogeneity has replaced the forces and destinies of the ideas of unity, continuous resemblance, and a world seamed together by self-identical reality. Thinking with disciplined care from the periphery of our culture consequently has a disclosive power for us all. As one parodies our serious commitments that are repeated now in fading principles of identity, for example, the parody itself articulates what is happening in our society. The weakness of our unconscious masks becomes apparent in the parodic process. One begins, in this genealogical discourse, to dissociate from the dominant but dying identities that have controlled people: the parody and dissociation themselves have forming power. They form identities different from those developed in the reverberations of metaphysical discourses. Both severing and formation go on in the processes of differencing and differentiating vis-à-vis the dominant, fading center.

This is a process of forming "counter-memory, a transformation of history into a totally different form of time" (p. 160). Our memories are traditionally dominated by continuities. We usually think of historical knowledge, for example, as a recognition of real connections that form something like a narrative, one that is rational, ordered, and made continuous by an unbroken series of causes that are interpreted in various ways. In the name of memory we look intuitively, by virtue of our dominant discourses, for origins and fundamental meanings and structures, and we expect historical sequences to be essentially similar. "The purpose of history, guided by genealogy," however, "is not to discover the roots of identity, but to commit itself to its dissipation. It does not seek to define our unique threshold of emergence, the homeland to which metaphysicians promise a return; it seeks to make visible all those discontinuities that cross us" (p. 162). As we develop various knowledges through genealogical work, the developing discourse's sense of time changes. The emphasis on networks developing through events of connection and dissolution and the emphasis on the powers that are suppressed by the dominant forces of a society—these emphases form texts and discursive connections without the control of those subjects that have dominated the traditional formulations and knowledges. A counter-memory takes effect in the language. A different network of feelings, intuitions, and powers emerges.

Discovery and analysis of heterogeneous systems form a counter-memory that is controlled by difference rather than by resemblance and the idea of same.[97] The one who counter-remembers plays out of a discourse that entertains a variety of approaches under the powers of what has been broken, subjected, or dispersed. The unitary subject of knowledge, lodged in the traditional discourses, is given up in the discursive process. One adopts masks, for example, those that are already present, if usually rejected or unrecognized, such as the buffoon, the unjust ridiculer, the open experimenter, the schizophrenic knower. Caprice, in this way of thinking, is never mere caprice, that is, just fooling around or turning things on their heads out of rebellion. It contributes, rather, to a way of thinking that is sensitive to acausal connections, relations without categorial unity, and the transgressions of those good senses that have dictated how things had to be joined. We come to think in the dissociations of identity that are suppressed in our tradition's longing for the dominance of synthesis. Counter-memory develops out of the peripheries and residues of our history to form a part of the discourse of difference.[98]

4. THE LOSS OF MAN: THE EMERGENCE OF A DIFFERENT LIFE

Ruptures produce relations, systems, and regional necessities. When Foucault speaks of event as a discontinuity with effects, he speaks also of what occurs in his own discourse. Ruptures are productive. They are like spaces of reformation as well as of disintegration. The break in the ordinary social continuity that occurred by the confinement of nonrational people in the eighteenth and nineteenth centuries, for example, both separated rational consciousness and nonrational consciousness in a social practice, and produced a process that formed the asylum. And in Foucault's own writing, separation from the traditional centers—by its repetitions of disenfranchisements—that has happened in modern practices and institutions as well as in Nietzsche's and Heidegger's work—that kind of separation has produced a style and language of difference. This language is formed in those dislocating tensions and departures that erupted in its own history. There are obviously continuities and connections. We are following some of them, and if one did an archeology of Foucault's discourse, the subject matter would include the rules of continuity and exclusion that function in it. But by using such ideas as event, counter-memory, repetition, acategorial thinking, and periphery, Foucault's work is in a descent that has come out of dislocations and self-disintegrating tensions that produced (yielded) a dominance of differences. We have seen that continuities and identities are transgressed by mere lack, that difference lines out continuity and identity in connections. Continuities and identities occur, but never with final authority for what happens, never with final authority for their own development. Networks develop, rather, that are crisscrossed by forces, happenstance, fleeting mirages, decay, domination, and no being at all. Foucault's own work shows the effects of networks as it recognizes them. It composes a way of speaking and thinking in which differences arbitrate the formation and distribution of concepts and feelings. It has given a dominant place to empty spaces, broken chains, passing vectors, and contingent necessities.

In this section we shall follow this discourse in Foucault's account of the displacement in modern times of "man" with "a counter-science of discernment" in which the account itself is written.[99]

Man is the subject/object of modern knowledge, a way of life that developed as people established a body of knowledge about themselves and nature. Classical structures of knowledge and belief, ordered by the representational unity of nature and history, lost their formative power. Natural history had been grasped by rationally governed classificatory schemes, for example. The justification for and the representational adequacy of these schemes were underwritten by the ideas of Time and God. Time and God were conceived to be external *to* the schemes and to the disciplines of knowledge as well as represented *in* the schemes and knowledge. God and Time were "a formless exterior." They spanned the separation between human history and nature, and they were known, if imperfectly, through the orders of classificatory schemes. With the breakdown of this way of knowing and believing, another being, man the knower, emerges as the unifying basis of knowledge. The gap between the Order of God and the Order of Nature, a gap that formerly could be crossed by a careful knowledge that represented God's Order, *that* metaphysical gap was filled by a being who took the gap within itself. Man is the knower/known who is constituted by the gap between nature and knowledge. The discursive history of man is the history of man's effort to overcome the distance between nature and knowledge. The history of man is one of man's own ascendency, man's subjecting nature as the subject of knowledge. Man represents nature in an order of knowledge that is man-founded. Man time thus replaces divine continuity in the developing discourse. Man is in and of time as well as outside of it. It is man's "story" that is now to be known; and history, rather than classificatory schemes, becomes the text of truth.

Not only is man the foundation of unitary knowledge, however; man is also in natural processes and is the object of knowledge. Man does not transcend either nature or time as object, but develops and behaves in it; nor does time as historical process transcend man the subject of knowledge. It has its unity in man. Historical truth and the truth of natural processes emerge as dominant problems. Man of modern knowledge founds what man partakes in. It both centers nature and is in nature in the absence of classical natural law, Time outside of history, and God the transcendent one who functions as the immediate continuity for all relations, movements, and change. Man as the knower/known embodies a gap that it is designed to overcome. Man consequently occurs as a *question* to itself. It is the knower/known, the subject that produces itself as a knowable object, the basis for the orders of modern knowledge in which it lives and develops.

The account of man given in the ninth chapter of *The Order of Things*, after the discussion of man's emergence, may be taken as a genealogical study of the death of man and hence of modern knowledge, a displacement that Foucault's study of man repeats. First we will note the results of Foucault's study, and then we will see how Foucault repeats the displacement of modern knowledge in his account of that displacement. In this way we will see how one type of counter-memory—that is, a counter-science of discernment—develops.

Man was formed in a discourse in which the idea of transcendental identity had discursive dominance. It developed as the basis for metaphysical resemblance weakened. In this sense man is a transmutation of God's unifying function in classical discourse. It emerges as an incorporeal body of subjective identity that founds all relations and constitutions and that links things in their multiple differences. Resemblance had been a fundamental quality of the world into which man came. Orders were established by similarities that were linked through their founded resemblance.[100] The fundamental resemblance of things had meant that their connections were never totally without meaning—things could be read, as it were, through their meanings. Signs gave contiguity, and the sign-signifier relation was based on deep resemblance. Things were never without an inorganic connecting tissue that let them be known and interpreted. In their fundamental similarity, things essentially made sense and spoke, if softly, of God's continuing, undergirding, sustaining presence.[101] In the space of man's emergence, however, unbroken continuity among all things had become doubtful. People began to recognize things in terms of organic functions: life, labor, and language, for example, formed different organons with their own rules and principles. By the eighteenth century the "whole cosmos" was breaking apart into organic, functioning fields that were separated—spaced apart—giving rise to the question of how these fields were related. How were things to be grouped, divided, and ordered? What were *their* organic regional similarities and differences?[102] Man, the knower/known, emerged with the discontinuities among organic fields. Those fields had in their turn emerged out of "great circular forms of similitude" that seamed the world with ordered likeness in a permanent—that is, only partially broken—space between Order and thought. The seams opened up as observation and formulation became more specialized. Broken spaces replaced unbroken connections of similarity. What fills the ruptures or ties the fields together? What laws do these fields commonly obey? What holds their truths in Truth? What overrides or undergirds the interstices of words, organizations, and disciplines?[103]

The idea of the transcendental subject responds to these questions: it provides a condition for the possibility of all representations, the unknowable subject of orders of knowable things. Accompanying this idea and quite different from it, however, is the idea of the organic integrity of what is known. Things are separated and self-same in their own lives and are never fully grasped in the orders that represent them.[104] Two kinds of transcendence thus emerge: the transcendental subject as the unknowable condition for the ordered representation of objects, and the transcending powers of things beyond their objectivity, their own forces of life. In nineteenth-century discourse the subject and the object moved away from each other, as it were, in their different transcendences, and the fracture of this difference is deeply embedded in the knowledge that this discourse produced, particularly because man the knower and the man the known was a part of this separation of transcendences. The conflict between transcendental philosophy and positivism, for example, or Hegel's attempted synthesis of the transcendental and empirical fields, or the emergence of right- and left-wing Hegelianism articulates these different emphases within the modern discourse of transcendence. On the one hand, people expected to develop a pure science of transcendental forms that would produce certain formal knowledge based on transcendental subjectivity, and on the other hand people expected positive knowledge of empirical domains that would tell us with scientific certainty about ourselves and our world: transcendental knowledge versus empirical knowledge, with the human being the focus of both.

Man is a discursive creature in this situation of double transcendence. It functions invisibly, but as a bifurcated invisibility instead of as a unified being. Man is characterized by the kinds of gaps that both classical deity and eighteenth-century reason functioned to bridge. Those gaps and divisions were definitive and largely unconscious in the earlier discourses as well as in the discourse of man. But the knowledges constituted within the discourse of man, the gaps on which similitude and classification had depended, become internalized, and "the very being of that which is represented [falls] outside representation itself" (p. 324), a process that began before the emergence of man's discourse and one that informs man's transcendental division. Exterior-interior, organic-inorganic, in-itself-for-itself: such gapped polarities demanded mediations, but the mediations themselves were characterized in turn by the gaps. Mediation gaps. God's serene, transcendent function in classical knowledge is dead and not replaceable in modern knowledge. The force of life, for example, that emerged in nineteenth-century biology is often thought of as will to survive, as threatened by death, as pervasive of organisms, and as immaterial; and the force of life does not show eternal coherence in this knowledge. The fall from God by human being that had functioned theologically in an earlier discourse is now invested in the foundation of knowledge without the possibility of appeal to God's revelation, which cures the fall. Contingency threatens the whole.[105]

Double transcendence functioned unconsciously by generating dispersion—by its doubling, separating, and gapping effects—and it thereby changed the idea of immediate origin. Everything occurs in historical mediation. Every knowing state mediates the known object and mediates to itself its own historical development.[106] Objects and subjects are mediations; they are historical processes that lack the original clarity, for example, of representation in a table of categories. The pristine state is always a complex mediation away. The very idea of a pristine state sends the knowing process into another spasm of representation and synthesis in a futile effort, in this episteme, to overcome its own mediational historical situation. The process of knowing continually finds man juxtaposed with non-man, with biological life, economic processes, and functions of language that reveal exteriority and difference from man, not essential, originary similitude or categorial likeness. Each origin is in a history of development and relations that moves "origin" away from man. Man is always made contingent in the process by which it knows itself. Man's "origin," for example, in this analysis is an emergence through the disjunctions and distances in discourses that preceded man. Man is not contemporaneous with its own emergence. The other-than-man is always with man, and shows man's life to be in life that is other than man's own. Man the subject of knowledge finds itself, as object of knowledge, to be outside of itself as subject. And in this episteme this finding is based on man, the historical subject of its own objectivity.

Man thus continually displaces itself because it is both the condition for the possibility of knowledge and the known that is ordered in life, labor, and language. Man is constitutionally a question to itself, a subject that is an object of scientific disciplines, a broken unity that produces the conflicts of the human sciences that strive in this conflictual state after an inherited ideal of knowledge without essential conflict. Man repeats itself in the growing fragmentation of modern knowledge.[107] It finds itself to be a physical object, the measure of all known things, and the interpreting commonality of all knowledges. The self-understanding, which functions as the goal of modern knowledge, repeats the fracture, the doubling, that constitutes man the emperico/transcendental doublet, this being "whose thought is constantly interwoven with the unthought . . . [who] is always cut off from an origin that is promised to him."

This doubling, this repetition of man, occurs not as the symptom of man, not as the simple presence of a self-limiting scheme or system. It occurs as "withdrawn presence." Man, the episteme of modern times, experiences things simultaneously coming forth and receding. The loss of the subject of occurrence, for example, in strictly controlled behavioral experimentation occurs in virtue of the experimental methods themselves. Or, modern reflection experiences the loss of the nonreflective dimension that it recognizes by making transcendental subjectivity the necessary condition for natural order. In the world of man, things occur as withdrawing presence or presencing withdrawn. The conditions for the possibility of things make empty spaces—fissures—in the conditions' distance from things in *their* lives. And the vitality of things, their force, is presented and withdrawn through the transcendental necessities of knowing. The totalities of facts, concepts, and experiences that indicate the transcendental subject indicate also an It, Something, out of reach and unthinkable. The unthinkable excites speculation about libidinous desire, an unreachable chaos of force without time, fundamental economic need, or a transcendental region of pure necessity: whatever is undoubted, noncontingent, final, or pure presence lacks, for man, that fundamental quality of man reality: consciousness. Man is a representing occurrence, and simple presence appears in re-presenting like a dream of something lost, primordial, and original.

Transitions away from the man-episteme developed as the nonconsciousness and non-re-presentable gathered force and attention. The movement was toward the excluded and the unthinkable in the discourse of man. Psychoanalysis, for example, linked sickness with repression of the unconscious. It developed a discourse that retained the idea of an unquestionable region of rules, systems, and necessity, but it found a region that was ruled by desire. An intelligent, complex discourse of desire developed that was attuned to will and force, and that cultivated suspicion of structures that seemed to function without desire. Further, in the transition out of man's episteme, death was experienced as qualifying norms and structures. Desire qualifies conflicts and encounters, and signification qualifies systems and laws. Finitude, in this network, emerges from man's dominated nonconsciousness and controls the transitions out of the man-episteme. Death-qualified life gives priority to possibility over substantive presence. Desire, which qualifies thought, gives dominance to power over disinterested truth. And law, qualified by signification, elevates regional structures and practices over the idea of primal, unknowable origin. What was unthinkable for man emerges as discourse-forming. What had been closed to man, the unthinkable that had circumscribed man, now begins to form the space of discernment and clarity, for example, discursive strands in which death, desire, and law show how things happen and how they are accessible to intelligence. Man perceived these reversals as madness: the emerging power of hidden death, hidden desire, and hidden contingent necessities disjoined the man-episteme, and the man way of knowing and living saw perversity and insane threat to its orders of life.

The emerging discourse, on the other hand, found through this "madness" a way for discursive development. Man's fracturedness, its doubling repetitiveness, served as the reference for retrospective accounts of the emerging discourse's lineage. Through the doubling fracture of man, the "unthinkables" emerged as powerful and thinkable. Not man's ideals of unity, union with a primal source, or completion, peace, and truth: not the thoughts and ideals by which man repeated its inevitable disunity, lack of primordial source, and impossibility of completion and peace: but its fracture, its sense of coming madness, its anxiety in its groundlessness, its repression-centered dread of death, its powerful suppression of its desire for power, its violent insistence on peace-giving laws, its finite demand for eternity: man in the light of its refusals and repressions, in the brightness of its fracture and unfillable space, this modern way of being, with its self-doubling methods for exactness, certainty, progress, and truth, *is*, in its fractures and repressions, the locale of development for a discourse that now speaks genealogically of man.

By this genealogy, the knower studies man as a network of desires, rules, and forces, as an episteme that could not know what is now knowable in the genealogy. The repressed inevitabilities of man are now clear in another grouping of rules, desires, and forces that is designed to think in the lineage of man's repressions and overturning. It is a discourse in which the death of man—the consequences of its doubling—is easily thought. What man repressed, *these* differences, have formed a discourse, one of whose primary repetitions is man's rupture, which led to its death. Its death led to a network of thoughts and feelings in which man's repressed differences are not a problem for living or knowing. Death, desire, and contingent necessities are coins of the genealogical realm.

Foucault's way of knowing has avoided the doubling move of man by analyzing human finitude in terms of constitutive, transgressing differences and gaps rather than in terms of a structure of identity. The idea of identity could have functioned in a transcendental claim such as "Man's essential identity is found in its finitude." Instead, Foucault found the epistemic and experiential oppositions and countervailing functions that rule in this particular discourse. Differences strive with and against each other, form continuities that cross each other and repeat each other without a higher Same to link them. Man is an optional epistemic region whose scissions have made possible other regions in which man no longer lives as a way of knowing and speaking.

5. THE STRIFE OF DIFFERENCES

The idea of difference has functioned to produce differences and destabilize its own idea—the idea of difference—in such a way that it cannot function as a metaphysical category. Rather than provide a stable categorial structure within which things are represented, differences repeat themselves and produce differences. The idea of difference has exceptional power in Foucault's discourse. It carries its power by disassembling its own power, as we have seen, by dispersing, merely repeating, offsetting, affirming its own transgression, and so forth. To think in this discourse of difference is to find and live through differences that have only regional, summary power.

This discourse, in and after man's reversal, also has an internal process of repeatedly inhibiting global theories.[108] The *fragility* in traditional foundations functions in Foucault's work to *attack* the discursive functions of the idea of foundation, sub-stance, and so forth. Nonregional totalities have been "curtailed, divided, overthrown, caricatured, theatricalized, or what you will" (p. 81). Noncentralized productions of theories, insurrection of subjugated knowledges, discursive reversals, attacks on institutions and practices, and the formation of counter-memories—these are some of the leading functions in this discourse of difference. Instead of a Whole or Being repeating itself endlessly and uncritically in discourses of similarity and resemblance, a limited organization—a region of thinking—is an image for what is repeated in the discourse. A region of thinking is repetition of organized power that makes truths, rules, and hierarchies of dominance. *This* incorporeal body of repetitions of Foucault's has appropriated its fragility and limits. It repeats them by increasing vulnerability to criticism on the part of those discursive wholes that have disguised their own repressiveness and are in the lineage of *this* discursive genealogy. Differences function in strife in a discourse that is attuned to struggle, hostility, exclusion, and repression; and its off-center aspect is developed by its speaking out of what has been discontinued, rejected, or made illegitimate. This discourse is made up of the effects of a group of insurrections against centralizing powers. As a de-centered region, it is not designed to succeed in reestablishing an overarching unity of knowledge. It "follows trails," wanders in various directions, trails off, plays with what it follows, or rejects coherences; it is a disturbing, regional discourse that lacks even the drive to contradict itself for the sake of achieving anarchy. It makes differences by making knowledges. Nothing more. By its meandering it emancipates discarded knowledges and ways of life from subjection, makes opposition and struggle, and refuses unitary tactics that create overwhelming subjects of knowledge (such as man or reason). It finds and makes regions of knowledge and practice. In this way it remains maximally attuned to the meanderings, effective events, and network changes in its environments.

The thinking of this discourse is nonmetaphysical in the sense that the discursive organization is formed and empowered by differences—not by difference-from-metaphysics but by the functions that have emerged from traditional conflicts and divisions, and that have their own developments. Those functions differentiate this discourse from metaphysics. This discourse is in the lineage and heritage marked by metaphysical thinking, but it is also made by the differences, spaces, repressions, failures, and transgressions that populate this history. One does not find in it that metaphysical power that laced *Beyond Good and Evil* or *Being and Time* and characterized their metaphysical ambiguity as they moved away from metaphysics. The counter-memory of this language, for example, does not form primarily by countering metaphysics, transvaluing it, or destructuring it. Counter-memory functions in ways of thinking in which that work already took effect, ways that continue to develop out of reversing, differencing processes and in which those processes, not metaphysical thinking or struggle against metaphysics, became its forming powers. The processes transform a mixture of metaphysical, nonmetaphysical, and antimetaphysical thinking into a nonmetaphysical way of thinking. In Foucault's work, counter-memory is a way of thinking about its own tradition after that tradition has lost most of its forming power in this discourse. A different organization is at work in relation to metaphysical organizations. In its counter-memory this discourse traces itself from the suppressions, spaces, and conflicting powers through which it emerged. It follows its own differences as it articulates its difference in relation to centralizing powers in its lineage. These powers are both in its genealogy and are contemporaneous with it in social and cultural life. Their differences characterize our time. Counter-memory maximizes its differences vis-à-vis these powers as it develops genealogical knowledges. Its attacks are ways of making differences, of continuing the decentering that has helped to form it in its meandering off-center ways.

We turn now to a different way of thinking, in which the idea of difference develops language, one in which *dwelling* and *gathering* rather than *transgression* and *counter-memory* will function as powerful words in the discourse. It too is in the language of difference, but in it thought takes place in an emphasis on tranquillity in difference rather than strife in difference.

5

The Coming of Time Has No Shape

In "The Ends of Man" Derrida speaks of two strategies for thinking. One might "attempt an exit and a deconstruction without changing terrain, by repeating what is implicit in the founding concepts and the original problematic, by using against the edifice the instruments or stones available in the house, that is, equally in language." The second strategy is to make a break with a discursive field by taking apart or eliminating rather than repeating what is implicit in the founding concepts. When the two strategies are combined, one changes the terrain by the way the founding concepts and problematic are repeated and thought.[109] We have seen that something like these two strategies took place in transvaluation and de-struction and in the language that developed out of them. *Strategies*, however, is probably not the best word. We have found that the developing language became different from the specific transvaluational and de-structive strategies of Nietzsche and Heidegger, and that Foucault's discourse, though characterized by strategies, involves combinations of words, reversals, moods, and so on, that take on a life of their own in their discourse. To think and speak in the discourse is to undergo not only strategies but also processes, orientations, and possibilities that emerge and develop in the discourse and that at times overturn the strategies that helped to form them. The terrain changes and shifts in the discourse as ways of thinking and speaking emerge and develop that were not available to the strategists.

Counter-memory, for example, formed in the strife of its inheritance, is not the same as a strategy. It is rather more like an environment for thinking that lacks the intuitions, interests, feelings, and dominant concepts of the metaphysical traditions, and that in this lack develops affirmations and effective bodies of knowledge about its own history. Heidegger's later way of thought, no more a strategy than is counter-memory, involves both strife and memory without the "counter." It develops words and feelings that are in distant kinship with those that articulated the joy of rightness with God or with Reason. The absence of both God and Reason, however, their various traditional functions, is part of his thinking, and this absence pervades his language and becomes a discursive space, an absence of filling, as it were, in which release and serenity emerge to give guidance without power in his language. Strife fades. Power language loses power, and a gathering of differrences occasions a nonmetaphysical way of thinking that makes both the dominance of power and the idea of strife through power appear strange and inappropriate.

Heidegger's later thinking also attempted to function with full awareness of the nonhuman dimensions of both thinking and speaking. How can a person think thoughts that are not his own and that are not simple repetitions of someone else's thoughts? Can thinking be the difference, think the difference, between a person and a discourse? Can the language of difference come to thought without being the object of thought? Can we think about Heidegger's thinking and also think in the language of difference? Our experiment is to see if we can follow Heidegger's thinking in such a way that the language of difference is thought in the process of following his thought, and to see if we can think in the difference of his discourse without violence, opposition, counter-memory, or objective agreement.

In Foucault's thinking the self-erasing image of the line of transgression and such words as *contestation, nonpositive affirmation, counter-memory,* and *episteme* address the orders and relations among things. Things happen in groupings and are ordered by intricate, regional networks of powers, practices, ideas, information, beliefs, and experience. The differences among things are not resolved by fundamental resemblance or by relation to something present to all things in common. Commonality is a regional characteristic of repetitions. Their "thin line of difference" does not reflect anything. Neither metaphysical commonality nor something abysmal, unthinkable, but still mysteriously present are meant by the line of transgression. The power of the idea of difference in Foucault's discourse is found in the transformation of the incorporeal element among things from metaphysical commonality to powers lined by mere nonbeing. Counter-memory and genealogy are ways of thinking that combine order and power with no hint of fundamental unity, order, identity, or will. In Foucault's own thinking the incorporeal element is not metaphysically contested. His thinking does not struggle with the kinds of transformation of metaphysical ideas that are in Nietzsche's transvaluational thinking or Heidegger's de-structive process in *Being and Time*. The "counter" of counter-memory refers to the counter-forces in our heritage that have ordering leverage in Foucault's thinking. He thinks about them, from them, with them, but their struggles have been changed by the places and forces they have in his discourse. They are now organizing powers rather than suppressed powers. Their marginality also produces order and hierarchy in his thinking. With such powers and the disciplines of knowledge that develop with them, he recognizes, for example, the optional nature of the most recent modern episteme ("man") and the thorough contingency (the replaceableness) of all centering powers. The suppression and pariah quality that have formed and empowered these traditional marginal ideas and practices have the power of insight and knowledge formation in Foucault's thinking.

One incorporeal element in Foucault's discourse is developed by the unresolvable play of differences. To play in differences and with them creates part of this discourse's sensibility, mood, and intuitive alertness. Just as a religious community understands itself and finds its identity in religious practices and worship, Foucault's discourse—this region of thinking—has for its element such nonresolving practices as discursive genealogy and archeology and those procedures that produce such differences as reversals, mockery, acategorial thinking, and regional descriptions with no expectation of a pervasive whole or a pervasive, teleological force. In this discourse, such elements of metaphysical thinking as the mystery of a pervasive force, a unifying whole, or sustaining presence, such elements as deep, meaningful coherence among radical differences, or longing for rational or affective appropriateness vis-à-vis something fundamental—those elements are gone, and a grouping of different incorporeal elements has emerged. The discourse's feelings, expectations, attractions and repulsions, uneasiness and pleasures, as well as its specific hierarchies and ideas, are formed not so much in opposition to traditional options as out of its own play, its own momentum, rhythm, and history of differentiation.

Heidegger's later thinking is also outside of the struggle with metaphysics that has characterized *Being and Time*. He experimented with a "dimension" of thinking that develops as time and being are rethought and decentered. His earlier de-structuring project transformed into a series of tentative efforts to rethink what remains when metaphysical ways of thinking no longer have discursive power. In contrast to Foucault, however, mystery, the language of giving and bestowing, and the affections of community life founded in commonality with differences remain in his discourse. How these elements—mystery, bestowal, dwelling together in common—are rethought and take shape in the language of difference is the issue of this chapter.[110]

1. A BEGINNING FOR THOUGHT WITH THE PASSAGE OF STRIFE

In the third chapter we identified Dasein, the subject matter of *Being and Time*, as a way of being that developed in a tradition driven by the forgotten question of Being. As the question of Being de-structures metaphysics in the course of *Being and Time*, we found that Dasein itself, in this discourse, is in question, not only because dying is its most characteristic quality, but also because its own forming history is in a process of radical transformation in the thinking and language of the essay. The end of philosophy, as Heidegger named the modern era of metaphysical thinking, is found in the transforming, de-structuring processes of the book titled *Being and Time*.[111] Dasein—human being—is the carrier of both metaphysics and its de-struction. Both the question of Being and suppression of that question are manifest in the formation and existence of Dasein. As the question of Being is rethought and brought to light in the descriptive account of Dasein, and as forgetfulness is highlighted in this process, the horizon for thinking—the shape of possibilities that arise in this process—changes in relation to the horizon of metaphysical thinking. The hidden question of Being transmutes into the question of the hiddenness of Being. Dasein, which is the disclosure of the question of Being, is found to be also formed in the concealment of Being, and with this discovery a beginning for different ways of thinking emerges.

Dasein is a disclosive region in the account of *Being and Time*. Description of its existential structures is description of how manifestness (or disclosiveness) occurs, not for human being, but as human being. The question of Being is moved in that essay from *what* is or could be to *how* Being shows itself in the self-showing of human being. This self-showing is in a historical process that has itself been formed by the question of Being and by how that question has been forgotten and suppressed. Being does not show itself as something behind the process, but as *the* question in the process that casts the process itself always in question. We have emphasized the intention of *Being and Time* to find a way of thinking and speaking that is alert and expressive in this questionableness that appears to pervade, usually unnoticed, the assertions, speculations, and agencies of our traditions.

The almost lost middle voice indicates both the difficulty of thinking without activity or passivity and the grammatical formation that is alert to self-showing of human being, and when Being is found as an unresolvable question in every dimension or aspect of the self-showing process, several discursive things occur: the language of substance, unity, and identity no longer centers thought; Being's difference, as self-showing questionableness vis-à-vis every determinate thing, begins to recast talk of essence and truth; the accustomed forms of certainty in our leading philosophical traditions are put into question; and the imagery of seeing accurately what is true is modified. This last modification develops through the use of *disclosed* and *concealed* to describe the occurrence of manifestness. Dasein is not a region of light that sees by its light what is really there in the world and beyond the world. Neither are essences shining realities that show themselves to be timeless verities. The emphasis falls rather on the showing process that both manifests and conceals in its process. Heidegger's descriptive claim in *Being and Time* is that that process is infused throughout by the question of Being, a question that "founds" the process that perpetuates it, and one that is not, in this process, designed to be answered. Recalling it, paying attention to it in its nonresolvability, learning to think with it and about it, and above all speaking and thinking in ways that manifest their own questionableness: those are the kinds of things that began a different way of thinking.

The analysis of Dasein has thus begun a development of language and thinking focused on the occurrence of self-showing. Dasein's self-showing is not a process leading to enlightenment, or one that functions in the hope of clear, unmixed vision based on formal entities; rather, it is woven in a texture of forgetfulness, distraction, and suppression as well as of communication, self-presentation, and alertness appropriate to its own situation. These differences do not dissolve by dint of disciplined effort into a larger harmony. They are part of the ideas and experiences of harmonies and of the ideals that come from those ideas and experiences. *Being and Time* shows that enduring stability, centered identity, or substantial presence are ambivalent ways of posing the question of Being in the historical process of disclosure that is Dasein. The question of Being is a continuously destabilizing element in human being as it has developed in its heritage. It is the element that shows Dasein as Dasein is. The strife of thinking in the question of Being, not perfection or harmony or a metaphysical teleology, is at the beginning of thought when thinking develops out of *Being and Time*'s discourse.

"A transformation of thinking, not . . . a propositional statement about a matter at stake" (p. 373) marks both the end of philosophy and the task of thinking. As human being is released for the questionableness of its own life, as it becomes alert in its mortality and is able to understand explicitly and with acceptance its thorough optionality—that it need not be—it experiences in this openness something like unlocking and release in its life. The *question* of Being, not the presence of Being, is manifest. A quite different sensibility develops in a human's thinking and desiring as this transformation takes effect. In our phrasing, a person is released for things as they show themselves, without the affections attendant to the suppression of deathliness, replaceableness, nonpresence, thorough questionableness. An alert, mortal release to the mortal and optional process of disclosure frees a person for the historical development of Dasein in the questionableness of Being. The releasing experience seems to be appropriate for Dasein's own self-disclosure. As one's traditional certainties fade out, for example, awareness of Dasein's own temporality sharpens; one has a clearer sense of being in and of a development that is questionable in all of its aspects. One experiences one's being like a middle voice, as neither an active nor a passive but a self-showing occurrence that is always in question and always constituted by relations with things past, present, and possible. *This* manner of self-showing, which Heidegger terms authentic or appropriate to one's own being, has become an issue for thinking; and although in *Being and Time* Heidegger wanted to make accurate statements about authenticity in order to differentiate it from other ways to be, he also wanted to orient his thinking around the issue of disclosure so that its occurrence, and not statements about it, gave thinking its orientation. We found that when thinking is transformed in this way, Dasein, the being developed in part through the suppression of Being, transforms. Its own being changes. The thinker is becoming a different being. The end of philosophy as Heidegger inherited it, and the task of thinking that emerges from this ending, occur as the question of Being ruptures the reflective procedures and certainties spawned of its suppression, offsets traditional, philosophical authorities, and makes the simultaneity of discourse and concealment, that is, questionableness, the issue for thought.

Being and Time is defined in part by establishing tensions and by de-centering metaphysical ideas, as we showed in chapter 3. Its de-structuring process is also a self-exhausting one in the sense that *its* way of posing issues moves toward a different way of thinking that is neither metaphysical nor de-structuring in relation to metaphysics. The task of thinking that comes out of *Being and Time* is not the same as the one that characterizes that book. If we continued to repeat the de-structuring process, we would repeat a process that has come to its own end. We could produce a technology for de-structuring, as it were, but that kind of thinking would repeat a process that has lived out its own possibilities. That kind of de-structuring discipline would not develop in the possibilities that come together as the de-structuring process finds and moves beyond its own limits.[112]

"A thinking which can be neither metaphysics nor science?" (p. 378). The thinker "first learns what remains reserved and in store for thinking to get involved in. It prepares its own transformation in this learning" (p. 379). The question of Being has given (or granted or yielded) the issues, anxieties, preoccupations, desires, ideas, and obscurities of the West. The question of Being, however, is not solely or even primarily the question of living with death. Something obscure lies behind that issue. Not, perhaps, a will to be, the fear of death, or a life force, but something that by being both present and forgotten has developed historically into such ideas and energy as will to be or life force. The analysis of Dasein showed that Dasein is a world-relational occurrence in which things are manifest. Dasein itself is manifest in the manifestness of things—but manifest not as subjectivity nor as a power that dialectically comes to expression in a process of self-showing and negation. Dasein happens in its region. Even the image of clearing obscures this occurrence that does not appear to be fixed by anything around that would demarcate its limits. It seems to withdraw from the images and ideas that define it, to be always like a horizon with the things that exist in it. Dasein is like a horizon that defines a thin line but is not fixed or held by that line. Dasein's being thus becomes more questionable as we push the analysis of Dasein. We are not at all clear about how this being is to be thought.

In his studies of Heraclitus and Parmenides, Anaximander and Plato, Descartes, Kant, Hegel and Nietzsche, and many others, Heidegger finds repeated the issue of obscure clearing with whatever is. "Unconcealment is, so to speak, the element in which Being and thinking and their belonging together exist" (p. 388). He explores ways of thinking that might be appropriate in this concealing unconcealment and that might articulate the affiliation of Being and thinking. He finds them—concealing/unconcealing, the affiliation of Being and thought—at the beginning of Western thought, and they are certainly things to which *Being and Time* led him, as to a puzzle or a peculiar obsession that functions in the simultaneous presence and absence of Being and that is repeated, usually without awareness, in the availability of beings. When the elemental, unpowered difference of concealment and unconcealment becomes the explicit issue for thinking, the pervasive obsession of Western thinking, as well as the basic affiliation of Being and thinking, comes to the fore in a discourse in which the idea of force has no priority or privilege.

Our traditional ways of posing questions and our deepest expectations regarding what constitutes satisfactory answers are transformed in a language of release, not of force. Release and difference combine. A different *Fragestellung* emerges in which the obscurity of Being, the free and open clearing, seems to provide the place for thought. The obscurity of unconcealment delimits the language of *Being and Time* as well as of metaphysics, and calls for a new beginning within the language and thought that have borne the obscurity and that have alerted us to the inadequacy of our thought in the question of Being. Play with this obscurity develops in Heidegger's language. There is no longer strife with metaphysics. Instead, thinking develops by allowing the difference of concealment and unconcealment to interplay in the elemental occurrence of the discourses that have given us to be as we are. One reads the traditional texts with reference to concealment and unconcealment. One is alert to how the texts themselves embody the interplay of concealment and unconcealment. Metaphysics is defined by its covering over this difference, in spite of its being formed by it. Heidegger's purpose is to think without overlooking the obscure difference of concealment and unconcealment, to think in it, to find its words, and to see what happens as this thinking goes on.[113] Releasing the traditional obscurity of unconcealment/concealment, being open and free with it, and letting it function to bring things together in a developing language is the way this exploratory thinking proceeds.

2. OUTSIDE THE QUESTION OF BEING

The transformations in *Being and Time* made evident that the ontological difference between Being and beings, a difference elaborated as the question of Being, and not ontological resemblance should guide thinking when Being and human being are the issue. The priority of question and of disclosure in that essay broke down the power of the ideas that have clustered around substance and subjectivity in traditional thinking. We find conflict in the essay's tradition around the idea-experience of Being as well as deeply ingrained forgetfulness of that idea-experience. The essay itself is in conflict with metaphysical thinking and its tensions and denials, and in this conflict a traditional, forceful stance regarding Being is evident. Instead of attempting to resolve those conflicts, however, Heidegger intensified them, and we followed a process of de-struction that took place in the language of the essay. That process appeared to move against its own destructive force and toward a way of thinking and posing questions that is removed from both metaphysical thinking and active conflict with it.

One way to state Heidegger's movement after the transition of *Being and Time* and away from *Being and Time* is: He is inclined to think with the obscurity of Being, not primarily about it, but to think with the obscurity of Being in such a way that the obscurity of Being—not substance, subjectivity, will, or reason—comes into view as he thinks. This obscurity seems to be a nonforcing element as he thinks. The question of Being, the transgressing difference of Being with Dasein, changes. Instead of beginning with human being in his effort to pose the issue, Heidegger experiments with ways to pose the issue for his thinking by approaching the question of Being directly. This means that Being is not followed primarily with regard to difference from human being or its being forgotten in its tradition; rather, Heidegger's language changes its emphasis to Being as concealed, self-withdrawing, and hidden, and hidden not because of human forgetfulness, but because hiddenness is a dimension of its disclosure. *This* thinking, this way of thinking Being in its history of difference as concealing and revealing, leads Heidegger to subordinate Being as well as time to "other-than-Being," which he terms *Ereignis*, "Event" or "Appropriation." We shall follow this development in Heidegger's thinking in order to see how the function of the idea of difference changes, and by changing, transforms the entire discourse.[114]

An unresolved issue for Heidegger's later work is whether interpreting can be thinking in his sense of the word. We shall attempt to follow his thinking and to interpret it in the language of difference. If this attempt succeeds, difference will be a gathering affect, a dimension of our thinking that is thought in our language about Heidegger. If his thinking and our thinking vis-à-vis difference work together, our interpretation and Heidegger's specific claims will recede in this thinking process in favor of something quite other vis-à-vis them both.

The power of Being as Heidegger finds it in our history is not like will power. Hence we have spoken of disclosure, manifesting, appearing, and horizon in the tradition of Being instead of force, movement, intention, teleology, or will. The emphasis on time in this discourse has dislodged Being from the language of timelessness and aseity. We followed some of the ways in which the question of Being is manifest in the tradition that has developed out of the idea-experience that has been calling Being. *Presencing* is the name Heidegger gives this idea-experience. Time is the determination of presencing, and one of Heidegger's projects in *Being and Time* was to rethink presencing so that a present moment or the present time does not control the meaning of time. By reorienting time around the horizon of the future and by finding this horizon *in* discourse, he de-structured time's domination by the present and opened presencing to a way of thinking that is not controlled by substance. Further, morality or perishableness—the passing of time, the temporal passing of all things—are metaphors that set the conditions for thinking about the endurance of things. Enduring is simultaneously passing away. Enduring is presencing, and presencing is also a process of passing away. So Heidegger speaks of "the constancy of time's passing away" in the context of presencing and being present (p. 3). How are we to think this process of coming-to-be-passing-away, this time-Being process? We have found the language of unity, foundation, and identity to be misleading, since time and Being are not unities or in a unity. They are not like a foundation. They are not identities. They are otherwise than beings as they function in the formation of our own tradition.

Instead of using the language of "it is," as in "time is" or "Being is," Heidegger plays with another grouping of words. "There is time," "there is being." Or, in German, *"es gibt Zeit,"* *"es gibt Sein."* In this play he associates such words as presencing, letting-presence, bringing into unconcealment, bringing to openness, giving, and giving presence to. He finds a way of thinking that lets the "there is" be experienced and heard as yielding and as clearing. If the "there is" can be heard, perhaps we, in the hearing experience, will be thinking presencing, the issue that seems to have moved our tradition in its depth preoccupation with the question of Being (p. 5). The question is: How are time and Being given or yielded, how are time and Being together in yielding and clearing? They have yielded a specific, broad tradition. They have brought it to presence in definite eras. Through the eras, "Being means presencing" (p. 5), but we are to speak instead of "letting presence," of unconcealing, as the clearing for presencing and as a dimension in which neither Being nor any being prevails. Is our thinking these words like a process of letting Being be present in a word-giving, tradition-yielding process? Is there a difference to be noted between the temporal process of presencing and the yielding of this process? If there is such a difference, we can move beyond the tradition that is molded by the question of Being by means of the clearing that gives, as it were, the clearing for this process.

The interplay of these words might yield a different thought from Being, one that is not reachable when the idea of presence dominates. Should that happen, the interplay and yielding rather than the temporal process of presencing could become the issue. A silent dimension that has accompanied the question of Being would come to the fore. The idea-experience of presencing would move to the side and a quiet, previously unheard dimension could gain prominence for a different . . . would it be a different idea-experience? a different thought? or would this transformation be on the scale of the transformation of Nietzsche's "last man" to a being other than man (the *Übermensch*)? Would it be a transformation in which the fundamental words, ideas, and experiences change to such an extent that even those words—"fundamental words, ideas, and experiences"—would yield to things that we can no more envision than Nietzsche could have envisioned the language that developed out of his transvaluations? Would it be a way of thinking that is free of the question of Being, free of the transformations of *Being and Time*? Is that possible?

"To think Being explicitly requires us to relinquish Being as the ground of beings in favor of the giving which prevails concealed in unconcealment, that is, in favor of the It gives" (p. 6). To ask what gives Being is extremely awkward. We are aware that when we speak of Being we are speaking also of tradition, of question, of a complex process of shaping words, ideas, and experiences in relation to presencing. This issue of presencing has given presence to a tradition of thinking and practices that not only reflects the deep preoccupation with presencing, but one that preoccupies the preoccupation by unconsciously and repeatedly expressing it, coming out of the questioning preoccupation and back to it, like a perpetual, if not an eternal, return. A being does not give Being. Our tradition, for example, does not give Being or create it. Our tradition is shaped out of it, by it, with it. The presencing process of our tradition shows the issue of presencing that forms it. But in another sense, *there is* Being in our tradition. Being does not produce itself. The language that has something's producing something is too narrow, too focused by a thing's doing something to produce or express presencing. Presencing is assumed rather than adequately explicated in the narrow formulation. In our speaking and thinking there is Being, which withdraws from our grasp and reveals a nongrasping process of presencing-in-continuous-passing-away, that is, the nongrasping process of time and Being together. If we work on the revealing-concealing dimension of presencing, we will be working on how *there is* Being instead of on the question of what Being is. That is our entrée to thinking Being in relation to the *dimension* for presencing rather than in relation to self-reflective presencing, that is, to presencing disclosing itself.

Heidegger uses *sending* rather than *self-disclosure* to speak of Being's history. *Sending* means simultaneous self-manifestation and holding back, and hence is not the same thing as self-manifestation (p. 9). Presencing, or the temporal discernibility of things, involves nonpresence, nondiscernibility, not like an indeterminate future or like horizon, but something like darkness or the imperceptible dimension of mere light or impenetrableness. *Holding back* is the word Heidegger uses. By this distinction, presencing is discernible. Our discourse allows the distinction, and in the aftermath of *Being and Time* we are able to give attention to discernibility, as Heidegger himself did, for example, in *On the Essence of Truth* or *The Letter on Humanism*. Being and time are found together—discernible, thinkable together—as the condition for the language and ideas that attend to them. They have been uncovered, as it were, and can be thought in various ways of being thought out and covered over.[115] Their discernibility and lack of discernibility now becomes an issue: how is Being "given"? How are we to think this "there is Being"?

Heidegger's initial move is to differentiate Being from the clearing dimension to which it belongs and which is hearable when one attends to Being (p. 10). If we think of this dimension as time, as the process of presencing-passing-away, or as mortality in the style of *Being and Time*, we can differentiate Being from whatever occurs in its process. Then we find ourselves with an account of a rich, versatile tradition in the question of Being—an *Überlieferungsgeschichte*, in Gadamer's language—governed by the metaphor of horizon.[116] That is a presencing process in the question of Being in which human being has come to be as it is in its formative element of Being-time. But how are we to think of Being and time's own coming together in being-yielding event? How do Being and time come together into their own, not as beings but as presencing-passing-away? We have learned not to pose the issue in such a way that explanatory causes are called for. We have learned not to ask, what is Being? We have sought ways to keep Being and time in their own element as we think about them. We have particularly attempted to let question and obscurity prevail in order to be true to the tradition that has, as it were, owned us by giving us our language, perplexities, and experiences. But Being-time too seem to have a sent and owned character. They yield clearings that are themselves disclosive, like Dasein. They give language and thinking, which give presence and duration. How are we to think of Being-time's yielding, giving, gathering, and differentiating? By posing the issue in this way, time is no longer suggested as the element of Being. Being-time are together as a process of presencing, and the element of difference is no longer within the hegemony of Being. "What is peculiar to Being is not anything having the character of Being" (p. 10).

Being is not something that gives itself or that determines itself. *Time* names the determining element. Further, the "it gives" names an other than the letting-be of beings or the determination of beings. It is the term that Heidegger uses to see if he can think of Being as presencing, as in a history of presencing, and as occurrence that is not a self-productive kind of thing. Rather than on passing away—that is, rather than on the temporal element—the emphasis falls on the lasting, repeating element in passing away. And rather than on letting-beings-be, the emphasis falls on the letting be of letting-beings-be, that is, on lasting and giving in letting-presence. Difference from both Being and time is gaining attention, and if time seemed to be the element of Being in *Being and Time*, that direction has been changed by virtue of the obscurity of Being, as we shall now see.

We have found that Being is obscure not only because it is displaced in its epochs by a variety of beings that are taken to be criteria for what is true, but also because it is not any specific thing. It occurs epochally as ways in which things are apparent and thinkable. None of those ways or their sum total are the same as presencing or letting-beings-be. They are instances of disclosive processes. When the defining elements of a way of presencing make claim to ultimate reality or to timeless identity, a displacement of Being occurs, a displacement that is nonetheless a temporal, disclosing situation. As Heidegger thought through the systematic forgetfulness of Being, Being's obscurity did not dissipate. The more our traditional ways of ignoring or suppressing the question of Being were retrieved and recalled, and the more the tradition's preoccupation that has let us be as we are was retrieved and recalled, the more questionable Being appeared. Language about Being did not become unambiguous, nor was Being to be thought as known clearly. The history of our coming to be in the question of presencing made clear only that the question did not dissipate into the presence of presencing. Our approaching the question of Being in the continuing approach of Being to us only heightened our sense of difference and withdrawal on the part of Being.[117] The suggested discipline is one of preserving the obscurity in order to preserve our alertness to Being and its question.

"There is Being" seems to mean: in the tradition of Being's question, Being withdraws in its approach. Within this way of thinking we do not have a quandary to be solved, but a clearing-unclarity to be thought and preserved. It appears to be preserved when we give place in our thinking for such words as "concealing-revealing" regarding a continuing sameness without identity or unity. This obscurity, in its difference from presentational clarity and self-disclosure, replaces the importance of time, and in this element, in the "there is," Being is displaced from the place our traditional preoccupation has given it. If Dasein, that is, "being there," is the being of the question of Being, Dasein is now being transformed by a different question. "There is Being" means that presencing is in question, not in reference to human being, but in reference to "there is," to *else* or some other word that suggests no temporal determination in the midst of temporal determinations. The de-structured unity of time that we noted in our discussion of *Being and Time* is transmuted into words whose combinations suggest no unity at all. But like time, this dimension without unity or identity—this difference—"reaches" throughout all presencing as giving or opening up, as *"es gibt"* (p. 15). It gives the difference of Being, the for us awkward continuity of presencing-passing away, a continuing that is more like a process of differencing than it is like some kind of identity, and it is no less de-centering and disconcerting than Foucault's line of transgression. Can we think of the "there is" without invoking the dominance of time or of presence? Can we think in and of this difference without setting the issue in terms of identity and difference from identity? Can we, that is, set the issue for thinking in relation to Being and its obscurity, and thereby recast our language in a difference that has apparently not found focused expression in our tradition?

An initiating move by Heidegger is to speak of the interplay of time's dimensions, past, present, and future. Their interplay is termed their fourth dimension. "Playing in the very heart of time" is Heidegger's phrase (p. 15). The concealing-revealing theme is phrased now in terms of distancing and nearing, and "interplay" suggests that concealing-revealing plays out in temporal relations. In contrast to Foucault, however, coming near has dominance over distance. Heidegger uses *Nahheit* to name the interplay of nearing and distancing. The *heit*, and the English *hood*, in *Nahheit* or "nearhood," as it is translated, have linguistic kinship to words connoting *head, manner, hence, clear, cheerful,* and *bright*.[118] The interplay of distancing and nearing among past, present, and future has a clearing, bright manner that enhances interplay, as distinct from dissipating it. They are apart and different in Difference that interplays, does not settle them or fix them, but, for example, "keeps open the approach coming from the future by withholding the present in the approach" (p. 15). In withholding and nearing, the temporal dimension enjoys a sameness of interplay. The sameness is like giving, in the sense that the dimension continues to be gathered and preserved in its differences, and continues to differentiate as it provides clearing for all events. In this phrasing, the alternatives to nearing-withholding would be collapse into nondifferentiation or spinning off into no relation. *Nahheit* is like a clearing that gives relation with no action, no act, but as . . . The . . . is what Heidegger is attempting to think through as his discourse moves with extended horizons for speaking and thinking.

Heidegger is attempting to avoid the "danger" of taking "there is" as reflecting "an indeterminate power which is supposed to bring about all giving of Being and of time" (p. 17). He gives free play to that aspect of his discourse that emphasizes temporal determinations. Epochs have their inevitabilities, and until epochal inevitabilities are able to undergo transvaluations or de-structions or de-centering, by processes like those we have followed, some thoughts *will be* thought and some things *will be* known. Our experiences *will* occur in certain ways. Other thoughts and things in other epochs will not be there. The "there is," this "else" that seems so indeterminate, is beginning to be thought in these words at this time with this history. This discourse, with its emerging emphasis on difference, houses, as it were, the horizon for thinking the giving of Being. We think this move beyond Being in the determinacy of an epoch that is emerging from the end of metaphysics. We are attempting to think what is coming out as the clearing of this attempt, a clearing that has emerged out of such de-structured ideas as *condition, foundation, identity*, and *historical possibility*. We are not positing a power outside of this epoch or a movement that undergirds or pervades this time. We are thinking in a language that has shifted and become unsettled and doubtful regarding its previously established limits. Even the idea-experience of presencing has moved off center. "The giving in 'It gives Being' [that is, '*Es gibt Sein*'] proved to be a sending and a destiny of presence and its epochal transmutations" (p. 17). We are trying to think through the epochal transmutation in which the ideas and words that de-structured metaphysics are themselves being changed. The closure of an epoch and the opening of another marked the concealing-revealing, and marked them in such a way that concealing-revealing are not associated with subjectivity, unity, identity, or subjective conditions for the possibility of their being thought. Transmutation, epochal shift, and opening into different thinking are not like specific structures or actions; they are like something else that we are trying to think out. We do not foresee a deep illumination toward which we are moving, or a vast and dark profundum that underlies our surface effort. We do not think of Something with which we seek communication. We are thinking in a clearing that is more like a line of difference, an else-than what we are traditionally able to think, than it is like something definite. It is like a clearing that comes without epochal differentiation and that seems to offer different time, different thinking, different speaking and feeling, but one that is obscure in its offering. The giving is not completed. Its possibilities and grammar are not clear. How it comes to speech is not certain. As else-than, it has an enticing aspect quite different from the repetitive exhaustion that can characterize thinking. It unsettles, hides, withdraws, perplexes, and calls into question most language in its regard. Nothing is promised. But "the destiny in which It gives Being lies in the extending of time," and time, the determining factor of our lives, seems itself to be given or sent, to be in that sense alterable and replaceable even though we are inscribed through it. Hence, our limit now appears to be the giving of the "*Es gibt*," the "there is" of "there is Being."[119]

One exploratory word to elaborate the "there is" is *Ereignis*. A function of this term is to name an emergence of "else" that has been silent in traditional philosophy. This "else" does not have an epochal history, "is itself unhistorical," in the sense that attention to it has never functioned to determine a period of time or to preoccupy thinkers (p. 41). Rather than think of it as an abyss or as something somewhere that has been overlooked, Heidegger thinks of *Ereignis* as "clearing the way for what is thought without itself being thought." It names the there-is of thinking. It is that thought that has not been thought, but is now to be thought.[120] Such words as *gathering, sheltering, presencing, sending, giving*, and *making place*, that is, *appropriating*, seem appropriate in speaking about *Ereignis*. Instead of the middle voice of appearing, becoming, and dying, we are dealing with something more like the occurrence of the middle voice as such, which makes way for all middle-voice occurrences, that is, which gives the letting-be of things. *Ereignis* is not revealed or exhausted in the language of time and Being. It is emerging as clearing difference that pervades the words, formations, and experiences that inscribe that language. There is sameness without identity—*die Gleiche*—for example, that pervades but has come neither to thematic expression nor to a self-disclosure. It is like a pervasive else-than-what-is-thought that seems now to be coming dimly to view through the processes that de-structure metaphysical thought and de-center our traditional preoccupation with Presencing and Being. Heidegger's attention to *Ereignis* is thus a movement away from the process of overcoming metaphysics.[121] We shall now follow one of his ways of trying out words and ideas to find a way of thinking that holds this strange obscurity in view, as it attempts to give the obscurity initial expression in his thinking. He is liking *Ereignis* to Being and time with the effect of thinking something not previously available to thought.

3. LOOKING BACK TO A SHAKY BEGINNING

By allowing Being—the preoccupying question in Heidegger's discursive heritage—to guide his thinking, a group of words come to prominence for him:

> To think "Being" means to *respond* to the *appeal* of its presence. The response *stems from the appeal* and *releases itself toward the appeal*. The responding is a *giving way* before the appeal and in this way an *entering* into its speech. But to the appeal of Being there also belongs the *early uncovered* has-been (*aletheia, logos, phusis*) as well as the *veiled advent* of what *announces itself* in the possible *turnabout of the oblivion of being* (in the keeping of its

nature). The responding must take into account all of this, on the strength of *long concentration* and in constant testing of this *hearing*, if it is to *hear the appeal of being* . . . [This thinking] is rooted in the essential *destiny [sending]* of Being, though itself *never compelling as a proposition*. On the contrary, it is only a *possible occasion to follow* the *path of responding*, and indeed *to follow* it in the complete *concentration of care and caution* toward Being that *language has already come to*.[122]

This thinking "*renounces* the claim to binding cultural achievement or a deed of the spirit . . . everything depends on the *step back* fraught with *error* into the thoughtful reflection that attends the *turnabout of the oblivion of being*."[123]

The interplay of *sending, giving, oblivion, responding,* and *stepping back* is especially important. Thinking and language now occasion—or, in terms that we have used, yield—more than philosophical positions have been able to say regarding Being. It is as though the sending of thinking and speaking has been covered over by what has been thought with care and discipline. One must step back from the disciplines of representational thought, the search for standards, the rigorous application of standards to specific situations, the systems of definitions of ideas and things, in order to hear something else in thinking and speaking. We have discussed the process of de-structuring ideas in order to hear the question of Being. We have followed Heidegger as he de-centered Being and time in his own thinking, as he stepped back from his own focus and made way for a difference that was nonthematically carried in this thinking and its heritage. The words and their combinations that have opened up this move are those that we noted above, and others like them. Although they are hard to comprehend because of their break from traditional philosophical speech, they are gentle words. In contrast to Nietzsche, Heidegger does not think with a hammer. He utilizes words from Judeo-Christian piety and meditation and from modern poetry in order to let a process develop that has already left behind the doctrines, thoughts, and intentions that structured that piety. That structure, concerned as it is for the presence of God, overcoming death, and appropriate response to divinity, is as absent in Heidegger's discourse as the metaphysics that informed and explained it. But these words nonetheless have bearing when he lets go of "destruction" and "overcoming." Linked to the absence of God, Christ, and metaphysics, they release a difference of thinking by which thinking and speaking come into a different light, a different hearing. The "else" of thinking and speaking, in its lack of clarity, seems to approach through a release from the dominance of the history of Being. In the renunciation and release that occurs in this newly forming speech and thought, a different gathering of words and ideas takes place. Thinking seems to come to itself, to come into its own, in an approach that is made possible through a release from the dominance of its previous formations.

If transvaluation and de-struction were the processes that provided a gathering place for new combinations and possibilities for thoughts and words in *Beyond Good and Evil* and *Being and Time*, release from such metaphysically related approaches appears to be the gathering place or "*ort*" for Heidegger's later writing, or *Eröterun*.[124] We have seen that his move from de-struction to what he calls thinking is at the same time his move to thinking without metaphysics, a thinking that we find to be moved by something recognized as obscure by it and something totally obscure to traditional ways of thinking. We now find Heidegger in a way of thinking that stays with the obscurity, the "else," with the hope of eventuating a discursive development that will be a place, a site, in which the unthinkable comes increasingly to word and thought. This is a considerable hope. Will a thinking situation that does not do violence to the unthought by insisting on traditional forms of clarification allow the unthought, the obscure, to emerge without violation or severe distortion? Is the situation of release, in this case release from violence done to the giving and sending of speaking and thinking, one in which something different can take place in thinking? Is this difference due in part to release, rather than to insistence or domination, that occasions the differences' being manifest?[125]

Language gathers, gives, and makes place for the writable and sayable. By following this dimension of language, by giving place to its place-giving dimension, Heidegger experiments with ways of thinking and speaking that release this releasing dimension from a more insistent, prescribing way to think. Perhaps by releasing, by allowing, stepping back, granting space and place for the grating dimension of language, combinations of words and thoughts will develop that carry and express this dimension rather than distort it or refuse it. If the experiment succeeds, a way of thinking considerably different from those that have formed us will develop, and what happens in withdrawal will begin to take place differently in the space for thinking and speaking granted by this appropriating release vis-à-vis "else."[126]

We shall consider first language's own speaking. We are to learn how to think with regard for language's own granting occurrence, rather than with exclusive regard for what is specifically said. Heidegger uses Trakl's poem, "A Winter Evening," because it lets the exhaustion of its religious symbolism bring nearer the eventuating site of poetic language. As a whole, the poem is alert in the granting dimension of language. In it the religious dimension is over—completed—and something else comes to expression. The something else is language's own speaking. What is completed—we could also say exhausted—is a group of traditional religious words and symbols. This poem releases the religious language from its heritage, and in this release becomes a poem of language's own poetic granting.[127]

The poem:[128]

A Winter Evening

Window with falling snow is arranged,
Long tolls the vesper bell,
The house is provided well,
The table is for many laid.

Wandering ones, more than a few,
Come to the door on darksome courses.
Golden blooms the tree of graces
Drawing up the earth's cool dew.

Wanderer quietly steps within;
Pain has turned the threshold to stone.
There lie in limpid brightness shone,
Upon the table bread and wine.

"The last two verses of the second stanza and the third stanza read in the first version" (letter to Karl Kraus, December 13, 1913):

Love's tender power, full of graces,
Binds up his wounds anew.

O! man's naked hurt condign.
Wrestler with angels mutely held.
Craves, by holy pain compelled,
Silently God's bread and wine.

The image of the tolling vesper bell is itself one that tolls within the poem in a sense of absence. Both calling and dying are meant. Traditional assurance is gone within the poem. The possible senses of belonging have changed. What can be said with deep feeling, what can be hoped and loved, what one can live for: these things have changed. There is a greater sense of "no longer" or of absence than of continuity and presence. But the poem itself also is. It speaks, takes place, and communicates—calls to language—in the midst of loss and passing. Nothing in particular other than the poem comes. Absence sounds in the evening tolling across the darkening, falling snow. The tolling is present in the poem, but it does not bring anything else to presence. The well-provided house and well-laid table are not to reveal or receive or entertain a known divinity, a group of old friends, or the presence of something else that fulfills or answers human need. "The verses bring the well-provided house and the ready table into that presence that is turned toward something absent" (p. 199). It is a silent house, vacated, waiting in absence. "Sheltering in absence" is Heidegger's phrase (p. 199). But it is not forbidding. As though some presence had been released and an arrival were welcomed, this inviting, vacant house is marked by a tolling that is not mournful or anxious, but calling, bidding. Without a dominating or defining presence, the house and table are sheltering, ready for whatever might eventuate, ready for a gathering of things into this earthy, homely site under the darkening sky. It suggests life—nurturing, protection from the cold, companionship, the hallmarks of human need and satisfaction, with a distant sense of divinity and mystery. In their lonely setting, the house and table do not speak of what has to be, but of a situation that lets people and things be in their place and time. "The first stanza speaks by bidding the things to come" (p. 200).

Wandering people, those who are unsure, who are on dark courses, find something remarkable and in stark contrast to the winter evening: a tree of graces in this empty, nourishing setting that tolls no presence and that is surrounded by silence. The golden richness of the tree, its rootedness, its drawing up moisture in the dead of winter give a shining quality to the empty dwelling, certainly not in the form of a cross, and not as decoration. Something splendid happens in the unexpectedness of this image. It could not be expected in the first stanza. A place just short of eerie—a vacant house with a full table, no one there, and a tolling sound of absence—has a radiant tree in bloom, golden and strange, unnatural, bestowing.

The poem speaks—"calls," Heidegger says—this interplay of difference. He uses the words "world" and "things" to speak of the play between the first and second stanzas. The house invites things into the shining of the golden tree. It is like a sheltering world in which things take place in open manifestness. There is intimacy—not fusion, but interplay—in which things are separate and distinct in the gathering element of the house with full table and golden tree. Our emphasis falls on his word *dif-ference*. The German is *Unter-schied* and carries the sense of intimacy (*Unter*, viz. the Latin *inter*, re *intimacy*) and separation (*Schied*). "The intimacy of the dif-ference is the unifying element..." (p. 202).

This poem, in its language that marks an opening through the released, exhausted religious symbols and meanings, provides a shelter for the granting, allowing dimension of language. Its "unity" is neither an idea nor an originary source. It is in difference, an exploratory name for the dimension of language that lets things be together in difference, that is, that lets things eventuate. The poem "carries out the intimacy" of "language speaking." Language speaks: we hear again that Heideggerian middle voice in which things happen in a dimension of allowance free of subjectivity and objectivity, of activity and passivity.[129] The poem takes place dif-ferentially in the sense that it both finds shelter and gives shelter in the sheltering-giving dimension of language, a dimension that is its dif-ference with all things in their connections and separations.

When "wanderer quietly steps within," the poem's tone changes. The movement into this sheltering place in the dif-ference of language is over a threshold that pain has turned to stone. The ground beam that holds the opening has petrified, has hardened, and in it the sedimented minerals have slowly become an enduring, transformed element. This image echoes the tolling absence in the first stanza. And the line "Pain has turned the threshold to stone" is no less striking than "Golden blooms the tree of graces" in the second stanza. The move into the sheltering dif-ference of language involves pain as unexpected in the poem as the tree of graces. "Pain is the joining element in the rending that divides and gathers." Although Trakl's early version of the poem suggested a longing for "God's bread and wine" to fill a painful void left, perhaps, by struggle with angels, the version at hand holds pain and entrance together as well as pain and the gathering closeness of differences. The rift between—the dif-ference—the gathering-giving dimension of language and the world outside of this dwelling, happens with both division and joining. This pain is to be felt in the poem. The poem is joined together in pain as it holds together and apart the tree of graces and the wintry outside, call and absence, sound and silence. To come into the poem and its austerity is to undergo a rift in our lives. In this work there is no brightness or deep sense of gift without the hard, strange entrance and the strange sense of absence. Rending and gathering, presence and absence, foreignness and intimacy, speech and silence, entrance and loss, gift and separation are inseparable in it. The poem in one sense is a threshold for entering a place of loss, separation, release, and in this difference, one finds strange nurturance and intimacy that holds no release from pain. Trakl's hard and severe language tears one away, quietly, from known patterns of experience. It has given up the comforts of redemptive pain. It strans by itself, a world apart, as a place of speaking and feeling, where wanderer—not *the* wanderer—has not yet eaten or drunk or warmed himself. As wanderer steps over the stone threshold, like a reader reading the poem, a clarity, a brightness, not unlike the poem itself, gives presence to bread and wine that wanderer does not touch in the poem. One would like, perhaps, to add a stanza, to present a next scene. But neither Heidegger nor Trakl finds the addition of a stanza fitting. The poem as it stands, in its foreshortened animation, is as much as can be said. The poem's stillness gives its images place. Its severity holds in place its dif-ference. The rift is held, not in stone, but in a poetic quiet that marks its own appeal to a place apart from what can ordinarily be said.

The stillness in this language speaks of what seems to be an otherwise unspeakable difference. It does not speak of fulfillment, of eating and drinking or of laughter and camaraderie, certainly not of mystic communion and worship. Nor does it speak against such things. It does not speak of despair over the exhausted symbols and practices, or of existential anguish. Sadness or anger are not its moods, nor gladness of heart and relief. It is not disturbed, and it is not serene. Something different, a gathering of things and world, says Heidegger, that is neither human nor divine, but like an intimacy among four differences: earthiness, skylike horizon, deathliness, and godlike strangeness. None of the four can interpret the others. Rather, the poem is like a gathering that forgoes everything but gathering. The poem is like dif-ference that brings near and divides at once. That is what language does in its speaking. It brings near and divides, and neither what it brings near nor dividing nor bringing near can interpret the other elements. Language speaks as dif-ferencing. The poem's own restraint functions to let this dif-ferencing go on with minimal disturbance in the absence of any dominant gathering center. It calls us to a different way of speaking and listening and leaves us with that call, letting the call eventuate as it may.

Can we come to think in a way that appropriates dif-ference and its stillness? Will our thinking come to listen to the gathering, allowing, withdrawing of language? Can it become a thought of dif-ference?

One intention in Heidegger's discussion of this poem is to raise such questions as these. The poem can be an occasion in which the end of our traditional philosophizing is experienced. Instead of experiencing the world in the names of certain kinds of beings—reason, God, or subjectivity, for example—one can be brought by the poems to the question, How, in the absence of traditional realities, are we to think of presencing? What does the pain of Trakl's poem mean? Are the opennesses of the poem and the openness of the dwelling like the "well-rounded" place of unconcealment of which Parmenides speaks?[130] Does the poem bring us to the experience of which we have already spoken, the overlaid and forgotten experience of unconcealment rather than to the question of which being is to interpret or found all other beings? When the poem raises questions for thinking, it has a transforming function. It occasions a new contact, a renewed awareness with the question that differentiated Western thought and that now seems to be able to recur in our language and thought only through their difference from traditional ways of thinking. The transformation occurs in the struggle to ask about unconcealment, about clearing, granting, allowing, and gathering, without meaning a deed or presence on the part of anything.[131] The poem's own occurrence, in which the clearing of language interplays with the clearing of the dwelling, with its full table and a tree of graces, shows, perhaps, a bond in our history between thinking and clearing. If Western thinking carries with it the sense that thinking is like an opening that grants things to be, if Parmenides were registering this kind of wonder in his poem, for example, this wonder over presencing and clearing, then Trakl's poem puts us in touch with considerably more than a poetic encounter with the exhaustion of Christian experience. It recalls something borne and concealed in our language: that clearing, concealment and unconcealment, uncertainty, presence, and deep puzzlement go together with the experience of thinking. As philosophy and traditional powers of interpretation end outside the poem's threshold, a difference from philosophy and the traditional powers emerges. This difference indicates the puzzle of language's and thinking's own concealing-unconcealing event. Dif-ference, a name for the concealing-unconcealing event, looks as if it might be thinkable in this time when things differentiate and hold together in a language that itself is differentiating out of the exhaustion of a tradition.

Heidegger is right to say that the task of thinking is a modest one. He does not have any specific reality or group of realities to define or analyze. The task is found in the effort to learn how to think in the ongoing clearing that is initially clarified rather than obscured by the painful loss of our thinking foci. The opening for thought is strange to us. Presence is uncertain, ill-defined. The discipline of beginning is severe. Heidegger's words on its own terms are exploratory, limited, and no haven for rest and confident repetition. Only the opening experience out of an exhausted language is to be repeated. "Strangely enough," he says, "we cannot even ask these questions always neglected in philosophy as long as we have not experienced what Parmenides had to experience: *aletheia*, unconcealment. The path to it is distinguished from the street on which the opinion of mortals must wander around."[132] Our thinking and experiences are in a language, of a language, that has a continuing preoccupation with presence and presencing, one that has not been lived out. As speakers and thinkers, we are in the mission of that preoccupation, which, to the extent that we are aware of it, makes us different from our dominant, centering heritage that has forgotten it and is nonetheless controlled by it. This separation from our heritage, as maddening as the separation is, with its sense of pervasive, unthinglike clearing through all the differences, is also an opening to the preoccupation that has been misappropriated in so many passions and thoughts. We can show how it has been missed. We can look for expressions like Trakl's that let language say far more than the writer as a person can mean. We can work with the words and names in a context that builds presence and presencing while at the same time giving them a different shape from traditional thought. We can rework the questions related to presencing. And we can learn how, perhaps, to let traditional speaking and thinking transform into a different way of speaking and thinking that can say what we cannot imagine. But this task for thinking also has a sense of its own meagerness, its lack of cultural and professional power, its own inadequacy. Nietzsche's "last man" would know that he was the last of his kind, that a way of being other than he, beyond him, is on the horizon. Presumably on Heidegger's transgressional horizon the transformational being is even more strange than the last man. This different way of thinking and speaking is accompanied by a sense of both loss of life and of new life in elements of thinking already refined by Nietzsche and by Heidegger's own early work.

One can also read Trakl's poem as the words of a "last man," and one can read Heidegger's reading of the poem as beyond Trakl's terrible loneliness. Trakl's separation and nostalgia have been turned by Heidegger's reading of his poem into a clearing for beings who wait no longer with alienation, but with a sense of being beyond the severe loss of faith and metaphysics. Heidegger's language speaks of presencing and obscurity rather more than of absence and loss, of a beginning, a task that is moved by experiences of renewal and discovery that are making way for something deeply and obscurely embedded in their own heritage. The language of difference that separated Trakl from his tradition occurs in Heidegger's language that speaks of the open clearing in language and thought, a clearing that bestows presence in a way yet to be thought. In that sense, Heidegger's language is beyond transvaluation and destruction and is beyond the limits that have defined the way of life produced by metaphysics. Heidegger did not get far beyond the questions raised by the emergence of the open clearing beyond Being. But he did find a way of speaking that seems to allow for this "else" of his thought. We turn now to a modest option for conversation, for a way of speaking together, that develops alertness for the middle voice of "it gives Being."

4. A MODEST OPTION

The idiosyncracy of Heidegger's way of thinking might seem to suggest a lonely, noncommunal pilgrimage. Trudging back to the experiences of early Greek thinkers . . . and so forth, Heidegger succeeds, however, in shifting the *Sache* of thinking away from subjectivity, with its potential for alienation and bifurcation that we have already seen in Foucault's analysis of "man," by rethinking and reworking the thought of his predecessors in the community of his heritage. Traditional connections and a community of passionate people working to understand who we are and how the world is pervade his work. His own differentiation from technology and from thinking dominated by methods of control includes appreciation of their limited appropriateness as well as the hope that something else can be heard in our culture other than a violence-prone intention to produce a better world by dint of conflictual effort. Production itself is to be rethought, reconsidered in the difference of letting things come to be in the yielding of language and thought. If the "free space of opening" could give us our thoughts and names, a world appropriate to our own deepest history and experiences might emerge.[133] But how is one to begin? How is one to face this dark obscurity, the free clearing, in common with other people? One option can be found in a way of speaking together.

Is it possible to converse in the domain of free and open clearing? If we renounce the functions of will, for example, without the intentions of asceticism or self-sacrifice, without the idea of God or the patterns of Law or Christ, but in the puzzling experience of things coming to presence, do words and thoughts form that carry with them not only our own release but the "release of presence" by language and thought? Can dif-ference happen with alertness as people converse together? Will something like a thought or poem take place through the release, a thought or poem for which the language of production seems inappropriate? "The Conversation on a Country Path" engages such an experiment.[134]

This conversation among three academics has a function analogous to Heidegger's discussion of Trakl's poem. The issue of their discussion is thinking. They probe to see if they can speak of thinking without at the same time speaking of willing or representation. They develop a slow, careful rhythm of finding words and names for nonvolitional occurrences. They work together to keep in mind primarily the word *Gelassenheit* (or clearing release), which names what they come to suspect is a dimension of speaking and thinking. They release themselves easily from Eckhardt's Christian assumptions and language, which gave context to *Gelassenheit* in his writing. They emphasize the word now by freeing themselves from the sense that they have to know exactly what they are talking about when they use it. The word and its namesake are equally available. They say the word in a variety of contexts and cultivate a waiting sense, listening to what the word can say in these contexts. They develop among themselves a state of mind characterized by uncertainty and waiting without despair or definite expectation. The image is one of being on a path, like wanderers. The path is already there, and they are already on it when they notice it, but it is not defined by having a specific destination as a highway or a road would have. They feel that they are alert and walking in the open, and the path they are on accentuates the openness around them. This openness is not like an infinite expanse, but like a region in which the path goes its way. The region pervades and rests in its path, its countryside, its fences and fields and buildings. It is like a language or a way of thinking that pervades whatever is said or thought. The three people use a variety of words to speak of this pervasive allowance: sheltering, abiding, re-sheltering, with drawing and returning, coming to meet us, regioning, release. They find that their own releasing uncertainty about thinking and *Gelassenheit*, their bearing of alert waiting and exploring, puts them in touch with the dimension of clearing release in their own conversation. Their lack of prescriptiveness attunes them to the nonprescriptiveness that takes place in speaking and thinking. The more they are released from demanding or insisting thought, the more a dimension of speaking and thinking emerges that is different from the language of force, drive, intention, system, or subjectivity. Their own attunement is puzzling to them. It increases their uncertainty and their alertness. It draws them into the conversation, encourages their speaking and thinking, gives them an issue for which their best prescriptions and methods are ill suited. Their *gelassene* attunement returns them repeatedly in their conversations to the *gelassene* region of thinking and speaking, and they do not know what that means. Something abides in their conversation that they can neither will nor represent. It neither solves nor resolves. It does seem to bring them together through release, however, and to occasion more interaction than Trakl's wanderer found outside the wintry house.

What the three academicians attempt to think happens among them. In the process of their conversation they find themselves increasingly attuned to each other through or in something else, for which they are trying to find fitting words. They find themselves getting closer to the nearing affect of language and thinking, and by the end of the conversation they are in sufficient accord with each other and their subject matter to complete appropriately each other's thoughts and sentences. They find that their ideas are formed in the situation of release, uncertainty, and the clustering of fitting words. The transformation that develops is in the process of which they find themselves a part. But the transformative process in this conversation is not like that of transvaluation or de-struction; the conflict and overcoming that characterize those processes are no longer present. This conversation is gentle in the sense that transvaluation and de-struction have themselves been left aside. Their overwhelming, undercutting, transmutation, and often violent recasting of words and thoughts have been released in this interaction, and this experience of release seems to be an opening into a dimension of thinking that was as closed to transvaluation and de-struction as it was to their progenitor, metaphysical thinking.

From a transvaluing or de-structuring point of view, this conversation on a slow walk is strange in its complete lack of contest, strife, and competitiveness. The conversation has no element of strife to overcome. It lacks the desires to cut (or slash) through disagreeable thoughts or to establish definitve word combinations. The pressure for academic success is gone. There is no need to establish dominance or to carve out an excellent achievement. There is no fear of thoughtful closeness and intimacy. Something else is taking place. Instead of being like a process of bifurcation, the time of the conversation is more like a nearing of differences. Instead of mortal care, the being of this conversation is like an open way to wait. Instead of the metaphors of seeing, those of hearing seem best suited to the released waiting. The activity of the three people, which is hard, concentrated work for them, does not reflect back on itself, but is more like the effort involved in stepping back from one's characteristic, intuitive hold on things so that something else can take place with more freedom and attention than is otherwise the case. The three participants find that words come together in this process and that different thoughts form that indicate the situation of release rather than a situation of determined and well-intentioned effort.

The idea of return that is significant in Nietzsche's thought is now elaborated in a serene language, with the thought not of will to power but of release. Will for Nietzsche immediately seeks itself, and the image of something's returning to itself in his language functions to show how will to power unseats all particular expressions of will by a reversal to pure force. The eternal return of will to power is lived out as a violent play of upsurge and disestablishment, centering and unseating. Gathering closeness is difficult if not impossible to think in his discourse. Return in the present context, however, is not like willing energy going out from and coming back toward itself. Language and thought, rather, are like "a region . . . where everything belonging there returns to that in which it rests" (p. 65). The region gathers "just as if nothing were happening, each to each and each to all" (p. 66). The region is not represented in clusters of expressions. It returns in the gathering interplay of differences. It is more like open dwelling than driving energy. It is neither active nor passive, and in that difference from our accustomed "voices" it returns us to a different task for thinking. Formation and de-formation, creation and de-struction, self and other: these shapes of differences have come together in the return of dif-ference by means of clearing without representable form. Thinking finds its own clearing in something other than form and its binary opposite, nonform. Heidegger's later work has as its modest task finding ways to ask how we are to think without representation those words that bring out the preoccupying experience, the difference of our heritage: the coming to presence of all things in a pervasive return of dif-ference.

The strand of discourse in which the idea of identity has lost its hegemony has developed in Heidegger's later work toward a way of thinking occurrence without form or substance. His way of thinking is unmarked by the violence that characterized the overthrow of identity's priority. It is beyond the functioning of transvaluation and de-struction, attuned to a type of serenity that is foreign to Foucault's discourse, and is nonetheless a way of thinking in the priority of difference. When one thinks within Heidegger's discourse, the idea of difference becomes an opening to obscure, forgotten experiences and language endemic to Western thought. These experiences and forgotten language function without the anxious concern of the discourses of identity. They continually differentiate, seek no center, and find thinking to be, perhaps, like a shapeless clearing that gives presence and occasions the demands of a discipline to learn how to speak and think beyond the limits of Being and beings.

6

"Différance" without Conclusion

We have followed the development of the influence of the idea of difference in the discursive functions of transvaluation, destruction, and such reversals of word dominations as "contingency's" control of "timelessness" or "disrelation's" control of "unity." Its influence was felt as centralized ideas, affections, and practices have been de-centered and transmuted in Nietzsche's, Foucault's, and Heidegger's thought. These processes may be followed in strands of discourses without appeal to the language of consciousness or subjectivity: discourses are characterized by developments and destinies of which groups of people are parts, but frequently are not controlling parts. The associations, rules, and interventions in discourses develop destinies of their own. Further, people can move among various strands of discourse, think and speak in different ones at different times, and find themselves in remarkably different perceptive regions. As one speaks and thinks, the strand of discourse speaks itself in its own functions, hierarchies, associations, inevitabilities, and characteristic ways of change.

In the language of difference the shift of discursive control from the idea of identity to the idea of difference has given expression to ideas, words, and functions that have been subjected to suppressive force in our heritage. The anger and fighting spirit of Nietzsche's language was, we found, alert to its own heritage of force and suppression. But experiences and processes of release from suppression were also active in his thought, particularly through the function of transvaluation, and we found that aspect at work in Nietzsche's imagery of overcoming, the overman, and eternal return.[135] We also found the heritage of release from suppression in Heidegger's account of authenticity, Foucault's account of affirmation and counter-memory, and Heidegger's later writing on language and thought. As the idea of difference and its multiple effects functioned without the negative force of those ideas and words that clustered around the idea of identity, we found a growing emphasis on differentiation without suppression or violence in response to deviations from overriding and "transdiscursive" entities and laws. Heidegger's language of release and dwelling is one momentary culmination of that emphasis. The affections, beliefs, and ideas, and the energy of their defense, that carried the sense that world order and human well-being depend on metaphysical identities, laws, and principles have passed away in this strand. Instead, differences without substantive grounding, gaps without meaning, contingent collections (or regions) of practice and thought, disclosure without formal identity: such "things" have brought together ways of thinking and speaking, as we followed them in Foucault and Heidegger, that develop with the experiences of release from suppression and release to affirmation of thoroughly historical differentiations. The language of difference carries the sense that in this release our language is returning to words and thoughts that it has borne repressively, anxiously, and usually without recognition, that in this strand of discourse new energy and directions for thinking and speaking are coming from outcast but preoccupying ideas and words in our heritage. Disconnection, absence of ultimate meaning, splintering, hidden discursive motives, uncertainty without judgment, time conceived in the metaphors of return, unreconcilable differences, and the experience of no being at all are parts of this gathering dimension. These hopeless things in our established discourses have led in their emergence in the language of difference to experiences of release without a violence that has characterized our heritage. They have begun to develop ways of speaking and thinking that repeat the releasing effect of the idea of difference with discourse-forming power.

We can see this "releasing effect" function as Jacques Lacan uses his own experience of "excommunication" from the International Psychoanalytic Association as an occasion for introducing his 1964 seminar on Freudian thought.[136] His work on "the fundamentals" of psychoanalysis, which was focused on training analysis and the desire of the analyst, had evoked outrage—"fury" is Lacan's word—on the part of the leading members in the International Psycho-analytic Association. It constituted a breach in psychoanalytic teachings, a violation of second- and third-generation language in the Freudian tradition. His writings were censored, not allowed to be published in official journals in that tradition, and his teaching was in effect banned. He was effectively excommunicated from the association, exited from the rights and privileges of communicating within the Association.

He was, he says, part of an exchange, a deal, in which a certain conceptual conformity, a constellation of linguistic agreements, is traded for the privileges of membership. But the *ex*-communication, the breaking of his membership, and not the identity of the affiliated language, occasions a noteworthy exhibition of something unconscious. In this case, Lacan says, the break in affiliation shows the unconscious of Freud's desire and hence the unconscious of psychoanalysis. The International Psycho-analytic Association, with its own sense of identity and autonomy, its power to organize and to bestow privileges as well as to exact punishment, lives out of Freud's language, discoveries, and practice of psychoanalysis, as well as out of Freud's own desires, which are deeply embedded in his work: this association is Freudian. Its own autonomy has covered over and profoundly obscured its Freudian origins, which, like the continuing presence of God vis-à-vis contingent being, according to some metaphysical accounts, supports and infuses the present moments of psychoanalytic language and practice. This obscurity of Freudian desire is in the functions of routine Freudian language, in the easily memorized concepts and metaphors, as well as in psychoanalytic practice. It particularly darkens the Freudian presence, however, in the functions of the association's identity as the association perpetuates itself, defines what is other than it, establishes its friends, and seeks to live out of its own language and interests. The association's identity covers over the already obscure desires that invest its work. How else, then, could the unconscious of psychoanalysis come out except through a rupture in its patterns of speech and thought?

When the obscure Freudian unconscious begins to be manifest, does not psychoanalysis, this practice of desire, find that its own desire is not given by its official identity, that is, not given by the association's subjectivity? It seems to come from elsewhere, from something too covered over to allow clear speech and thought regarding even its obscurity. The desire of Freudian analysis began, perhaps, to disrupt the official and guarded serenity of psychoanalysis as Lacan's analysis of training analysis brought into question the certainties of the established tradition. The obscurity of this desire, whatever it might be, became apparent through the expelling action of the official body; an unconscious part of the established communication of the association, and one that breaks that communication, became apparent in the *ex* of the excommunication of Lacan in the context of his analyzing the desire of psychoanalysis. And in this situation of expulsion, in which Lacan's communication was officially banned, Lacan's now other-than-official communication became something like a release from repression and a gathering point for what is active and obscure in the established communication. Excommunication, release from an official and repressive identity, becomes a symbol of something obscure in psychoanalysis. Something already there but hidden and carried by psychoánalytical search for the unconscious seems to be coming out, something "stricken by something like oblivion," says Lacan. Lacan's excommunication brings with it, and with greater than usual apparentness, the obscurity of desire that is present and hidden in the tradition and its practitioners.

Lacan's language in his excommunication address speaks out of the releasing division from the International Psycho-analytic Association. His exclusion is an opening through which something suppressed and unknown begins to emerge.[137] His analysis of his excommunication articulates a sense of something unanalyzed both in his own language and in the very transmission of psychoanalysis. He calls this unanalyzed element Freud's desire. But that name functions to signify something that is sensed, not known, something guessed to be originary for psychoanalysis and in psychoanalysis as an unconscious and powerful component. Lacan's language maintains the difference between its own consciously articulated meanings and structures and something else, desire-like probably, that will not fit into Lacan's articulation. *His* alertness in and to this obscurity is signified by the *ex*communication. And the obscurity itself emerges in the release of his excommunication. Violation of the association's identity, casting into doubt its certainties, a transgressive sense of difference, a sensed relation between an obscure else-than and a developing, highly energized language: these are elements in Lacan's address. The effects of his address are to disturb the very sense of professional identity by means of a dominant, pervasive sense of difference and to suggest an opening for a quality of exploration and communication available with the obscure, if disturbing, opening. The hallmarks of psychoanalytic process become operative in a broadened discourse in the language of difference. In a psychoanalytic context, it is a process of opening to the unconscious. Release to nonrepressive communication occurs through the ex-ing of patterns of suppression vis-à-vis the unconscious. Through the transgression of the Psycho-analytic Association's identity, a new sense of responding happens in relation to something hidden but present, something obscure but motivating, something unknown in the tradition and yet to-be-said. Lacan is "embarked" on "a new phase" by this occurrence, and one is led to think that as this new phase happens in psychoanalysis at its best, Lacan and his students might undergo a quality of exchange that is not, for a while at least, based on the maintenance of repressing patterns, but is exploratory with a dimension that is unfixed, freeing, and disclosive (p. 1). In that case the experience of release from repression and openness to the Freudian unconscious would mold the communication, and release rather than repression would exercise a new influence on how people speak and think.[138]

The distance in this aspect of Lacan's thought, and, as we shall see, of Derrida's, from Nietzsche's Preface for the second edition of *The Gay Science* has developed as "deprivation" in traditional thinking has become a peculiar richness in the language of difference. Nietzsche says that for some ways of thinking, "it is their deprivations that philosophize; in others, their riches and strengths" (p. 33). Nietzsche means that some thinking is moved by an oppressive, resenting will to power that attempts to eliminate that exuberance of spirit that the discourse cannot tolerate, while another kind of thinking is moved by a flowing, creative affirmation of will to power. Nietzsche's words have been changed. What was traditionally deprived of influence has become, in its release from traditional suppression, peculiarly rich. As the idea of difference has functioned to develop its own discourse, the repressed, left out, and obscured words and ideas have gained organizational, idea-developing power. Part of this power has occurred as the discourse has let go of the language of force and given freer rein to releasing occurrences. Instead of the Nietzschean words of force, the suppressed words and ideas clustering around released differences have moved language to emphases and configurations that Nietzsche foresaw broadly in *The Gay Science* in the image of Dionysus as a free and glad way of thinking in the mood of gratitude. *Différance* and *play* in Derrida's writing carry out one direction of the gay science by a way of writing that releases the unwordable in language from the domination of presence, connection, self-expression, and even momentary completion.[139] In this writing the irony has come full circle by which Nietzsche identified the traditional, dominant ways of thinking as deprived. Now the deprived richness of the completely obscured idea of radical difference comes to expression as a word that cannot be said and as a spelling that in its violation of correctness sets in motion a way of writing that excludes one kind of traditional suppression and violence from its play.

Derrida does not intend merely to coin a new word when he introduces différance. By its use he puts in his writing a "playing movement that produces" the "effects of difference" (p. 11). The playing movement takes place, for example, as this word appears to name "the movement according to which language, or any code, any system of referral in general, is constituted 'historically' as a weave of differences" (p. 12). This movement named by différance at first seems to be a process of relations. But this name—*différance*—is deferred in its naming function. "What" it seems to name is not properly nameable, and it is designed to indicate that it does not do what it seems to do, that is, name something nameable. In Derrida's writing this word "marks" what defies the function of naming. It thus defers or puts aside its own function. It marks no present or presence. It marks instead intervals that separate by lack of sound, sense, signification, or action. It names no action or thing, but it marks nonetheless the "becoming-space-of-time and the becoming-time-of-space," that is, it marks spacing and timing without presence. Spacing and timing (are) "without subject, substance, and cause." We reach a now familiar difficulty. How are we to write of the different-from-what-one-can-say-or-grasp as we write of timing and spacing? The lack of activity and passitivity drives us to writing without active or passive voice. We keep the relation of active and passive "undecided" by the nonmeaning of the -*ance*. Différance functions in Derrida's writing as a kind of middle voice by which difference differences in the functions of continuous deferral and differing. It keeps everything in its play undecidable. It "produces" differences, for example, by deferring its own naming function. In seeming to name, it cannot name. In seeming to signify, it has no signified. It cannot be said unambiguously, since différance and différence sound the same. It offsets consciousness, since the consciousness of writing or reading the word is deferred by the word's nonmeaning in the discourse. The deferring and differing are repeated, but with no buildup of significance. As it functions in Derrida's writing, there is only the continuing trace of silent, wordless breaching.[140]

The play of différance in Derrida's writing "shakes the dominance of beings" that impress themselves as a continuing presence over, under, or through all movements and relations (p. 21). By making all verbal directions undecidable, holding them in animated but nonconclusive play, différance offsets a strange and powerful type of violence in our tradition. Call it the violence of presence. Traditional preoccupation with presenting, with which we are familiar, the obsessive concern for coming to be with purpose, with continuing and ceasing to be with relation to some way of being that is continually self-presencing, has violated the gappy historicity, the fissures, and the conflictual, network quality of the traditional discourse. This violence has been lived out in reflective insistence on presence—in a relentless effort housed in our language and thought to make presence and to preserve presence. When presence as such is made undecidable and, as presence, replaceable by no presence at all through the function of différance, this kind of violence is itself deferred. The difference of nonpresence offsets the violence of overriding presence in language, since language is billed, as it were, with no presence at all and continuously defers presence. One of Derrida's major accomplishments has been to write without this violence and to further a way of thinking in which the disposition toward it, if not erased, is deferred by functions that have self-erasure in their discursive occurrences.[141]

Has our discussion of the function of différance given us a conclusion? Do we conclude that the language of difference, born in an intense anger of massive, unconscious repression, borne through transvaluation, de-struction, and the processes of differing, transformed by discursive releases and repeated plays of nonconclusive differences: do we conclude that the language of difference harbors hope for freedom from that peculiar Western emphasis on force plus rightness? Is the recognition that all syntheses and conclusions are dangerous for human beings unless they are repeated in discourses of counter-memory, release, and undecidability—is that recognition a sign of a different way, a different *ethos*, that will function without the anxious force of obsession over presence? Is a new being coming to be in this language that will not repeat the resentment and presence-oriented spirituality of our tradition? It would take only a small step, motivated doubtlessly by interest in human well-being, to make these discursive traits into conclusions and to reinstate the dominance of presence. But the risk of no conclusions, of continuing undecidability, of criteria so cut and splintered that they can no longer incite passion, but can only solicit conviction through uncertainty and tolerance: would that not risk anarchy? Perhaps some of the massive suffering of our history has come from the functions of Laws, Principles, and Beings that could not be aware of their own replaceability. Absolutes do generate their opposites when differences are polar and opposition is part of the structure of speech. Non-therefore, non-hence, non-purpose seam . . .

Notes

1. Any discourse will be experienced as heavier or lighter in its demands on hearer/reader. There can also be in the discourse a play of the senses of heavy and light, dense and clear, obvious and obscure. In some instances the lightest of expressions will have heavy density in its context, such as "truth is transgressive." The play of heavy and light senses is particularly active in the language of difference. As the idea of difference functions to break connections of identity or to offset the centers of traditional comprehension, the language can seem heavy, demanding unaccustomed effort on the part of those following it. But in its function an unaccustomed sense of lightness also develops, a release of force that has held words and ideas in certain patterns of intelligence and feeling, and also a light movement, often called play, that allows alignment and realignment of words and ideas in combinations that lighten and brighten as they proceed. This kind of play takes place in the following discussion, not as a technique of presentation or as a style grafted on to certain texts, but as part of the discourse that is followed and written. It is an aspect of the language of difference that has a peculiar affinity for the metaphors of weight and surface, not unlike the play of seriousness and frivolity in Nietzsche's writing, and a play that changes some of the functions of "force" in our traditional speech. This lightness is frequently called play without purpose, but it occurs in discursive movements that have discursive consequences. One consequence that we shall follow particularly in the latter part of this book is a releasing effect on thinking, one that influences how words and ideas are combined, and one that lacks a particular kind of violence as it finds expression through its own way of offsetting itself.

2. We speak of thinking and speaking within a discourse or a strand of discourse throughout the book. Part of the genesis of this essay is in the experiences of speaking and thinking in the jurisdictions of very different ideas, associations, and images. Things are often different in different discourses. One often feels differently in different discourses. The senses of satisfaction and inadequacy are often different. When a person is thoroughly within a way of thinking and speaking, he or she will often experience anxieties and frustrations that are different from those characteristic of people within other discourses. We shall see, for example, that lack of being is associated with life-affirmation for Foucault and Derrida, and that the anxiety associated with mortality in *Being and Time* transforms in Heidegger's work into moods closely associated with serenity. The shift from one discourse to another is not unlike shifting fluently from one language to another. As this kind of experience sharpens in focus and awareness, one discovers that "neutrality" of language and thinking is an ideal in one way of thinking, not only because of specific interests, such as interest in objective observation, but also because the ideal of neutrality is formed in association with many other discursive interests and values. As one thinks and speaks inside other strands of discourse, one comes to know that an ideal of transdiscursive neutrality is a characteristic of one influential strand in our tradition. It too has associated with it many feelings, rankings of ideas and ideals, fears and desires, and so forth. It too is in a way of thinking and speaking.

As we learn to speak and think in different discourses, their differences become significant. The present essay does not attempt to override these differences either by the idea of continuity or by judgments that rank the differences. Our interest is in following the unresolved differences in such a way that the ideal of resolution does not have synthesizing power in our discussion. In that sense we are thinking through the idea of difference, as we shall call it, and not through metaphysical principles of judgment. We want to see what is hearable, believable, feelable, and knowable in the strand of discourse ruled by difference.

3. "Within the Microcosm of 'The Talking Cure,'" *Interpreting Lacan*, eds. J. Smith and W. Kerringan (New Haven: Yale University Press, 1983), p. 41.

4. Unless otherwise noted, all references in this chapter are to *Beyond Good and Evil: Prelude to a Philosophy of the Future*, trans. W. Kaufmann (New York: Random House, Vintage Books, 1966). We will follow closely several sections of *Beyond Good and Evil* in order to see how Nietzsche's discourse involves such ideas as transcendence, eternity, being, and essence in functions that transvalue them and create the conditions for their elimination. We will emphasize these functions and their transvaluing power in forming an antimetaphysical discourse that moves toward a nonmetaphysical discourse.

5. The directions of instincts are "valuations," that is, *forces* of will (I.3). These are forces of life preservation that are expressed as "estimates" (I.3). Estimates are interested in preserving our kind of creature. The kind of creature we are is a product of the conflicts, fears, punishments, successes, and so on, that make up the creature's history. "Life-promotion" is the interest of a judgment, not particularly what it claims or sees. We live by judgments, by the "estimates" or "fictions" of cognition. We determine our lives by them. That they claim to be true or false, that they expect to reveal the connections among things just as the connections are, that they claim a priori or apodictic rightness: that is part of their own life-promoting efforts. That is part of their fiction, their insistence, their happy folly (I.4).

6. See, for example, I.6: "For every drive wants to be master—and it attempts to philosophize in *that spirit.*"

7. Other characteristics of distance: inner independence (II.29), total misunderstanding (II.30), distaste for unconditional statements (II.31), avoidance of those pleasures native to the passing organization (II.33), attention to the erroneousness of the world as organized by the other discourse (II.34).

8. One can also show, particularly in *Genealogy of Morals*, that Nietzsche thought in more naturalistic terms about the transformation of sickened will into robust energy through a process of reversion. Nietzsche thinks then of will and reversion as though they have some kind of law of development that we might expect in any similar historical situation. The purely historical emphasis that we are now seeing is in tension with the naturalistic ideas of will, sickness, and health.

9. The "superiority" of this force may be read either as "more basic and hence fundamental for the power of saintly power," or as "gaining dominance through a process of pious self-sacrifice and the consequent development of a different kind of power." In the first reading will to power is *the* energy base for an inauthentic expression of saintly piety. In the second, will to power continues its strictly historical development through the conflicts and suicides of pious power. On this second reading, one need not assume a metaphysical entity, will to power, at the base of things, although one could say that will to power is effectively there and is becoming evident through the designated process. As we saw in the last section, all

of these readings are possible, and giving will to power a metaphysical standing is in severe tension with Nietzsche's critique of "reality," "being," "metaphysics," and "substance." Nietzsche's *use* of will to power in this context frees thinking from the traditional hierarchy, however, as well as from the intuitive and nonvoluntary attractions of the saint. His discourse thus loosens the hold of metaphysical convictions, including those that have a positive function in his own thinking.

10. One could also show an analogous development through the "continual suicide of reason" that characterizes part of the Christian tradition (III.46). Nietzsche is not saying that all of Christianity includes rational suicide. But the part that does, exemplified in this particular paragraph by Pascal and related to earlier Roman Christianity, *this* part leaves the space of rational power open for the emergence of power without rational formation: a willpower with a transvaluational process that replaces self-denial with self-affirmation. A willpower emerges that is neither rational nor Christian, one that is without "enslavement and self-mockery, self-mutilation" (III.46). This willpower can be the basis for very different states of mind and discourses, for instance, like the discourse operating in III.46. Nietzsche also finds affiliation between "a genuinely religious life" and the leisure of aristocratic classes: the religious life has transvalued the good conscience of some aristocratic life into the bad conscience of Christianity, and that bad conscience has prepared the way for a different leisure of free-spirited withdrawal from the main stream. This leisure is a half-hearted version of "free-thinking" found in the basically nonreligious Lutherans and Calvinists (III.58–59). In these and other of Nietzsche's genealogical connections one finds instances of historical generation of "things" that can also be taken to be nonhistorical and transtemporal.

11. This mediocrity believes that it has enormous staying power, Nietzsche observes: "The mediocre alone have a chance of continuing their type and propagating—they are the men of the future, the only survivors" (IX.262). So says the discourse of mediocrity. But that means primarily that this leveling discourse lacks sense for its own contributions to the opposites and differences that it hates. Its "survival power" is in its concealments from itself, and its concealments will allow other forces to outstrip the mediocre states of mind and spirit, take them over in another interplay, and transform them while they are busy "surviving."

12. The following remarks, unless otherwise noted, are based on IX.258–260.

13. We note the use of the language of essence, necessity, ultimate goals, foundation, and energy with a single nature. In light of earlier sections of this chapter, we recognize also that the issue is what happens to this language, how it is appropriated and overpowered, in this discourse. In an often ragged and unsure way Nietzsche's thinking shows that the language of essence and so forth, is itself in a transformative process that will incorporate that language into a different discourse.

14. "It was this morality itself that dammed up such enormous strength and bent the bow in such a threatening manner; now it is 'outlived' " (IX.262).

15. "All sorts of new what-fors and wherewithals; no shared formulas any longer; misunderstanding allied with disrespect; decay, corruption, and the highest desires gruesomely entangled; the genius of the race overflowing from all cornucopias of good and bad; a calamitous simultaneity of spring and fall, full of new charms and veils that characterize young, still unexhausted, still unwearied

corruption. Again danger is there, the mother of morals, great danger, this time transposed into the individual, into the neighbor and friend, into the ally, into one's own child, into one's own heart, into the most personal and secret recesses of wish and will: what may the moral philosophers emerging in this age have to preach now?" (IX.262).

16. *On The Genealogy of Morals*, trans. Kaufmann (New York: Random House, Vintage 1967), Chapter II.

17. *The Will to Power*, trans. Kaufmann and Hollingdale (New York: Random House, 1968), p. 7.

18. *Being and Time*, Introduction. Unless otherwise noted all quotes from *Being and Time* will be from Joan Stambaugh's unpublished translation. Only her translation of the Introduction to *Being and Time* has been published, in *Martin Heidegger: Basic Questions*, ed. David F. Krell (New York: Harper & Row, 1977). The number of the section in *Being and Time* from which the quote is taken will be noted parenthetically.

19. "And so we must first of all awaken an understanding of the meaning of this question [of Being]. The intention of the following treatise is to work out concretely the question of the meaning of Being" (Krell, p. 40).

20. Hence, in our preceding note Heidegger is quoted as saying "awaken." The German is *zu wecken*. Below we shall see that for Heidegger, the history of metaphysics has its beginning in Plato and Plato's influence. Heidegger begins *Being and Time* with a quote from *The Sophist*. Not only does Plato state the issue of *Being and Time*; his discourse also sets in motion the thinking that will be offset by Heidegger's maintaining the *question* of Being in relation to metaphysical thinking. The initial quote is: "For you have evidently long been aware of this (what you really mean when you use the expression 'being'); but we who once believed we understood have now become perplexed." The perplexity is to be maintained in the question of Being, that is, *Being and Time* goes behind Plato's and our metaphysics to the question that helped most to give rise to metaphysics. We shall see the fulfillment of this perplexity in Heidegger's use of the word *strife* at the end of *Being and Time* (cf. the last section of this chapter).

21. "Our provisional aim is the Interpretation of *time* as the possible horizon . . ." (Krell, Intro.).

22. If we penetrate to the "origin," we do not come to things that are specifically obvious for "common understanding"; rather, the questionableness of the obvious opens up for us.

23. "Author's Preface to the Seventh German Edition," in Martin Heidegger, *Being and Time*, trans. John Macquarrie and Edward Robinson (New York: Harper & Row, 1962), p. 17.

24. Macquarrie and Robinson translate *Wiederholung* as *restating*. Stambaugh translates the word as *recapitulation* (2). Heidegger's emphasis is on getting back to and reasking a question that is in Dasein's history, and one that consequently is a part of Dasein but has been overridden and, though constitutive, forgotten. To bring it back and give it expression—"einer ausdrücklichen Wiederholung" (1)—is to reintroduce the question explicitly into Dasein's speaking and thinking.

25. In the course of this discussion we shall see a development similar to the process of transvaluation that goes on in Nietzsche's thinking. The indefinable and self-evident character of Being will be transmuted into Heidegger's idea of the self-disclosiveness of Being. Universality will transmute into the different idea of

"whole," and "self-evident" will transmute into the different idea of disclosure. Metaphysical thinking will again be transformed through its own influences into a way of thinking that develops away from metaphysics.

26. "... the question of Being is nothing else than the radicalization of an essential tendency of Being that belongs to Dasein itself, namely of the pre-ontological understanding of Being" (4).

27. "The de-struction of the history of ontology essentially belongs to the formulation of the question of Being and is possible within such a formulation. Within the scope of this treatise, which has as its goal a fundamental elaboration of the question of Being, the de-struction can be carried out only with regard to the fundamentally decisive stages of this history." Heidegger would not have said in *Being and Time* that Dasein fundamentally changes as de-struction goes on. One of the purposes of this chapter is to show that on *Being and Time*'s own terms, however, Dasein does change fundamentally in this process, so fundamentally, in fact, that the idea of fundamental change itself will become suspect. This effect is a function of *Being and Time*'s discourse in spite of Heidegger's intentions and convictions.

28. If, for example, one attempts to take the explicit question of Being out of *Being and Time*, emphasizing perhaps the regional, ontic descriptions of tools, speech, and so forth, one loses the essay's de-struction of its own language and tradition. Such an approach would reduce *Being and Time* to a metaphysical episode without significant discursive power or effect. One would think outside the essay's own effect, and to that extent the interpreter would miss the thinking that goes on in this essay. If this discursive strand is to be thought through, one must work through *Being and Time* in the question of Being and let the effect of thinking out this question empower the ongoing thought. The jump over the question of Being is another kind of forgetfulness in which one overlooks the historical power of that question in the jump. It is a serious misevaluation of the history of human being and the part played in it by what one jumps over.

29. "In its factual being Dasein is always as 'what' it already was. Whether explicitly or not, it is its past." "Dasein is its past in the manner of *its* being...." "Dasein is determined by its historicity in the ground of its being." "... it is inevitable that inquiry into Being, which was designated with regard to its ontic-ontological necessity, is itself characterized by historicity" (6).

30. "... de-struction of the traditional content of ancient ontology which is carried out along the guidelines of the question of Being. This de-struction is based upon the original experiences in which the first and subsequently guiding determinations of Being were gained." The metaphysical "resolutions" of the question carry the question—maintain it—by suppression or by building a theoretical superstructure that hides the question. Although the context is significantly different from Nietzsche's, Heidegger's account uses the same idea used by Nietzsche: the hidden issue is historically carried by what hides the issue.

31. "The de-struction of the history of ontology essentially belongs to the formation of the question of Being and is possible solely within such a formulation" (6).

32. Perhaps Heidegger's closeness to Nietzsche through the power of discursive functions is becoming evident. Although Heidegger does not think in terms of will to power, and thinks rather that that idea is a capstone of the Western metaphysical edifice, he expects that through de-structuring a transformation in thinking and speaking will take place, a transformation that is similar to the kinds of transformations we found in *Beyond Good and Evil*. In his interpretations of

NOTES

Nietzsche, Heidegger defines and criticizes Nietzsche's concepts in relation to traditional concepts without addressing adequately their transforming (de-structuring) functions and effects. He consequently tends to abstract Nietzsche's ideas from their thinking-effectiveness and not to associate will to power or eternal recurrence with the transvaluations that they enact *because* of their attachment to their heritage and their reversal of it. The *metaphysical* nihilism in Nietzsche's thinking occurs discursively also as nonmetaphysical freedom and departure from metaphysical interests and affections, a departure that makes possible other ways of thinking. Heidegger's critique of Nietzsche involves another way of thinking not available to Nietzsche, but one that follows in the wake of the transformative power and effect of Nietzsche's discourse. As we are in the process of discovering, *Being and Time* de-structures metaphysical ideas and beliefs by probing its own metaphysics in the suppressed experience of the question of Being. Heidegger's interpretation of Being by temporality and not by power is a major shift away from Nietzsche and Western metaphysics. But de-structuring processes that happen throughout *Being and Time* are like the transforming processes in Nietzsche's thinking. Heidegger is now able to think outside the language of power. Something of Nietzsche's Child-Metaphor (in *Zarathustra's* "The Three Metamorphoses") seems to be embodied in this post-Nietzschean language. Heidegger's language is more removed from the Lion than Nietzsche's, and like the image of the Child, it is more innocent of power than Nietzsche's language could have been. Heidegger's discourse is a clear development beyond anything Nietzsche's language could have accomplished. But the power of Nietzsche's discourse and its transformations is at work in the de-structuring processes of *Being and Time*. While the ideas are significantly different, the discourses, by virtue of the breaks and oppositions among the different ideas, are similar: there is a similarity of discursive effectiveness, in spite of the ineffectiveness of Nietzsche's specific concepts in Heidegger's thinking, because of the functions of transvaluation and de-struction. Heidegger's work on Nietzsche may be found in his four-volume *Nietzsche* (Neske: Pfullingen, 1961), volumes 1, 2, and 4 of which are available in David F. Krell's translation New York: Harper & Row, 1979). See also Heidegger, "The Word of Nietzsche: 'God Is Dead,'" in *Holzwege* (Frankfurt: Klostermann, 1957). One might note particularly in *Nietzsche*, Volume 2, Heidegger's discussion of the indebtedness of *Being and Time* to Nietzsche, an indebtedness he also acknowledges in *Holzwege*, p. 195.

33. "The analysis of Dasein is not only incomplete but at first also *preliminary*. It only brings out the Being of this being without interpreting its meaning. Its aim is rather to expose the horizon for the most original interpretation of Being. Once we have reached that horizon the preparatory analysis requires repetition on a higher, genuinely ontological basis" (5). The "horizon" for the question is developed through the preliminary steps of de-struction. Then temporality, not substance or eternity or some other interpretation of extra-temporal Being, will define the arena of thinking.

34. "Dasein is in such a way that, by being, it understands something like Being. Remembering this connection, we must show that *Time* is that from which Dasein tacitly understands and interprets something like Being at all" (5).

35. ". . . we must show, on the basis of the question of the meaning of Being . . . that—and in what way—the central range of problems of all ontology is rooted in the phenomenon of Time correctly viewed and correctly explained" (5). *Correctly* here means viewed and explained in a language and thought no longer controlled

by metaphysical beliefs and categories. Correctness concerning Dasein's fundamental question comes from metaphysical de-struction.

36. What, then, does Heidegger mean when he says that "temporality is at the same time the condition for the possibility of historicity as a temporal mode of Being of Dasein itself, regardless of whether and how it is 'in time'" (60)? Historicity, he says further, is a determination that is "prior to what is called history (world-historical occurrences)" (6). On the one hand, historicity is a "temporal mode of the Being of Dasein." On the other, temporality is "a condition of the possibility of historicity" *in the context of discussing how research by Dasein regarding itself is possible.* One way to read this language is this: Dasein is a self-reflecting being. It can study itself in many different ways because *it* is essentially temporal. If Dasein were not temporal and thus not historical, such study, given the vast number of different ways of living, would not be possible. Temporality is Dasein's meaning: it is that factor of Dasein that gives it universality in all of its particularities—and in this context, it gives universality with regard to multiple self-interpretations. But Heidegger's claim does not mean that temporality has a transhistoric status. He says only that it is a common factor in the historical being, Dasein. Another way to read the above quote: temporality is transhistorical in the sense that it characterizes Dasein in all of Dasein's historical appearances. While temporality is clearly not a structure of subjectivity, it has a yet-to-be-determined status in Being that is never defined by historical origins and parameters. Both readings can be defended by textual appeal. Our discussion will show that both readings are de-structured before the essay is finished. Heidegger is clear from the beginning, however, that Dasein is elementally historical, that *its* being is historical (6). From this position will come the further interpretation that temporality is understood in its relation to history as a pervasive part of Dasein's history. If it has transhistorical status, that status is part of a history that has not come fully to terms with itself. "This elemental historicity of Dasein can remain concealed from it"; ". . . Dasein is determined by historicity in the ground of its being"; ". . . the essential historicity of Dasein . . ." (6).

The inquiry into the question of Being is founded in historicity and is an historical process. Once the full power of this idea is developed, historicity will gain dominance over temporality, and a major de-struction of the correlation of temporality and transcendence will take place. The history of Being and all the aspects of Dasein's being—temporality, meaning, disclosure, and so forth—will be seen in a process that circumscribes them.

37. I am following Stambaugh's translation of *verfallen* by *ensnare*.

38. The de-struction of Dasein's foundational, nontemporal self-interpretation involves a recasting of Kant's "obscure doctrine" of the schematism. Although Heidegger's *Kant and the Problem of Metaphysics* carries out this project in detail, he does not need that analysis in *Being and Time*, since recovery of the question of Being in the language of time and the consequent offsetting of the priority of subjectivity and transcendence provide the beginning necessary for his rereading of Kant. "The ontology of Dasein" sets the course of a discourse different from Kant's. It destroys the "new and secure foundation for philosophy" that Descartes offered and Kant accepted. "Being-in-the-world" offsets both the *cogito sum* and the idea of pure reason as well as its schematism. Modernity is not reversed in *Being and Time*, but a language and way of thinking take shape that recast the questions that dominate modern thought and suppress that experience of *Being* that moved our tradition and continues to move in the tradition's subterrain (6).

39. Derrida's early writings—for example, "The Ends of Man," "Ousia and Grammé," and the essays of *Writing and Difference*—look for the origins in the history of Western philosophy of both the dominant metaphysical way of thinking and of the nonmetaphysical traces that accompany metaphysics in unsayable ways. He was then working with a central idea about historical origin and another central idea about traces that are obliterated in the dominant language. He thought that metaphysical language was the only possibility for linguistic communication and that it would always violate the traces by the dominance of presence in it. Both the overwhelming power of metaphysics and the unsayableness of the utterly different were lodged in these two central ideas. Together they function for him, however, like a metaphysical absolute, and perhaps knowing that, he was all the more puzzled at that time about how to speak nonmetaphysically. Derrida's options appeared to him to be either to think metaphysically or to so construct his own discourse that something that could not be said would begin to happen in its unsayableness—not as absent, but something like an unsayable tracing.

For example, at the conclusion of "Ousia and Grammé," he says that a trace, which is "beyond metaphysical closure," cannot be simply absent. If it were absent, either it would furnish us nothing to think of or it would still be a negative mode of presence. Therefore it is necessary that the sign of this excess be both absolutely transcendent (*excédant*) with respect to all possible presence-absence—all production or disappearance of a being in general—and yet *somehow* still self-signifying. *Somehow*: in a way unformulable by metaphysics as such, "to surpass (*excéder*) metaphysics, a certain trace must be imprinted in the metaphysical text, yet one that points toward a wholly different text—not toward another presence or another form of presence" (p. 91). "*Wholly* different text" deemphasizes that texts of themselves merge and flow and shift continuously in their processes. The phrase means, rather, that there are metaphysical texts and that "something" wholly different from them is crushed out of sight and sound by their power. In this way of speaking, Derrida underplays the play of discourses, their own nonmetaphysical aspect that occurs as they develop, transform, transmute, and differentiate. Discourses, as we are finding, make ideas and wordplays that override, undercut, or offset the ideas and wordplays that are dominant within a given discourse. We are, for example, following a group of discursive developments that have made the philosophical and linguistic environment of differences in which Derrida reads and speaks.

"The way such a trace is inscribed in the metaphysical text is so inconceivable that it can only be described as an effacing of the trace itself. The trace comes to be by its own effacement. The trace erases itself; by its own action it removes what might maintain it in presence. The trace is neither perceptible nor imperceptible" (p. 92). The trace "does" something that makes possible Derrida's powerful insight—self-effacement, for example. Effacement is borne, "inscribed," in the metaphysical text; inconceivably so for metaphysics, but not absolutely inconceivably so in Derrida's emerging text. This way of thinking is not *in* metaphysics. Derrida's language is part of a language that is breaking away from metaphysics. Metaphysics is not as absolute as Derrida thought, nor are the traces so totally inconceivable. But Derrida is also right: texts, discourses, are not merely present or absent. When the idea of presence is used to interpret texts, including the *texts* of presence, it loses—forgets—the textuality, the discursiveness. The text in its happening is other than what is said about it, and cannot properly be said to be either present or absent.

If the text is not *present*, but is something that witnesses against its interpretation as metaphysical presence, how are we to speak of it? The text speaks, produces, interplays. Effacement goes on, differencing goes on, the imperceptible goes on, and the metaphysical polarity of presence-absence fixes too quickly, rejects too fixedly, gives status and station too routinely, and encompasses too thoroughly. Presence is, always, but never wholly. Absence is and is not, but never absolutely. In texts differing, effacing, and presenting are neither presences nor absences. Texts produce in their presence, in their gapping and differencing, in their discontinuing and obstacling. As texts intermingle, different wording, doing, conflicting, and feeling come about. These differences emerge out of the interplays, are interplayed, fade in and out, produce and yield and leave some marks, some differences, some presences in the continuing interplay that soon drops "interplay" for other images (no longer "images") and other metaphors (no longer "metaphors").

Derrida applies his thought of trace, his trace-thinking, to Heidegger without considering the transmuting, de-structuring processes of Heidegger's own discourse. "It is in this way that the difference between Being and beings—that which has been 'forgotten' in determining Being as presences and presences as the present—is so deeply concealed that *no trace of it remains. The trace of difference* is expunged.... It is the trace of the trace which has disappeared in forgetting the difference between Being and beings" (p. 82, emphasis added). We have remaining for thinking "the trace left by the removal of the trace." But if we "name" the trace, "give it determination," we by that action revert back to metaphysics. We make it into a presence. That would appear to be so only if the naming were in a discourse totally dominated by "presence" or if the discourse did not override or ride through the presencing specificity of names and determinations. The presencing of names is not final or total: discourses de-presence. Names can override determinations. In their discursive functions they can produce nonpresencing options, as we have seen, for example, the self-effacing idea of trace, the self-overcoming idea of will to power, the de-founding idea of foundation, the undeterminable idea of Being in the horizon of temporality, the offsetting idea of regions of significance. They present, re-present, de-present, perhaps in the same movement. The "thing itself" too is played through and out. As the emerging language of difference functions, there is as-such, none-such, de-such, no-such.

As we follow our selected texts in their transistory, disclosive, forever deferring and differenciating manner, the inconceivability of traces may be thought of as a border phenomenon—not only the border that demarcates identity, but the borders that crisscross discourses and line out passing names and emerging differences. Borders differ. And at borders, as transmuting goes on, traces of the transmuted occur. At and in borders, through them, language traces both the passing and the emerging. In this language now, and in Derrida's, the dominance of identity and presence is overridden as "border" and "trace" come into play.

When Derrida wrote these early essays he subtly gave identity dominance over transition and transmutation as he read our traditional texts, and he consequently thought that metaphysical discourses were as total as *they* thought they were. At that time he thought that our task was to write the unthinkable, while Heidegger came to think in a different discourse in which "the early trace (*Spur*)" was coming to thought and not to presence. This idea is developed in Chapter 5.

40. In Old Sanskrit as well as in Greek, the middle voice could express reflexive action, such as "he washed his hands." Even then, however, in Old Sanskrit, for

example, only two words were needed—*pānt nēniktē*—so that the nominal and pronominal functions are expressed in the verb and the inherence of the nominal in the verbal is indicated. In nonreflexive instances, however, such as the middle voice of die—*mriyáte*—or of born—*ayáte*—a different situation is stated. The German *es wird gestorben* or *es wird geboren* are probably close to the intended middle-voice meaning. In these cases no one performs an action or receives an action, and the situation itself does not refer back to itself in a way that allows a noun or pronoun to act or be acted on. Dying or borning is going on. In the case of *phainesthai*, like *gegonesthei* (becoming becomes), no one and no thing is acting or receiving action.

41. Many *sta* words, derived from the Sanskrit *stha* (to stand), undergo rethinking in *Being and Time* as well as in post–*Being and Time* works. They include not only *history, stance, substance,* and *understanding,* but also *consist, constancy, constitution, destiny, ecstasy, existence, subsist,* and *system. Dastehen, entstehen, Gestalt, Stelle, stellen, stehen, Stand, Verständnis, verstehen, vorstellen* are also prominent in this family. Generally these words are destabilized in Heidegger's discourse relative to their traditional metaphysical uses. Insofar as the question of Being is the *Stelle* of thinking, for example, and the temporal occurrence of Being is the "stance" of *Being and Time,* an "understanding" emerges in the discourse in which there is no *substance.* "To come to stand" is of a larger nonstanding event, and the tradition's intuitive correlation of "stand," "found," and "ground" is changed. "Stand" no longer addresses the question of how things are together in common. Scott Abbott's "*Stunde, Stelle, Gestaltung,* and *stehen*: An Etymology of Time, Place, Figuration, Part I, and Being in Rilke's *Duino Elegies*" (unpublished) is a particularly fine discussion of a transformation of the *sta* words.

42. "The logos of the phenomenology of Dasein has the character of *hermeneuein,* through which the *proper* meaning of Being and the basic structures of the very being of Dasein are *made known* to the understanding of Being that belongs to Dasein itself" (7.c) (italics for "proper" added).

43. With that era will pass also the "historical humanistic disciplines" that have developed out of the "meaning question" (7.c). Our discussion of Foucault will show the extent to which the historical humanistic disciplines are founded in a metaphysical history whose passage means their passage as well.

44. Stambaugh's translation includes Heidegger's marginal notes from his copy of *Being and Time.* With regard to understanding of Being, Heidegger writes marginally that this understanding is to be taken "as hearing." This means that "Being (qua the Being of beings) qua difference is 'in' Dasein as what is thrown by the (throw)." Earlier in section 39 Heidegger says, "thrownness is the kind of being of a being which *is* itself its possibilities, in such a way that it understands itself in them and from them (projects itself toward them)." To be an understanding occurrence "in the throw" means that Dasein's difference from Being occurs in and as its primordial alertness. It is not thrown, plunk. It is always in the throw. It never has a complete grasp of Being or of itself in its lineage vis-à-vis Being. When we see more clearly that Being is *the* question of the tradition that has produced human being, we will see that this difference, far from being a metaphysical difference, is in Dasein's history. Both the *lack* of grasp and *Being,* which is outside of the grasp, are in and of Dasein's history. Further, this primordial alertness, which has its own history in the idea of immediate awareness, means neither presence nor absence. It means being in question, a kind of occurrence that is not adequately interpreted by presence-absence language. That language, which is

sometimes used about *Being and Time*, needs to be in a process of destructuring to avoid being wholly metaphysical.

45. "The term existence formally indicates that Dasein *is* as an understanding potentiality of being which is concerned in its being about its being" (39).

46. "If we are to have a fore-sight of Being, we must see it with respect to the *unity* of the possible structural factors belonging to it. Only then can the question of the meaning of the unity that belongs to the totality of the Being of all beings be asked and answered with phenomenal certainty" (45).

47. "Our previous interpretation [i.e., Part I] was limited to an analysis of indifferent or inauthentic existence, starting out with average everydayness.... As long as the existential structure of authentic potentiality of being is not incorporated in the idea of existence, the fore-sight guiding an *existential* interpretation lacks primordiality" (45). Authentic existence is attuned to the primordial unity of Dasein and provides the existential basis for speaking and thinking that are attuned to their own primordial possibilities. Prior to authentic existence, "one thing is unmistakable. *Our existential analytic of Dasein up to now cannot lay claim to primordiality.*" This recognition is authentic. Further, "fragmentary" and "inauthentic" are paired by Heidegger: "its fore-having never included more than the *inauthentic* being of Dasein, of Dasein as fragmentary" (45).

48. The horizon of time gives the context for interpreting the meaning of Being as such, Heidegger says toward the end of section 45. In a gloss at that point he notes, "Presencing (*An-wesenheit*) (arrival and Appropriation)." The *Entwurf* (project) is accomplished (*vollziehen*) in the horizon of time, and that may be taken to mean that Being arrives, occurs, in how it is given space and time in a discourse that the question of Being has made possible. Being is not present, but "continuing to arrive," that is, the historical discourse lacks what preoccupies it, and its preoccupation is constitutive of Being's occurrence. The project's accomplishment is itself an occurrence of the question of Being, one in which the meaning of Being as a question in Dasein's being is apparent. Being arrives in the throw of Dasein.

49. One can see a clear analogy with Aristotle's "the soul's knowing itself" or with absolute knowledge in Hegel. Here, however, nothing that Dasein is like is "found." Nothing else that is whole or absolute shows itself to or through authentic Dasein. The wholeness of Dasein does not reveal a greater whole or anything in the image of which Dasein is. Further, *Eigenlichkeit* (authenticity) is not conceived as completing a process or fulfilling a telos. To say that Dasein is *fulfilled* as it learns to hear and to be in accord with its mortality can be meant ironically—it is fulfilled in the absence of "real" fulfillment. Or it can be a way of de-structuring the idea that human being has fundamental purposes that can be completed in a state of wholeness. Basically, however, the idea of fulfillment falls away from the idea of wholeness through the work of Heidegger's discourse.

50. I translate *Entschlosseinheit* as "release" or as "open to." Resoluteness and resolution are not able to carry those intended meanings in Heidegger's word.

51. "To expose the *structure of occurrence* and the existential and temporal conditions of its possibility means to give an *ontological* understanding of history" (72).

52. "When Dasein, anticipating, lets death become powerful in itself, as free for death, it understands itself in its own *higher power*, the power of its finite freedom, and takes over the *powerlessness* of being abandoned to itself in that freedom, which only *is* in having chosen the choice, and becomes clear about the chance elements in the disclosed situation." When he says that "authentic being-to-death, i.e., the finitude of temporality, is the concealed ground of the historicity of Dasein," he

means that mortality is the meaning of all events. He is showing that Dasein's wholeness is centered in mortality, and not, for example, in presence. Finitude and mortality immediately mean the up-coming end, that is, authentic futurity (74).
53. For example: "Only if death, guilt, conscience, freedom, and finitude live together equiprimordially in the being of a being as they do in care, *can* that being exist in the mode of fate, i.e., be historical in the ground of its existence" (emphasis added). "Only authentic temporality that is at the same time finite makes something like fate, i.e., authentic historicity, possible" (74). In these examples, the transcendental overtone has been so qualified by the ideas of finitude and mortality, as we have seen, that speaking of the transcendental status of Dasein's ontological structures has become awkward and counterintuitive. But these types of formulation point out that Heidegger's de-structuring of transcendental phenomenology involves his reliance on that way of thinking.
54. "The historicity of Dasein is essentially the historicity of the world which on the basis of the ecstatic and horizontal temporality belongs to the temporalizing of that temporality" (75).
55. Section 83 of Stambaugh's translation. Heidegger also wrote to a young and anxious Karl Löwith, when the student feared that his departure from his *Doktor-Vater*'s ideas in *Being and Time* might prevent his advancing, that he, Heidegger, had no interest in schools of agreement. His work, he said, prevented such a traditional desire. Rather, difference and disagreement are to be developed. Thinking has its many ways. "My work is unique in a limited way and can only be done by me—on account of the uniqueness of this constellation of conditions." Further, "whether one goes along with *Being and Time* is a matter of complete indifference to me...." His indifference came from the recognition that misunderstanding and trivialization are inevitable, and that agreement and disagreement are incidental to the work of thinking with and through the essay. His recognition of the limits of his own way in that context of Dasein's history with Being is consonant with his recognition, and welcome, of strife, departure, and difference. The quotations are from Löwith's "The Nature of Man and the World of Nature: For Heidegger's 80th Birthday," in *Martin Heidegger In Europe and America*, eds. Ballard and Scott (The Hague: Nijhoff, 1973), pp. 37–38.
56. "... The beginning of the strife already needs preparation. This investigation is solely *underway* to that" (83).
57. *Language, Countermemory, Practice* (Ithaca: Cornell University Press, 1977), p. 49. Hereafter, L CM P.
58. Contrary to what Foucault suggests in chapter 9 of *The Order of Things*, the power of Heidegger's discourse in *Being and Time* is found rather more in the way it fractures assumed connections in our tradition than in the specific formulations of "forms of finitude." When Dasein's finitude is thought *in* the question of Being, its discursive effect rather than the explicit, formal claims taken in separation from the question of Being provides the locus for its formative power.
59. "Let us imagine ... an ontology where being would be expressed in the same fashion for every difference, but could only express differences. Consequently, things could no longer be completely covered over, as in Duns Scotus, by the great monochrome abstraction of being, and Spinoza's forms would no longer revolve around the unity of substance. Differences would revolve of their own accord, being would be expressed in the same fashion for all these differences, and being would no longer be a unity that guides and distributes them, but their repetition as difference. For Deleuze, the non-categorial univocity of being does not directly

attach the multiple to unity (the universal neutrality of being, or the expressive force of substance); it allows being to function as that which is repetitively expressed as difference. Being is the recurrence of difference, without any difference in the form of its expression." L CM P, pp. 186–187.

60. This section is based on "Theatrum Philosophicum," in L CM P, pp. 165–196. In this article Foucault discusses Gilles Deleuze's *Différence et Répétition* and *Logique du sens*. Deleuze's work is, of course, prominent throughout the article. But Foucault picks out specific ideas, adds his own emphases, and presents his own thinking. It is a series of thematic variations and plays on Deleuzian themes, always appreciative of Deleuze and always Foucault's own. Given our interests we shall comment only occasionally on Foucault's use of Deleuze, and shall emphasize the discursive function of "difference" in this writing.

61. *The Birth of the Clinic* (Vintage, 1973), for example, follows the body of medical knowledge and practice in the imagery and function of the dead body in recent medical history: the corpus of the corpse. Deleuze's and F. Guattari's *Anti-Oedipus* (U. of Minnesota Press, 1977) uses the ideas of "body without organs" and "desiring-machine" to analyze both capitalism and psychoanalysis; the order of representation in *The Order of Things* is an organized body.

62. Foucault continues with reference to Deleuze: "Phantasms do not extend organisms into an imaginary domain; they *topologize* the materiality of the body. They should consequently be *freed* from the restrictions we impose upon them, freed from the dilemmas of truth and falsehood and of being and nonbeing (the essential difference between simulacrum and copy carried to its logical conclusion); they must be allowed to conduct their dance, to act out their mime, as 'extra-beings' " (p. 170, emphasis added). The relation between *topologize* and *freed* is important in this language, which "liberates the simulacrum" from its own event.

63. See *The Birth of the Clinic*.

64. Foucault's irony in this discussion of metaphysics involves Deleuze as well as traditional metaphysical thinking. Deleuze has enough of the idea of being left in his thinking, primarily in his idea of body, to have his own ambivalent relation with the metaphysical tradition. Body for Deleuze is more dense, less cultural than for Foucault. Hence "incorporeal materiality" suggests play on bodily surfaces for Deleuze, whereas for Foucault bodies themselves are incorporeal materialities. Hence, Foucault speaks of Deleuze's thought as a metaphysics that accepts what metaphysics rejects—"Phantasma-physics, i.e., metaphysics as phantasma without illusion." His irony in speaking of Deleuze is not less appealing for its expression of both amused rebuke and admiring enthusiasm.

65. Our attention is on how Foucault speaks of Deleuze. Foucault's own language about bodies does not have illusions in this "epi" or "meta" position in relation to bodies; rather, bodies are made up of the effective forces that constitute their histories. "The body is molded by a great many distinct regimes; it is broken down by the rhythms of work, rest, and holidays; it is poisoned by food or values through eating habits or moral laws; it constructs resistances" (L CM P, p. 153). See also section 3 of this chapter. Bodies, as Foucault understands them, are unstable loci that are describable and traceable. He is freer of the heritage of the idea of "thing-in-itself" than Deleuze (and also than Lacan).

66. We shall discuss in greater detail this network. *The Order of Things* is also an extended discussion of the orders of resemblance and representation.

67. Deleuze speaks of totalities that are peripheral to one another and of multiple

groupings that function "at the same time, but amid hiatuses and ruptures, breakdowns, and failures, stalling and short circuits, distances and fragmentations, within a sum that never succeeds in bringing its various paths together so as to form a whole" (*Anti-Oedipus*, p. 42). Other phrases in this context: wholes that do not unify the parts, paths that suddenly come to an end, noncommunicating juxtapositions, presence without belonging, fragmented universe, a world of explosions, vibrations, rotations.

68. In this discourse, break, dissolution, and separation are not opposed to continuity. These words speak of how continuities develop and are juxtaposed with each other. A break can occur as part of an object is sliced off from one grouping to join another grouping. Or breaking happens as replacement, for example, a clock replacing a tree on a desert in a dream, or the madman replacing the philosopher in Nietzsche's work. A break can be an interruption in a flow of things, for example, religious practices being detached from religious meaning. Dispersions, lesions, violations, proximate patterns without meaningful connections: these are breaks in continuities that can develop other continuities. As we shall see, this idea of break elaborates the idea of event in this writing. It functions to show that parts have relations in fragmented regions. Processes of detachment can be also processes of constellation—the constellation articulates breaks rather than a part-whole relation.

69. ". . . Three systems fail to grasp the event. The first, on the pretext that nothing can be said about these things which lie 'outside' the world, rejects the pure surface of the event and attempts to enclose it forceably—as a referent—in the spherical plentitude of the world. The second, on the pretext that signification only exists for consciousness, places the event outside and beforehand, or inside and after, and always situates it with respect to the circle of the self. The third, on the pretext that events can only exist in time, defines its identity and submits it to a solidly centered order. The world, the self, and God (a sphere, a circle, and a cylinder): three conditions that invariably obscure the event and that obstruct the successful formulation of thought. Deleuze's proposals, I believe, are directed to lifting this triple subjection which, to this day, is imposed on the event: a metaphysics of the incorporeal event (which is consequently irreducible to a physics of the world), and a logic of neutral meaning (rather than a phenomenology of signification based on the subject), and a thought of the present infinitive (and not the raising up of the conceptual future in a past essence)" (L CM P, p. 176).

70. The idea of return, for example, that functions in this language of event, though directly related to Nietzsche's idea of eternal return, makes no appeal to a force that returns to itself and is never fully expressed in what it produces. In this language, surface repetition elaborates the idea of return. A pattern, for example, returns by repetition. It is repetition without origin, as we shall see in detail below.

71. We note the difference between Foucault and Heidegger on the history of metaphysical thinking. For Heidegger in *Being and Time*, the question of Being is the continuing origin of metaphysics and is primordial. Hence he follows this question. For Foucault, "primordial" is itself a function of modern discourse. In the discourse in which he writes, scissions and incorporations eradicate the possibility of primordiality.

72. "Determining an event on the basis of a concept, by denying any importance to repetition, is perhaps what might be called knowing; and measuring the phantasm against reality, by going in search of its origin, is judging. . . . Thinking,

on the other hand, requires the release of the phantasm in the mime that produces it at a single stroke; it makes the event indifferent so that it repeats itself as a singular universal" (L CM P, pp. 177–78).

73. "Common sense extracts the generality of an object while it simultaneously establishes the universality of the knowing subject through a pact of goodwill. But what if we gave free rein to ill will? What if thought freed itself from common sense and decided to function only in its extreme singularity? . . . What if it conceived of difference differentially, instead of searching out of common elements underlying difference? The difference would appear as a general feature that leads to the generality of the concept, and it would become—a different thought, a thought of difference—a pure event" (L CM P, p. 182).

74. "The freeing of difference requires thought without contradiction, without dialectics, without negations; thought that accepts divergence; affirmative thought whose instrument is disjunction; thought of the multiple—of the nomadic and dispersed multiplicity that is not limited or confined by the constraints of similarities; thought that does not conform to a pedagogical model (the fakery of prepared answers), but that attacks insoluble problems—that is, a thought that addresses a multiplicity of exceptional points which are displaced as we distinguish their conditions and which insist on the play of repetitions" (L CM P, p. 185).

75. For Deleuze, the univocity of being is transformed into the recurrence of difference. Being does not distribute things; difference distributes. For Foucault's less metaphysical thinking, one does not generalize differences even in Deleuze's paradoxical way of putting generalization itself in doubt. One follows differences and the processes of emergence, separation, division, collapse, and so forth. One can, for example, analyze the principles by which subjection of difference produces sub-jects and ob-jects or domination by categorical identity (for example, by office, status, class) or by knowledge combined with authority (for example, profession, expert). But one does not make difference a transdiscursive principle. It is a function empowered in *a* discourse.

76. Although Foucault would not speak, even with Nietzsche's irony, of cosmos or of a faith that all is redeemed and affirmed in the whole, the following report by Nietzsche is close in spirit to Foucault's own affirmation: "Such a spirit who has become free stands amid the cosmos with a joyous and trusting fatalism, in the faith . . . that all is redeemed and affirmed in the whole—*he does not negate any more.* Such a faith, however, is the understanding of all possible faiths: I have baptized it with the name of Dionysus" (*Twilight of the Idols*, section 49).

77. Or, as he states it in the imagery of the theatre regarding Deleuze's appropriation of various philosophers: "This is philosophy not as thought, but as theatre; a theatre of mime with multiple, fugitive, and instantaneous scenes in which blind gestures signal to each other. This is the theatre where the explosive laughter of the Sophists tears through the mask of Socrates; where Spinoza's methods conduct a wild dance in a de-centered circle while substance revolves about it like a mad planet; where a limping Fichte announces 'the fractured I $\neq$ the dissolved self'; where Leibnitz, having reached the top of the pyramid, can see through the darkness that celestial music is in fact a *Pierrot lunaire.* In the sentry box of the Luxembourg Gardens, Duns Scotus places his head through the circular window; he is sporting an impressive mustache; it belongs to Nietzsche, disguised as Klossowski" (p. 196). So much for the singularity of an Idea or a Group of Ideas forming a history. The fissure breaks in ceaselessly.

78. Foucault's line and space imagery has one function similar to that of Heideg-

ger's use of the middle voice. Both disrupt the discursive structures of continuity and familiarity by the image or the grammatical function that communicates something that, while sayable, is thoroughly counterintuitive. In both instances, what is to be said is nonmaterial. The to-be-said seems at first to be properly in the realm of spiritual discourse, but it functions to set aside the idea of spiritual discourse.

79. The following discussion is based on "A Preface To Transgression" (L CM P, pp. 29–52), which is a discussion by Foucault of Bataille.

80. Foucault says in relation to Hölderlin that the poet found that he could no longer write in order to hold death away. Writing, which at one time functioned to provide an author with a work that was deathlessly true, that was, as a work, in touch with deathless creation: such writing was found alien by Hölderlin. He found that "he could only speak in the space marked by the disappearance of the gods and that language could only depend on its own power to keep death at a distance" (p. 59). Like the thinker, this poet found that the possibility for poetic speech was radically different from the centering, lordly discourses or eternity and Truth.

81. *Madness and Civilization*, for example, is a study of the noncommunication, the silence, existing between the dominant discourse of seventeenth-century France and the discourses of the mad. At that time, one apparently could not think in or out of that difference. Normal and intelligent language could not imagine that its own identity had to be transgressed in order to communicate intelligently with the vast difference of insanity.

82. "This experience forms the exact reversal of the movement which has sustained the wisdom of the West at least since the time of Socrates, that is, the wisdom to which philosophical language promised the serene unity of a subjectivity which would triumph in it, having been fully constituted by it and through it. But if the language of philosophy is one in which the philosopher's torments are timelessly repeated and his subjectivity is discarded, then not only is wisdom meaningless as the philosopher's form of composition and reward, but in the expiration of philosophical language a possibility inevitably arises . . . : the experience of the philosopher who finds . . . at the inner core of [his language's] possibilities the transgression of his philosophical being; and thus, the nondialectical language of the limit which only arises in transgressing the one who speaks. The play of transgression and being is fundamental for the constitution of philosophical language, which reproduces and undoubtedly produces it" (pp. 43–44).

83. The following section will detail the processes of investigating and transgressing limits.

84. "Transgression forces the limit to face the fact of its imminent disappearance, to find itself in what it excludes (perhaps, to be more exact, to recognize itself for the first time, to experience its positive truth in its downward fall . . .). Perhaps it is like a flash of lightning in the night which, from the beginning of time, gives a dense and black intensity to the night it denies, which lights up the night from the inside, from top to bottom, and yet owes to dark the stark clarity of its manifestation, its harrowing and posed singularity; the flash loses itself in this space it makes with its sovereignty and becomes silent now that it has given a name to obscurity" (L CM P, pp. 34–35).

85. The affective contrast between Foucault and Heidegger in relation to images of homeland seems at first stark. Heidegger frequently thought of Being with

images of belonging and rootedness in order to show that "home" is where human being is in the tear (*Riss*) of difference between Being and human being. (See particularly "Language," in *Poetry, Language, and Thought* [New York: Harper & Row, 1971]). Foucault rejects images of home. Instead, he moves from the line image to the language of descent and heritage, as we shall see in section 3. Heidegger uses the affections associated with home and homeland, however, particularly as he makes the withdrawal of Being the focus for his thinking. Since this withdrawal has no center and disrupts everything that it "centers," the discursive function of Heidegger's home imagery is not greatly different from Foucault's line imagery, as we shall see in the next chapter.

86. See *The Birth of the Clinic*.

87. See *The Order of Things*, particularly chapter 9, "Man and His Doubles."

88. See particularly Foucault's "Afterword" in *Michel Foucault: Beyond Structuralism and Hermeneutics*, H. Dreyfus and P. Rabinow (University of Chicago Press 1982), pp. 327ff. Also "Truth and Power," in *Power/Knowledge*, (New York: Pantheon, 1980), pp. 109ff.

89. The line image pluralizes and disperses the idea of linear development when that kind of development is taken as showing the unitary development of phenomena. A line of development within the power of the line image is transgressed by no line at all, that is, by a repeating line of no development, no movement, no purpose, no being. The idea of singularity of purpose in "linear development" is removed in favor of intersecting lines with multiple directions and jagged, interrupted trajectories. Lines of development crisscross. Within them there are displacements, distributions and redistributions, multiple juxtapositions, dominations, subversion, and so forth. A genealogy follows the track of this or that power group, which by its repetitions establishes a dominant line of development along with many other parallel lines of intersecting processes. Also, for the genealogist, the dominated powers within a particular development are as important as the dominating powers. A dominant regularity, teleology, or grid of significance is naturally de-structured in this emphasis, since it is seen as merely a dominating power that is always optional. The noncontrolling powers in a region may have voice and effective play in a genealogical study that is designed to subvert the controlling powers and give the noncontrolling ones organizational influence in the study. *Madness and Civilization* is a good example of this aspect of the approach, although Foucault had not articulated his genealogical method when he wrote that book. The voices of the excluded and dominated mad were given a significant degree of discursive control through Foucault's emphasis on silence and gap in that study of the voices of sanity and enlightenment.

90. In *Archaeology of Knowledge* (New York: Harper & Row, 1972), Foucault follows the divisions, dispersions, groupings, common objects, and repeated concepts that form knowledges. Discursive formations are his subject in that book. One can distinguish between archaeology of discourses and a genealogy of descents and heritages. In that case, our interest now is in genealogy as a way of giving difference priority over identity as genealogy generates knowledge about human orders. An archaeology of knowledge complements genealogical study and need not be taken as an alternative to genealogy. See *Archaeology of Knowledge*, p. 234. See also his "The Structure of Genealogical Interpretation," a section in "On the Genealogy of Ethics," in *Michel Foucault: Beyond Structuralism and Hermeneutics*.

91. While the founding of Plato's Academy or the institutionalization of Aristotle's philosophy for theological reflection, for example, repeats and develops the power of its ideas, the discourse that develops in Nietzsche's, Heidegger's, and

Foucault's work does not lead to institutionalization. They lead to differencing processes in the form of discourses that disenfranchise established centers for thinking or as random genealogical studies. They disperse rather than centralize powers. This characteristic of the language of difference makes it odd in institutional frameworks. It also suggests an option that was barely imaginable in traditional discourses: the positive, affirmative functions of confederations without drives for overwhelming power. Perhaps ever since Roman organization conquered Etruscan lack of organization, the advantages of centralizing power have seemed obvious in the West. What could be more important than powerful control with right and true principles?

92. "Let us say that the philosophy of event should advance in the direction, at first sight paradoxical, of an incorporeal materialism. If, on the other hand, discursive events are to be dealt with as homogeneous but discontinuous series, what status are we to accord this discontinuity? Here we are not dealing with a succession of instants in time, nor with the plurality of thinking subjects; what is concerned are those caesurae breaking the instant and dispersing the subject in a multiplicity of possible positions and functions. Such a discontinuity strikes and invalidates the smallest units, traditionally recognized and the least readily contested: the instant and the subject. Beyond them, independent of them, we must conceive—between these discontinuous series of relations which are not in any order of succession (or simultaneity) with any (or several) consciousness—and we must elaborate—outside of philosophies of time and subject—a theory of discontinuous systematization. Finally, if it is true that these discursive, discontinuous series have their regularity within certain limits, it is clearly no longer possible to establish mechanically causal links or an ideal necessity among their constitutive elements. We must accept the introduction of chance as a category in the production of events. There again we feel the absence of a theory enabling us to conceive the links between chance and thought" (*Archaeology of Knowledge*, p. 231). Foucault uses *chance* here to destabilize the idea of category; or, he uses the category of chance to point toward acategorial thinking.

93. "Essences are fabrications in a piecemeal fashion from alien forms." Stated by Foucault in relation to Nietzsche, L CM P, p. 142.

94. By contrast, the interest in origins that has dominated our various interpretations and senses of history has sought intuitively "the exact essence of things," the "primordial truth fully adequate to its nature," and the removal of masks, covering, and descent in order to show a virginal origin (pp. 142–43). Foucault finds probable Nietzsche's observation that our Western search for truth, rather than founded on a pure origin or a transcending presence of Truth, has been formed in the dissensions of scholars, "their reciprocal hatreds, fanatical and unending discussions, and their spirit of competition—the personal conflicts that forged the weapons of reason" (p. 142). The quest for the lost origin or origins— "an adolescent quest"—involves a language that knows that what is essential is both lost and present. Foucault has eliminated this pairing of loss-presence as well as that of absent-present by shifting from origin to descent.

95. ". . . to follow the complex course of descent is to maintain passing events in their proper dispersion; it is to identify the accidents, the minute deviations—or conversely, the complete reversals—of errors, the false appraisals, and the faulty calculations that gave birth to those things that continue to exist and have value for us; it is to discover that truth or being do not lie at the root of what we know and what we are, but the exteriority of accidents" (p. 146).

96. "History becomes 'effective' to the degree that it introduces discontinuity into

our very being—as it divides our emotions, dramatizes our instincts, multiplies our body and sets it against itself. 'Effective' history deprives the self of the reassuring stability of life and nature, and it will not permit itself to be transported by a voiceless obstinacy toward a millennial ending. It will uproot its traditional foundations and relentlessly disrupt its pretended continuity. This is because knowledge is not made for understanding; it is made for cutting" (p. 154). This discourse, in its cutting effect, is transgressive. It offers no solid function of understanding, but is in its function destabilizing. Its effectiveness is in yielding differences where there has been sameness, unity, and continuity. Its effect clears the way for analyses of power relations in a way of thinking that is free of their power.

97. "In a sense, genealogy returns to the three modalities of history that Nietzsche recognized in 1874. It returns to them in spite of the objections that Nietzsche raised in the name of the affirmative and creative powers of life. But they metamorphosized; the veneration of monuments becomes parody; the respect for ancient continuities becomes systematic dissociation; the critique of the injustices of the past by a truth held by men in the present becomes the destruction of the will of the man who maintains knowledge by the injustice proper to the will to knowledge" (p. 164).

98. Counter-memory forms in texts and practices, not in a subject or subjectivity. We shall discuss this point in detail in the following section. If one thinks of counter-memory in terms of subjectivity, that is, in a modern post-Kantian discourse that intuitively gives primacy to the subject, the discourse of counter-memory is lost. Derrida and Foucault agree in their rejection of a fundamental ground that provides a coherence of desire or structure "underneath" the free plays of historical events. "The concept of centered structure is in fact the concept of a free play based on a fundamental ground, a free play which is constituted upon a fundamental immobility which is itself beyond the reach of free play." For both Derrida and Foucault, the lack of an immobile center means that possibilities are found in whatever discourse and practices—that is, in whatever networks—there are. Derrida notes, for example, "the appearance of a new structure, of an original system, always comes about—and this is the very condition of its structured specificity—by a rupture with its past, its origins, and its cause. One can therefore describe what is peculiar to the structural organization only by not taking into account, in the very moment of this description, its past conditions: by failing to pose the problem of the passage from one structure to another, by putting history into parenthesis." His use of *always* indicates the power of *differences* in developing this idea. "Structure, Signs, and Play in the Discourses of the Human Sciences," in *The Structuralist Controversy*, eds. R. Mackey and E. Donato (Baltimore: Johns Hopkins Press, 1972), pp. 248, 263.

99. The following account is based on "Man and His Doubles" in *The Order of Things*.

100. See chapter 2 of *The Origin of Things*, particularly pp. 18–24, for Foucault's account of four "principal figures that determine the knowledge of resemblance": *convenientia, aemulatio*, analogy, and the play of sympathies. Part I of this book follows the descent in which man developed. For our purposes, we assume that account. In it, Foucault shows how man emerges from the dissolution of the dominant discourses of the classical period in Western Europe, although the dominance of the idea of identity continues now in an unconscious bifurcation of knower/known. The function of this idea occurs in man as divided, as question

rather than as a serene transcendence. Man is the modern identity, one that is ruptured and hence self-representational in its structure, a clefted Same that pervades all known things and is the condition for disciplined, well-ordered knowledge. Through its rupture, its doubling as both the foundation of knowledge and the object of knowledge, this identity loses its unifying discursive power. Man is a broken center from which Foucault's own discourse develops. Whereas in the classical period "resemblance was the invisible form of that which, from the depths of the world, made things visible" (p. 26), now man's internal difference as the knower/known makes things visible. Classical representation articulates resemblance-based-on-Same. In man, representation articulates a subject/object that cannot overcome its difference.

101. But: "Resemblance never remains stable within itself; it can be fixed only if it refers back to another similitude, which then, in turn, refers to others; each resemblance, therefore, has value only from the accumulation of others, and the whole world must be explored if even the slightest of analogies is to be justified and finally taken on the appearance of certainty. It is therefore a knowledge that can, and must, proceed by the infinite accumulation of confirmations all dependent on one another" (p. 30). By the eighteenth century, self-referential reason had become the common ground underlying this rich profusion of similarities. This common ground, and not an external deity, could still be thought and known in its self-expressed unity. The self-enclosure of reason, however, meant that what was not reason—for example, the nonrational, God, or nature—was external. The beginning of a pluralizing and splintering process was taking place.

102. During the course of this essay, Foucault also shows how space functioned in classical and modern thought in the establishment of order. As a genealogy that traces the functions of space from classical discourse to his own discourse, Foucault's account resembles Nietzsche's genealogy of morality, which shows how his own views are developed in the decline and self-destruction of morality. In both cases, the author's concept emerges from the disruptions of its genealogical predecessors. Disruptions rather than continuities form the subjects of each account.

103. As an archaeologist of knowledge, that is, as one who studies what holds together the various epistemes, Foucault details the rules that establish the various orders and arrangements of knowledges. Our interest is in man's descent, and hence our emphasis falls on the development of the ruptures and fissures rather than on what held the epistemes together.

104. "It was the dissolution of this homogeneous field of orderable representations, in the last years of the eighteenth century, that brought about the correlative appearance of two new forms of thought. The first questions the conditions of a relation between representations from the point of view of what in general makes them possible: it thus uncovers a transcendental field in which the subject, which is never given to experience (since it is not empirical), but which is finite (since there is no intellectual intuition), determines in its relation to an object = X all the formal conditions of experience in general; it is the analysis of the transcendental subject that isolates the foundation of a possible synthesis between representations. Opposite this opening to the transcendental, and symmetrical to it, another form of thought questions the conditions of a relation between representations from the point of view of the being itself that is represented: what is indicated, on the horizon of all actual representations, as the foundation of their unity, is found to be those never objectifiable objects, those never entirely representable representations,

those simultaneously evident and invisible visibilities, those realities that are removed from reality to the degree to which they are the foundation of what is given to us and reaches us: the force of labor, the energy of life, the power of speech" (pp. 243–44).

105. In *The Order of Things* Foucault shows that some kinds of madmen and some poets gave expression to the gaps and differences that functioned unconsciously in premodern discourses (see pp. 48ff). In the language of each, difference qualifies (poet) or erases (madman) resemblance. Both spoke on the periphery of the overwhelming discourses, and in their differences from them helped to define the discursive centers. The language of both forecasts directions of discursive development that could not be seen in the dominant modes of discernment. The madman attempted to erase differences by wild, disordered groupings as though everything resembled everything; he thus erased resemblance by denying difference. The poet spoke out of the differences and held them in his language; he thus qualified the language of resemblance by the language of difference.

106. Man, for example, finds itself to be a living being that comes from a nonman biological process, an instrument of production that comes from economic processes that are not man's own. Man is a vehicle for words that say themselves and are not under the subject's control. Man is displaced by its own development and is shown by its own sciences to be differentiated over against itself as a thing that is outside its own knowing subjectivity.

107. The fragmentation, for example, among mathematics, physical sciences, the social sciences, and philosophical reflection. Math and the physical sciences develop orders of knowledge based on deduction and established connections among verified propositions. The social sciences look for causes and constants among discontinuous behaviors. And philosophical reflection looks for a Same that underlies and pervades all knowledges.

108. See particularly "Two Lectures," in *Power/Knowledge*.

109. *Margins of Philosophy* (Chicago: University of Chicago Press, 1982), p. 135.

110. We will also find that the metaphors of seeing and light that controlled metaphysical ways of thinking have changed. Particularly in the Platonic tradition, the shining of something essential through individual things defines the things' presence. Hence the close association of light, vision, wisdom, truth, timelessness, and agency. This confederation of metaphors has engendered in this discourse an elemental belief that without something shining, as it were, pervasively through all present things, there would be no presence at all. Since knowing is also closely associated with *seeing* things as they are, the light of knowing and the light of reality are deeply linked, and that linkage gives an essential affiliation of the light of knowing/believing and the light of Being. This elemental affiliation is not present in Heidegger's later thinking. His way of thinking about metaphysics lacks this metaphysical element, and although he often raises questions about metaphysics, his way of posing those questions and thinking with them is not, as we shall see, metaphysical or antimetaphysical. Questioning and hearing rather than seeing assume an elemental discursive role.

111. This section is based primarily on "The End of Philosophy and the Task of Thinking," tr. Joan Stambaugh, *Basic Writings* (New York: Harper & Row, 1977), published also in *On Time and Being* (New York: Harper & Row, 1972). Page numbers noted in this section will refer to the essay in *Basic Writings*. In this essay, Heidegger follows metaphysical thinking in the dominance of Plato. *Being and Time* is also a work in which the end of metaphysics takes place, not only because

Platonism is unseated, but also because Dasein is unseated at the central focus of thought. In the process of this unseating the forcefulness of de-struction also changes. The dominance of human being for thinking, the importance of existential identity, and the way the question of Being in relation to time is shaped are all transformed through the impact of the discursive processes that develop in *Being and Time* and are consequent to it, an impact that can be measured in part by the growing role of "release" in the language. Heidegger locates the completion of metaphysics in Hegel's thought and the exhaustion of metaphysics in Nietzsche's reversal of metaphysical thinking. The conflict—the strife—that develops when the priority of human being for thought is put into question in *Being and Time* comprises the most recent discursive development that creates, as a way of ending metaphysical thought, the questions and possibilities for Heidegger's later thinking. The function of forceful thinking in *Being and Time* changes in this process.

112. Once de-structuring has had its effect in Heidegger's discourse, more tentative and exploratory thinking begins to develop in his work. Although he remained preoccupied after *Being and Time* with the history of philosophy and explored in a de-structuring way the thought, both in its explicit and its suppressing dimensions, of most of the major Western philosophers, the turn of Heidegger's own thinking is the subject of our interest. Hence we emphasize the end of metaphysics in relation to *Being and Time* as far as Heidegger himself is concerned, and the development of a distinct and different way of thinking after *Being and Time*. He uses the forgetfulness of Being in the Western tradition as his major phenomenon to show how forgetfulness developed and how its essential issue—its *Sache*—was forgotten. We are interested specifically in how difference functions in his own exploratory thinking, and assume his work on the history of metaphysics. Consequently we will occasionally report his observations and claims about that history without repeating his studies in detail.

113. In "On Time and Being" he states: "To think Being without beings means: to think Being without regard to metaphysics. Yet a regard for metaphysics still prevails even in the intention to overcome metaphysics. Therefore our task is to cease all overcoming, and leave metaphysics to itself" (p. 24). When overcoming ceases, one may approach metaphysical thinking nonmetaphysically. In that case, metaphysics is left to itself even when one considers metaphysical thinkers.

114. Unless otherwise noted, all page references in this section are to *On Time and Being*. We shall retain the word *Ereignis* in order to underscore the difference Heidegger names by it. Its meaning will develop in the course of the discussion.

115. "Only the gradual removal of those obscuring covers—that is what is meant by 'dismantling'—procures for thinking a preliminary insight into what then reveals itself as the destiny of Being" (p. 9). These thoughts come out of the de-structuring process of *Being and Time* and the work that was possible because of that process.

116. Hans-Georg Gadamer, *Truth and Method* (New York: Seabury Press, 1975).

117. Derrida's discussion and use of *différance* and undecidability are creative elaborations of Heidegger's discussion of revealing/concealing, as we shall note again in the next chapter. Derrida has developed a context and way of speaking that differentiate themselves from this aspect of Heidegger's thought, while also deriving from Heidegger's thinking.

118. AS *had*, ME *had*, OHG *heit*, GOTH *haidus*, ON *heithr* and G *heiter*, as well as skr *Ketu*, which means *brightness*. Webster's *New International Dictionary*, Second Edition, Unabridged.

119. In the seminar discussions that followed the lecture "On Time and Being," two verses by Trakl are quoted. First, from "Psalm":

> It is a light which the wind has extinguished.
> It is a jug which a drunkard leaves in the afternoon.
> It is a vineyard, burned and black with holes full of spiders.
> It is a room which they have whitewashed.

The second is from "De Profundis":

> It is a stubble field on which a black rain falls.
> It is a brown tree which stands alone.
> It is a hissing wind which circles around empty huts.
> How said this evening.
> . . .
> It is a light which is extinguished in my mouth.

The repeated "it is" is like the "there is" and "does not name the availability of something which is, but rather precisely something unavailable" which we have termed the "else" or the "else-than." The word and phrase connotes nothing "mystical," but an other-than-speakable that is now concealed and manifest, that is also available for address, but only obscurely so. The depression contained in Trakl's verses in association with their remarkable language also suggests exhaustion in association with a dark, fragile, and obscure beginning. The verses themselves are like clearings in which the "*es gibt*" comes tentatively to speech. In the next section we shall see that the exhaustion of the "It is" in Trakl's poems is transferred into a language of dwelling and bestowing by Heidegger. That is a transmutation of the bereftness in the epochal shift to a gift of dwelling of new thought (p. 39).

120. "The entry of thinking into *Ereignis* is thus equivalent to the end of this withdrawal's history. The oblivion of Being 'supersedes' itself in the awakening into *Ereignis*" (p. 41).

121. "Yet a regard for metaphysics still prevails even in the intention to overcome metaphysics. Therefore, our task is to cease all overcoming, and leave metaphysics to itself" (p. 24).

122. *Poetry, Language and Thought* (New York: Harper & Row, 1975, p. 184), emphases added.

123. Ibid., p. 185.

124. In *On The Way to Language* (New York: Harper & Row, 1982 p. 159), for example, Heidegger develops this relation of *ort*, translated as *site*, and *Erörterung*, translated as *discussion*. We shall use *eventuate* in the context of *Erörtern* and *Ereignis* to indicate Heidegger's thought that speaking and thinking let things come to be, that they let things belong together. Language and thinking eventuate.

125. In the case of the poet: "But when the issue is to put into language, something which has never yet been spoken, then everything depends on whether

language *gives or withholds* the appropriate word. Such is the case of the poet. Indeed, a poet might even come to the point where he is compelled—in his own way, that is poetically—to put into language the experience he *undergoes* with language" (Ibid., p. 59, emphasis added).

126. The following discussion refers to "Language" in *Poetry, Language and Thought*. Page notations in this section refer to this essay unless otherwise noted.

127. "What is spoken purely is that in which the completion of the speaking that is proper to what is spoken is, in its turn, an original" (p. 194). The "purity" of the speaking involves the exhaustion of one kind of religious purity and the beginning of the purity of language's speaking, of language's letting speech come to speech, of language's gathering *Ereignis*. Such a poem makes possible by its poetic event a use of language that eventuates thinking in the element of *Ereignis*, a thinking that Heidegger's discussion of the poem attempts to be.

128. Quoted, pp. 194–195. We shall discuss the poem in the context of Heidegger's language and thought regarding it.

129. "The dif-ference carries out world in its worlding, carries out things in their thinging. Thus carrying them out, it carries them toward one another. The dif-ference does not mediate after the fact by connecting world and things through a middle added onto them. Being the middle it first determines world and things in their presence, i.e., in their being toward one another, whose unity it carries out" (p. 202). "The dif-ference is *the* dimension insofar as it measures out, apportions, world and thing, each to its own. Its allotment of them first opens up the separateness and towardness of world and thing. Such an opening up is the way in which the dif-ference here spans the two . . . in the bidding that calls thing and world, what is really called is: the dif-ference" (p. 203).

130. *On Time and Being*, p. 167.

131. "But above all, the thinking and question remains slight because its task is only of a preparatory, not of a founding character. It is content with awakening a readiness in man for a possibility whose contour remains obscure, whose coming remains uncertain. Thinking must first learn what remains reserved and in store for thinking to get involved in. It prepares its own transformation in this learning" (Ibid., p. 60).

132. Ibid., p. 68.

133. Ibid., p. 67.

134. *Discourse on Thinking* (New York: Harper & Row, 1969). Unless otherwise noted, page references in this section will be to this text.

135. Nietzsche's way of showing, for example, that revenge is ill will regarding time, and that by speaking of time in the images of a circle or of return and in a genealogical way of knowing one might experience release from resentment: that way of thinking has had a powerful effect in the language of difference. He hoped that by coming to know resentment genealogically we might be able to avoid repeating resentment in our ways of knowing and thinking, and that hope is echoed in both Heidegger's de-struction in *Being and Time* and in Foucault's own genealogical work. Resentment, this kind of suffering, has generated desires for punishment and suppression. The differences of strength without resentment transgress the carefully constructed identities and interests of resenting spirituality. Those differences mean within the traditionally dominant discourse obscure strength, enjoyment, hidden and threatening power, perhaps even evil spiritual power; they are closely associated with punishment and suppression in the discourses of resentment. The language of difference has repeatedly generated

desires to overthrow resentment, this kind of suffering and its attendant affections, by thinking of temporality in terms of human kinship and friendly nearness. Mortality and change are not the enemies of human being. The intention to rethink time has as part of its investment the Nietzschean hope to replace something like resentment with affirmation and to transmute the intention to suppress and punish those aspects of human being that disclose finite temporality in such concrete instances as violations of certainty and deathliness among transcendently conceived beings. The different, replacing desire in the language of difference, is to cultivate discourse—speech and hearing, writing and reading communication—in the occurrences of difference. Transgressing differences, instead of calling up associations of threat, wrongness, suppression, and punishment, instance obscure opportunities for discourse and communication.

136. *Four Fundamental Concepts.*

137. "Rupture, split, the stroke of the opening makes absence emerge—just as the cry does not stand out against a background of silence, but on the contrary makes the silence emerge as silence" (p. 26). This language of opening and absence is close to Heidegger's language in the "Conversation on a Country Path" in spite of obvious differences. In both instances the emphasis falls on the emergence of a dimension without identity about which we are ill-suited to speak, and on the changed quality of communication when one stays attuned to this obscure dimension.

138. Lacan and Derrida, in their different ways, write what they do not write about. Lacan tightens his schemes, his definitions and "laws," around a slash (S/s) that gaps and tears every relation. The tighter his conceptual relations, the sharper the cut as he ironizes, jokes, plays, and obscures his way through very serious matters. These ploys play off the slash, this idea that refuses itself as it functions in Lacan's discourse. It is a play of refusal and indefinite differencing. In the immediate incompleteness and severance that happens in his speaking, nothing quite sayable makes its difference and refuses even Lacan's own desire for completeness and explanatory sufficiency. In straight talk, the unconscious happens in its vast other-than-what-can-be-said. Lacan is a clinician as he does honor in all of his speaking to the unconscious in whose service his speaking occurs.

Derrida also found his "different writing" that disallows centering and totalities as centers. Totalities play off each other and off the grammar and meanings that have traditionally made sense by giving manageable presence to things. When one reads *in* his discourse an unspeakable happens that disjoins whatever he says. Difference-from-presence interplays, and nonsense refuses our desires for meaning. These things will not mean. We are to wonder how to speak, how to let-speak, how to read without presence or absence.

139. The following discussion refers to Derrida's "Différance" in *Margins of Philosophy* pp. 1–28. Unless otherwise noted, page references will be to this essay.

140. Derrida uses *différance* to inscribe this deferring-differing movement in his writing, a movement that is not an idea and that cannot exercise a force of control. By contrast, we have said that the idea of difference has a traceable organizing influence in the discourse of which Derrida is a part. The function of the idea of difference develops into the function of différance in his writing, and différance offsets the idea of idea. This move on Derrida's part makes différance, the movement of deferring and differing, a word for an unworded, ongoing, else-than that has no opposite. Différance is like a negative descriptive word in the sense that it describes as it defers and differs. Like the phrases "line of transgression" or "the

coming of time," and "description" (when the word is taken in the sense of "a line describing a circle") is self-erasing: by its description it will not tolerate any inclusive image or definition. This lack of toleration, similar to self-erasure, is part of its description. But Derrida's language and thought are also part of a developing history and are in a continuing discourse. It is one culmination of the idea of difference, one that makes sense in this discourse, as the idea of difference defers itself and puts itself in question. It is an original move on Derrida's part. And of course it is replaceable. The replaceability of différance, its nonnecessity and its discursive development, are kept in view when Derrida is read within a given history. The function of placing différance in *a* history radicalizes its own play in Derrida's writing by marking it as a discursive term that has no place or time, no life, outside of a functioning and replaceable development that we are calling the language of difference. So the inclination to think that différance (or, in Heidegger's writing, Being and *Ereignis*) is like a nonsubstance that is outside of time is mitigated by following discursive strands that weave their way as plays of words, and that promise complete silence when the strand unravels.

141. An astonishment over no being at all that is found in the language of difference is written into Derrida's emphasis on fissure, undecidability, deferral, and differing. This astonishment has helped to make apparent an unrecognized array of violences in our traditional language. Derrida's effort to write without polar opposites is one way to make this astonishment functional. The idea of categories, for example, fades out as a basis for organization and order. Instead, orders of interplay come to the fore in which there is compassion for differences without the ordinary categorial hierarchies. His discourse makes spaces and times for differences and for enjoyment of differences without polarization. At best there are always possibilities to effect different interplays when dangers or suffering develop, as when people of good will give the conversation a new turn if it begins to sour. One functioning purpose of the astonishment over no being at all is to avoid that kind of opposition that generates fights for domination, that effects dominations and unconscious processes of violence and suppression. One of Derrida's strategies is to show how writing is "structured" by difference, distance, and deferral. Astonishment over no being at all is written into that strategy by eliminating violence toward the missing, the hidden, and the undecidable.

Index

Abbott, Scott, n41
agency, 24–26, 36, 68, 69, 78, 125, n110
Anaximander, 127
antimetaphysical discourse, 5, 6, 10, 12, 19, 49, 50, 90, 119, n4, n110
  see also metaphysical discourse
apophainesthai, 68–70
  see also phainesthai
apophansis, 68–69
archaeology, 111, 123, n90, n103
aristocracy, 25, 44, n10
Aristotle, 65, 107. n49, n91
artist-philosopher, 20, 28, 32–33
asceticism, 23, 24, 27, 33, 39, 41–42, 47, 145
atheism, 37–42
authenticity, 72, 78–82, 90, 126, 150, n9, n47, n49, n52, n53

Bataille, Georges, 103, n79
Being, chap. 3, 91, 92, 100, chap. 5, n25, n29, n30, n32, n33, n34, n36, n38, n39, n41, n42, n44, n46, n48, n55, n140
  see also question of the meaning of Being
being, n2
  in Deleuze, 95, n75
  in Foucault, 98, 99, 100, 101, 117, 118, n59, n62, n64, n82, n94
  in Heidegger, chap. 3, 91, 95, 123, n39, n44, n47, n53
  in Nietzsche, 11–13, 15–16, 44–45, n4, n9
  of Dasein, 83, 88, 90, 127, n47
being-in-the-world, 61, 62, 71, 75, 77, 81, 85, n38
biology, 115, n106
Blanchot, Maurice, 104
body, 13, 93–94, 96, 99, 103, 106, 118, 122, 151, n61, n64, n65, n96

capitalism, n61
care, 64, 71–73, 78, 81, 83–84, 147, n53

category, 45, 47, 92, 99–100, 104–105, 107, 111, 115, 118, n35, n59, n75, n92, n141
cause, 17, 29, 37, 39, 69, 110, 111, 154, n92, n98, n107
certainty, 4, 7, 14–15, 17, 18, 21, 55, 69, 71, 75–76, 78, 84, 91, 114, 117, 125–126, 151, 152, n46, n101, n135
chance, 108, n92
Christianity, 10, 27, 36, 38–42, 43, 49, 104, 137, 143, 145, n10
classical discourse, 112–114, n100, n102
  see also modern discourse
Confucianism, 40
consciousness, 12, 82, 91, 109, 116, 149, 154, n69, n92
contestation, 104, 122–123, 147
contingency, 13, 16, 19, 34, 35, 36, 51, 56, 96, 104, 115, 117, 123, 149, 150, 151
  see also necessity
continuity, n2
  in Foucault, 89, 100, 104–105, 108–110, 111, 112–113, 117, n68, n78, n96, n97
  in Heidegger, 61, 75–76, 80, 85, 86–87, 134, 139
  in Nietzsche, 13, 22, 45, 53
conversation, 145–147, n141
counter-memory, 110, 111, 113, 118, 119, 121, 122, 123, 150, 155, n98
  see also memory

Dasein, chap. 3, 90, 124–127, 129, 132, 133, n24, n26, n27, n29, n33, n34, n35, n36, n38, n42, n44, n45, n48, n49, n52, n54, n58, n111
death, 7, n135
  in Foucault, 96, 113, 114, 116–117, n80
  in Heidegger, 73–74, 75, 77–78, 80–85, 124, 126, 127, 136, 137, 139,

182

142, 144, n52, n53
  in Nietzsche, 15, 21, 30, 38, 40, 41, 42–44
  see also God, death of
deconstruction, 121
Deleuze, Gilles, 93–97, 99–101, n59, n60, n61, n62, n64, n65, n67, n69, n75, n77
  Différence et Répétition, n60
  Logique du Sens, n60
Deleuze, Gilles, and F. Guattari, *Anti-Oedipus*, n61
Derrida, Jacques, vii, 1, 6, 91, 95, 121, 153–155, n2, n39, n98, n117, n138, n139, n140, n141
  "Différance," n139
  "The Ends of Man," 121, n39
  "Ousia and Grammé," n39
  Writing and Difference, n39
Descartes, René, 107, 127, n38
descent, 13, 16–17, 25–26, 30, 36, 37, 91, 105, 108, 111, n85, n90, n94, n95, n103, n110
  see also genealogy
desire, 7, 9, 12–13, 16, 21, 28–29, 38, 48, 90, 94, 116–117, 126, 147, 150–152, n2, n15, n55, n135, n138
de-struction, 3–6, chap. 3, 89–90, 92, 97, 106–107, 108, 119, 121, 123–124, 126–127, 128, 133, 134, 136–138, 144, 147–148, 149, 155, n27, n28, n30, n31, n32, n33, n35, n36, n38, n39, n44, n49, n53, n89, n111, n112, n115, n135
différance, in Derrida, 149, 153–155, n117, n140
dif-ference, in Heidegger, 140–143, 145, 148, n129
  see also unconcealment
Dionysus, 3, 38, 44, 48, 153, n76
disclosure, 68, 70, 71, 74, 75, 76, 77–79, 81–83, 87–88, 124–126, 128, 129, 131, 133, 136, 150, n25, n36, n39
  see also unconcealment
Duns Scotus, n59, n77
dwelling, 119, 124, 142–143, 148, 150, n119

economics, 116, n106

episteme, 115–117, 122, 123, n103
  see also knowledge *and* man
epistemology, 4, 28, 54, 78
Ereignis, 129, 135–136, n114, n120, n124, n127, n140
es gibt, 130–135, 138, 141, 144, n119
essence, 15–16, 19, 37, 44, 47, 63, 91, 125, n4, n13, n93, n94, n110
  see also substance
eternal recurrence, eternal return, 13, 30, 34–36, 41–42, 48, 50–51, 101, 106, 109, 147, 150, n32, n70, n135
  see also recurrence *and* repetition
eternity, 16, 42, 51, 74, 85, 117, n4, n33, n80
ethics, 4, 37
ethos, 155
event, 29, 30, 39, 59, 78, 85, 91, 95, 96–98, 100, 105, 107, 108, 110, 111, 119, 129, 134, n41, n52, n68, n69, n70, n72, n73, n92, n95, n98, n127
exhaustion, 3, 7, 85, 91, 126, 135, 136, 138–139, 141–143, n111, n119, n127

fate, 97, 100, 106, n53
Fichte, Johann Gottlieb, n77
finitude, 4, 57, 61, 64, 74, 78–87, 116, 117, n52, n53, n58, n135
force, 12–13, 29, 44, 46–47, 127–128, 129, 146–147, 149, 153, 155, n1, n5, n111, n140
forgetfulness,
  in Heidegger, 57, 59, 62, 64, 65, 72, 73, 74, 78, 87, 91, 124, 125, 128, 129, 133, 144, n24, n28, n39, n112
  in Nietzsche, 15, 23, 45
Foucault, Michel, 1, 5, 6, chap. 4, 121, 122–123, 134, 145, 148, 149, 150, n2, n43, n58, n60, n62, n64, n65, n71, n75, n76, n78, n79, n80, n85, n88, n89, n90, n91, n93, n98, n100, n102, n103, n105, n135
  Archaeology of Knowledge, n90
  Birth of the Clinic, n61, n63, n86
  Language, Countermemory, Practice, n57

Madness and Civilization, n81, n89
The Order of Things, 113, n58, n61, n87, n99, n100, n105
Power/Knowledge, n88
"The Structure of Genealogical Interpretation," n90
foundation, 16, 30, 48, 51, 61–62, 65–69, 71, 72, 73, 75, 79–82, 84, 104, 112, 118, 121, 130, 135, 143, n13, n38, n39, n41, n96, n100, n104, n131
free will, in Nietzsche, 16–17
freedom, 155
  in Heidegger, n52, n53
  in Nietzsche, 20–22, 32–33, 38, 42, 44, 48, 91, n10, n32, n76
Freud, Sigmund, 150–153

Gadamer, Hans-Georg, 132, n116
gathering, 88, 119, 122, 129, 132, 134, 136, 138, 140–143, 147–148, 150, 152, n127
genealogy, 57
  in Foucault, 91, 105–107, 108–110, 113, 117, 118, 119, 122–123, n89, n90, n91, n97, n102
  in Nietzsche, 9, 13, 16, 19, 36, 37, 43, 44, 46, 48, 52, n10, n135
God, 11, 14, 18, 20, 21, 24, 27, 37–44, 96–97, 112, 113, 114, 122, 137, 139, 141, 142, 145, 151, n69, n101
  death of, 38–42, 97, 107
Greek culture, 145
  in Nietzsche, 36, 38, 40, 44, 56
  see also Heraclitus *and* Parmenides

hearing, 3, 74, 75, 86, 130, 132, 137, 147, n2, n39, n44, n49, n110, n135
Hegel, 56, 57, 114, 127, n49, n111
Heidegger, Martin, 1, 3, 6, chap. 3, 89, 91, 95–97, 102, 107, 111, chap. 5, 149, 150, n25, n27, n32, n36, n39, n49, n50, n53, n55, n58, n71, n78, n85, n91, n110, n111, n112, n114, n117, n124, n127, n128, n135, n137, n140
  Being and Time, 1, 4–6, chap. 3, 89–90, 92, 100, 107, 119, 123–133, 138, n2, n18, n20, n23, n27, n28, n32, n38, n41, n44, n48, n55, n58, n71, n111, n112, n115, n135
  Kant and the Problem of Metaphysics, n38
  The Letter of Humanism, 132
  Nietzsche, n32
  On the Essence of Truth, 132
  On the Way to Language, n124
  On Time and Being, n111, n114
  Poetry, Language, and Thought, n85, n122, n126
  Time and Being, 6
  "Building, Dwelling, Thinking," 6
  "The Conversation on a Country Path," 145, n137
  "The End of Philosophy and the Task of Thinking," n111
  "On Time and Being," n113, n119
  "The Word of Nietzsche: 'God Is Dead'," n32
Heraclitus, 24, 52, 127
hermenuein, n42
historicity, 154
  in Heidegger, 76, 78–84, 86, 91, n29, n36, n52, n53, n54
  in Nietzsche, 13, 16, 19
history, 2, 3, 13, 26, 35, 36–37, 42, 43, n5, n9, n10
  in Foucault, 100, 110, 112, 115, 122, 123, n77, n94, n96, n97, n98
  in Heidegger, chap. 3, 124–125, 131, 133, 135, 136, 138, n27, n28, n36, n39, n41, n43, n51, n120
  in Nietzsche, 21, 25–26, 32, 36–37, 39
  of Dasein, 58, 60, 64, 67, 72, 75, 77–78, 80, 85, 88, 124, n24, n36, n44, n55
  of discourses, vii, 4, 6, 21, 26, 34–36, 44, 45, 48, 49, 51, 89, n140
Hölderlin, n80
home, 32, 110, n85
human nature,
  in Nietzsche, 19, 20
humanistic disciplines, 106, 115, n43

immortality of the soul, 14, 15, 17, 18
incorporeal materiality, 93–95, 122–123, n64, n92
insanity, 111, 117, n81, n101, n105

INDEX

instinct, 12–14, 29–30, 45, n5, n96
interpretation, 99
  in Heidegger, 54, 61, 62, 64, 66, 70, 72–73, 76, 78, 79, 80, 82, 87, 129, 142–143, n32, n33, n36, n38, n39, n42, n47, n94
  in Nietzsche, 17–18, 19, 25–26, 29, 30–31, 36
introductions, 1–4, 75
irony,
  in Foucault, 93, 95, n64
  in Heidegger, 79, n49
  in Lacan, n138
  in Nietzsche, 3, 9, 19, 20, 22, 24, 29, 30, 91, 153, n76

Judaism, 10, 27, 38–43, 137

Kant, Immanuel, 65–66, 127, n38, n98
Kierkegaard, Soren, 56
knowledge, 11, 21, 23, 31, 32, 36, 61, 94, 110, 112, 113, 114–115, 118, 119, 122, 123, n49, n90, n96, n100, n101, n103, n107
Kristeva, Julia, 7

Lacan, Jacques, 1, 150–152, n65, n138
law, 145, 150, 155
  in Foucault, 104, 105, 108, 112, 113, 116, 117
  in Nietzsche, 12–13, 18–19, 21, 23, 101
Leibniz, Gottfried Wilhelm von, n77
limit, 7, 59, 61, 76–77, 94, 95, 102, 104, 106, 118, 127, 135, 144, 148, n55, n83, n84, n92
line, image of, 101–102, 104–107, 109, 111, 122, 127, 134, 135, n39, n78, n85, n89, n140
logos, 68, 88, 136, n42
Löwith, Karl, n55
Luther, Martin, 39

Macquarrie, John, n23, n24
man, 32–33, 36, 39, 106, 111–119, 123, 144, n100, n103, n106
  see also Übermensch
Marx, Karl, 56
meaning, 2, 4, 7–8, 89, 90, 96, 98, 150, n68, n69
  in Foucault, 104, 107, 109, 113
  in Heidegger, 55–57, 60–63, 66, 70, 71, 75, 78, 80, 84–87, n33, n36, n43, n48, n52
  in Nietzsche, 41, 51
  see also question of the meaning of Being
medicine, 56, 94, 106, 108, n61
mediocrity, 42, 43, n11
memory, 45, 55–56, 87, 91, 110, 122
  see also counter-memory
metaphysical discourse, 3–7, 33, 54, 90, 92, 100, 147, 150, 151, n2
  in Deleuze, 95–96, n64, n75
  in Derrida, 95, n39
  in Foucault, 92, 95–96, 97, 101, 104, 109, 110, 112–113, 118, 119, 122–123, n64, n69, n71
  in Heidegger, 54–58, 59, 60–62, 64, 66–67, 70–72, 74, 75, 76, 78–80, 100, 107, 124–126, 128–129, 135–138, 144, n20, n25, n28, n30, n32, n35, n39, n41, n43, n44, n71, n110, n111, n112, n113, n120
  in Nietzsche, 5, 10–20, 27, 29, 34–36, 43, 45, 48–51, 89, 107, n9
  see also antimetaphysical discourse and nonmetaphysical discourse
middle voice, vii, 67–68, 70–72, 75, 78, 81–86, 125, 126, 136, 141, 144, 154, n40, n78
mime, 94–95, 96, 97, 98, 100, n62, n72, n77
model, 20, 33, 36, 93–94, 96, 98, n74
modern discourse, 114, 115, n102, n104
  see also classical discourse; biology; and economics
morality, 11, 12, 17, 19–22, 24, 25–26, 28, 34, 36, 37, 38–39, 42–45, 106, 109, n14, n15
mortality, 15, 56, 58, 64, 70, 72, 73–74, 75, 78–80, 81, 83, 85–87, 126, 130, 132, n2, n49, n52, n53, n135
multiplicity, 15, 29, 45–46, 51, 56, 82, 87, 91, 94, 98, 100, 101, 103, 106, n74, n77, n92
mystery, 74, 86, 91, 97, 124, 140, 142

mysticism, 41, 76, 86, 104, 145, n119

natural selection, 16
nature,
  in Foucault, 112, n96, n101
  in Nietzsche, 14, 16, 18–19
necessity, 4, n140
  in Foucault, 100–101, 108, 111, 116–117, n92
  in Heidegger, 64, 82
  in Nietzsche, 16–17, 19, 22, 27, n13
  see also contingency
negation, 51, 102, 104–105, 127
network, 9, 24, 63–64, 96, 107, 116, 117, 119, 122, 154, n98
Nietzsche, Friedrich, 1, 3, 4–6, chap. 2, 53–54, 56, 57, 75, 89–92, 97, 99, 101, 106, 107, 109, 111, 121, 123, 127, 131, 137, 144, 147, 149–150, 153, n4, n8, n10, n25, n30, n32, n68, n70, n76, n77, n91, n93, n94, n97, n102, n111, n135
  Beyond Good and Evil, 4–6, chap. 2, 56, 89–90, 107, 119, 138, n4, n32
  The Gay Science, 1, 3, 153
  Genealogy of Morals, 48, 50, n8, n16, n102
  Joyful Wisdom, 38
  Thus Spoke Zarathustra, 34, 48, 49, 51, n32
  The Will to Power, 46–47, 51, n17
nihilism, 48, n32
nonmetaphysical discourse, 5–6, 12, 19, 36, 54, 67, 76, 90, 95, 119, 122, n4, n25, n32, n39, n110, n113

objectivity, 28, 84–86, 90, 114, 115, 141, n2
obscurity, 62, 129, 132–134, 136, 138, 144, 151–152, n138
ontology, 28
  in Foucault, 92, 109, n59
  in Heidegger, 54–55, 62, 63, 64, 65, 70–72, 76, 79–82, 83, 86, 87, 128, n26, n27, n29, n30, n31, n33, n35, n38, n51, n53
  see also metaphysical discourse
origin, 151, 152

  in Foucault, 90, 95–97, 102, 104, 105–107, 108, 115, 116, n70, n72, n94, n98
  in Heidegger, 61, 62, 64, 74, 77, 83–85, 141, n30, n36, n39, n71
  in Nietzsche, 11–12, 16, 19, 24–25, 48, n22, n33
original, 95, 96, 116, n127

Parmenides, 127, 142–143
parody, 3, 109–110, n97
Pascal, Blaise, n10
periphery, 55, 68, 81, 108, 109, 111, 123, n105
phainesthai, 67–69, 82, 84, 87, n40
  see also apophainesthai
phantasm, 94–96, 98, n62, n64, n72
phenomenology, 54–55, 66–71, 82–83, 85, n42, n53, n69
philosopher,
  in Foucault, 102, 108, n82
  in Nietzsche, 11–19, 23, 33, 35, 43–46, n15, n67
philosophy, 4, 7, 13, 20, 23, 33, 35, 43, 54, 56, 89, 91, 96, 102–103, 106, 124, 125–126, 136, 137, 142, 143, n6, n38, n39, n77, n82, n92, n107, n112
Plato, 93, 107, 127, n20, n91, n110, n111
play, 1–3, 5, 6, 9–10, 12, 13, 14, 15–16, 20, 22, 27, 28, 32, 36, 46, 49, 53, 87, 93–94, 96, 97, 98, 100, 104, 109, 111, 118, 123, 128, 130, 134, 140, 143, 147–148, 153, 154, 155, n1, n39, n74, n89, n98, n138, n140
poetic speech, 30, 137, 138–143, 145, n80, n105, n119, n125, n127
positivism, 114
postmodern language, 2
power, 3–4, 9–10, 12–13, 15, 16, 20, 23–27, 30, 32, 33, 35, 37, 38–44, 48, 51, 54, 57, 68, 76, 90–94, 102, 106, 107, 109, 110, 116, 117, 118, 122–123, 127, 129, 144, 151, 153, n9, n32, n36, n52, n89, n91, n96, n135
  see also will to power
presence, 65–68, 70, 71–74, 77, 91,

104, 113, 116, 122, 123, 125, 126, 129–137, 139–144, 148, 153, 154–155, n39, n44, n48, n52, n67, n94, n110, n129, n138
pseudesthai, 69, 82, 84, 87
psychoanalysis, 7, 116, 150–153, n61
psychology, 19
punishment, 37, 45, 108, 151, n5, n135

question, 5, 10–13, 23, 29, 31, 54–55, 58, 115, 128–129, 142–143, 144, n100, n131, n140
   of the meaning of Being, chap. 3, 89, 90, 91, 92, 124–130, 132–133, 136–137, 143, n19, n20, n26, n27, n28, n30, n31, n32, n33, n35, n36, n38, n41, n43, n44, n48, n58, n71, n111

reason, 11, 20, 28, 62, 66, 76, 91, 119, 122, 129, 142, n10, n38, n94, n101
recurrence, 89, 100–101, 104, n59, n75
   see also eternal recurrence *and* repetition
release, 5–8, 20, 43, 51, 68, 73–75, 122, 126, 128, 136, 137–141, 145–147, 149–150, 152–153, 155, n1, n50, n111, n135
   see also force *and* repression
religion, 104, 123, 138–141, n68, n127
   Greek, 36, 38, 40, 44
   in Nietzsche, 24, 26–27, 34–45, n10
   see also Christianity *and* Judaism
repetition, 3, 5, 50, 92, 93, 97, 98–101, 104, 106, 107, 108, 111, 115, 117, 118, 121, 122, 131, 135, 143, n33, n59, n72, n74, n89, n135
representation, 5–6, n39
   in Foucault, 89, 93, 95, 96, 98–99, 101, 112, 114, 115, 116, n66, n100, n104
   in Heidegger, 55, 57, 68, 137, 145–146, 148
repression, 3, 5–8, 10, 19, 21–23, 35, 38, 39, 45, 48, 50
   see also release
resemblance, 16, 94, 96, 98, 109, 110, 113, 118, 122, 128, n66, n100, n101, n105
resentment, in Nietzsche, 3, 23, 27, 33, 34–35, 39, 45, 47, 153, 155, n135
reversal, 53, 89
   in Foucault, 93, 116, 118, 121
   in Heidegger, 57
   in Nietzsche, 9, 24–27, 34–35, 147, 149, n8, n32
Robinson, Edward, n23, n24

saint, in Nietzsche, 37, 40–42, n9
Sartre, Jean-Paul, 80
science,
   in Foucault, 106, 115, n107
   in Heidegger, 61, 127
   in Nietzsche, 18, 31, 36, 46–47
seeing, 3, 32, n39
   see also hearing
singularity, 32, 100, n77, n84, n89
   see also multiplicity
Socrates, 56, n77, n82
soul, 15, 21, n49
space, 67, 95, 96, 101, 154, n48, n102, n141
Spinoza, Baruch, n59, n77
Stambaugh, Joan, n18, n24, n37, n44, n55
strife, 51, 87–88, 90, 109, 118–119, 121, 122, 124–125, 128, 147, n20, n55, n56, n111
subject, 15, 16, 25, 61, 62, 73, 74, 81, 84, 90, 99, 103, 106, 107, 108, 110, 112–113, 114, 116, 119, 154, n92, n98, n104
   see also man
subjectivity, 149, 151
   in Foucault, 103, 113, 114, 116, n82, n98, n106
   in Heidegger, 54, 57, 58, 62, 71, 76, 78, 81–82, 84, 86, 90, 127, 128, 129, 135, 141, 142, 145, 146, n36, n38
   in Nietzsche, 10, 15, 17, 25, 28, 30, 46
substance, 4, 90, 150, 154
   in Foucault, 94–96, 98, 100, 104, 108, 118, n77
   in Heidegger, 69–70, 73, 74, 75, 76,

78, 81, 85–86, 125, 128, 129, 130, 148
 in Nietzsche, 10, 14–16, 19, n33, n41
surface, in Foucault, 93–95, 96–97, 98, 106, n1, n64, n69, n70

tear, 89, 92, n85, n138
temporality, 16, 54, 57, 58, 61, 62, 63, 64, 65, 66, 67, 70, 71, 72, 73, 75, 77, 78–84, 86–87, 126, 133, n32, n33, n34, n36, n38, n39, n41, n51, n52, n53, n54, n135
things,
 in Foucault, 99
 in Heidegger, 66–70, 77
time, 13, 27, 51, 54, 57, 63, 64, 65, 66, 76, 78–79, 83–84, 86–87, 101, 110, 112, 123, 129–130, 131–137, 149, 150, 154, n21, n34, n35, n36, n38, n48, n69, n92, n110, n111, n135, n140, n141
 see also temporality
totality, 29, 46–47, 62, 69, 71, 73, 77, 87, 103, 104, 116, 118, n39, n46, n67, n138
 see also whole
trace, vii, 77, n39
Trakl, Georg, 138–146, n119
transcendence, 4, 94, n135
 in Foucault, 112, 113, 114–116, 117, n94, n100, n104
 in Heidegger, 54, 55, 65, 66, 71, 74, 78–83, 85, 87, n36, n38, n39, n53
 in Nietzsche, 16, 19, 42, 107, n4
transgression, 6, 17, 89, 91, 100–102, 104–107, 111, 117, 118, 119, 122, 129, 134, 144, 152, n81, n82, n83, n84, n89, n96, n135, n140
 see also line, image of
transvaluation, 3–6, chap. 2, 57, 68, 89, 92, 101, 107, 119, 121, 123, 131, 134, 138, 144, 147, 148, 149, 155, n4, n10, n25, n32
truth, 4, 7, 14, 17, 56
 in Foucault, 90, 98, 99, 106, 112, 113, 116, 117, 118, n62, n80, n84, n94, n95, n97
 in Heidegger, 125, 133, n110
 in Nietzsche, 11–12, 17, 21, 23, 27, 32, 91, n5
 primordial, of Dasein. 74–75, 78
 see also will to truth

Übermensch (overman), 36, 44–45, 47, 50, 131, 144, 150
 see also man
unconcealment, 127–131, 133, 134–135, 136, 142, 143, n117
 see also disclosure
undecidability, 91, 154, 155, n117, n141
unity, 10, 45–47, 93, 149
 in Foucault, 92, 100–101, 103, 106, 109, 111–112, 115, 117, 118, 123, n59, n82, n96, n101, n104
 in Heidegger, 55, 71–73, 75, 76–77, 80–84, 86–87, 125, 130, 133–134, 135, 141, n47, n129
 in Nietzsche, 15, 29, 34, 44
universality, 60, 98, 101, n25, n36, n73

value, 8
 in Foucault, 101, 107, n95, n101
 in Nietzsche, 11–12, 13, 21, 22, 25, 33, 38, 56, n5
violence, 3, 5, 6, 8, 21, 41, 43, 117, 122, 138, 145, 147, 148, 150, 153–155, n1, n141

whole, 4, 41, 46, 57, 63, 71, 73–75, 80, 113, 118, 123, n67, n68, n76
 of Dasein, 61, 71–72, 74, 75, 77, 80, 83, n25, n49, n52
will, 11, 13, 15–17, 21, 29–30, 39, 40, 43, 44, 48, 91, 94, 114, 116, 123, 129, 145–147, n8, n15, n97, n135
 to be, 12, 127, n5
 to knowledge, n97
 to power, 13, 14, 18–19, 20, 22, 25–30, 34, 35, 37, 39, 41, 43, 45, 46–51, 109, 147, 153, n9, n10, n32, n39
 to truth, 11–13